The Uses of Charity

Published under the auspices of the
Shelby Cullom Davis Center for Historical Studies
Princeton University

Gerald L. Geison, ed. *Professions and the French State, 1700–1900.* 1984

Sean Wilentz, ed. *Rites of Power: Symbolism, Ritual, and Politics since the Middle Ages.* 1985

Peter Mandler, ed. *The Uses of Charity: The Poor on Relief in the Nineteenth-Century Metropolis.* 1990

Anthony Grafton and Ann Blair, eds. *The Transmission of Culture in Early Modern Europe.* 1990

The Uses of Charity

The Poor on Relief in the Nineteenth-Century Metropolis

Edited by Peter Mandler

upp

University of Pennsylvania Press
Philadelphia

COPYRIGHT © 1990 BY THE UNIVERSITY OF PENNSYLVANIA PRESS
ALL RIGHTS RESERVED
PRINTED IN THE UNITED STATES OF AMERICA

Library of Congress Cataloging-in-Publication Data

The Uses of charity: the poor on relief in the nineteenth-century
metropolis / Peter Mandler, editor.
    p. cm.
  "Published under the auspices of the Shelby Cullom Davis Center
for Historical Studies, Princeton University"—
   ISBN 0-8122-8214-0
   1. Urban poor—Europe—History—19th century. 2. Poor—New York
(N.Y.)—History—19th century. 3. Charities—Europe—History—19th
century. 4. Charities—New York (N.Y.)—History—19th century.
I. Mandler, Peter. II. Shelby Cullom Davis Center for Historical
Studies.
HV4084.U84 1990
362.5′8′094091732—dc20

               90-30496
               CIP

In Memory of
Michael Harrington

Contents

Acknowledgments

This collection originated as a symposium, "Down and Out in Paris, London and New York: Charity and Welfare in the Metropolis, 1700–1900," held at Princeton University in April 1986 as part of a two-year program of seminars and symposia on charity and welfare under the auspices of the Shelby Cullom Davis Center for Historical Studies. Although the symposium had a wider ambit, discussion centered on the separate identities of giver and receiver in the charitable transaction, suggesting the theme for a volume that includes versions of papers read at the symposium, papers read at other Davis Center seminars, and one paper solicited specifically for the volume.

As with any project emanating from the Davis Center, the two principal debts owing are to Lawrence Stone, for his intellectual leadership, and to Joan Daviduk, for her administrative wizardry. Ellen Ross, a Davis Center Fellow in 1985–86, also played an absolutely vital role. It was her contribution at the symposium, dovetailing with the paper read by Christine Stansell, which later appeared as chapter 10 of her book *City of Women*, that galvanized the discussion and sowed the seed for the book. Her enthusiasm for the project persuaded me to persevere with it. And her work has served as a model for many of the contributors and for others in the field.

I have also to thank a fleet of historians for holding my hand while I ventured into territories I had never imagined existed, much less explored. The contributors to this volume were my first resource. I thank them, and in particular Lynn Lees and Michael Katz. Among my colleagues at Princeton, I am grateful to Gary Gerstle, Liz Lunbeck, Dan Rodgers, Christine Stansell, and Lawrence Stone for reading drafts of my introduction and helping fill my great gulfs of ignorance, especially in the history of my native land. Pat Thane made the most searching and scorching—and thus, probably, the most helpful—criticisms. A still wider network helped me trawl the world for additional contributions, pulling up one big fish, the essay by Catharina Lis and Hugo Soly on Antwerp, to add an extra dimension to the London–Paris–New York axis with which we began. I would have liked to go further afield, to Rome and Berlin especially, and Christoph Sachsse, Stuart Woolf, and Marta Petrusewicz encouraged me in my quest; but the German and Italian historiography does not yet appear to have found or exploited the quasi-anthropological sources that case studies of this sort require. There is clearly room for a good deal more work on the themes that we explore below.

Finally, the staffs of the Princeton University Department of History, especially Peggy Reilly, and of the University of Pennsylvania Press have turned our manuscripts into a book.

Peter Mandler

Princeton University
May 1989

Peter Mandler

1. Poverty and Charity in the Nineteenth-Century Metropolis: An Introduction

ANTHROPOLOGISTS ASSUME that the poor understand the rich better than the rich understand the poor because for the rich social knowledge is a luxury and for the poor it can be essential to survival. Historians have tended to assume the reverse, not for any comparable analytical reasons, but simply because the rich have left behind them so many more (and more articulate) evidences of their social knowledge whereas the poor remained comparatively dumb. Although historians have progressively been bringing the poor to life by exploring new sources, reconsidering old ones, and, indeed, importing anthropological models, the places where rich and poor interacted—where social knowledge was acquired and put to use—remain the most difficult to penetrate. Although considerable headway has been made in fathoming relations in the workplace, other places are still largely rich man's territory.

Charity—the gift of the rich to the poor—is a classic case in point. The donors have left behind such rich documentation of their motives and achievements that the study of charity has been considered almost solely as a chapter in the cultural history of the upper classes. Given this tradition, and given their own preoccupation with labor relations, social historians of the poor have relinquished the field, virtually agreeing that charity was a business of giving but not receiving, a self-interested obsession of the rich that hardly figures in the lives of the poor.[1]

This volume aims to rectify the omission and to contribute to a social history of charity from below. Its contributors argue that poverty and charity went hand in hand as integral parts of urban life in nineteenth-century Europe and America. Although the supply of charity might vary with political and intellectual fashion, economics and demography meant that the demand for charity was more constant and pressing. Furthermore, at no point did the forms in which charity was offered match the forms in which it was needed. The task of the recipients was to fit themselves into the positions required by the donors at the moment of the transaction and then to apply the gift (so far as they were able) to their own real needs. The uses of charity, in other words, were different from its purposes, and the essays that follow seek to measure that difference. This introduction provides an overview of our main themes: the extent of urban poverty; the survival strategies of the urban poor; the place of charity in those strategies; and, finally, the degree to which the need for charity was superseded at the end of our period by the emergence of the modern welfare state. Whereas the individual essays tell stories full of national and local texture, revealing differences in the experiences and strategies of the urban poor, here the emphasis will be on the striking parallels in the problem of poverty and the provision of charity to be found in the great cities of America and western Europe.

Poverty in the City

Making a living in the Western city has never been easy. Long before proletarianization, the relatively high incomes available to skilled men in urban crafts and trades were constantly threatened by the disastrous instability of the premodern economy. War, plague, famine, clumsy state interventions, and primitive financial and commercial mechanisms all conspired to make the urban worker's position uniquely precarious. There was, indeed, a remarkable constancy in the *inconstancy* of urban artisanal work throughout early modern Europe: skilled artisans in late medieval Paris, in seventeenth-century Milan, and in eighteenth-century Lyons all averaged between 250 and 290 days of paid work per annum.[2]

Agricultural labor—the mainstay of these premodern economies—had its own built-in unreliability, its natural seasonality compounded by crop failures and limited marketing opportunities. But rural society had built up elaborate support systems to cope with this unreliability. At its heart was the household economy, making use of the entire family's labor resources year-round to achieve self-sufficiency in food, clothing, and shelter. Even where agricultural labor was already commercialized, as in England, the rural economy provided remunerative labor for most family members in season and well-established migratory and self-help routines to offset seasonality.[3] In emergency, extended families could provide additional resources, and even where coresidence was not the rule, the relative immobility of traditional society ensured that kin were never far away. As a last resort, assistance from social superiors was available. Whether it took the form of *ex gratia* private patronage, as in Italy, or the formal institutional relief of France's *hôpitaux généraux*, or the cash doles of England's legal system of poor relief, charitable assistance from the rich to the poor was seen by both parties as an essential part of the social order.[4]

Viewed in the starkest light—and we will see later how this view can be mellowed—urbanites had few such resources to sustain them. In towns, even before industrialization, the household economy was giving way to the family wage economy, in which ability to earn wages in the labor market determined a family's fortunes. The necessity for wage earners to leave the home to work and the inability of children to contribute to family subsistence until of wage-earning age subjected urban families to the "poverty cycle," first so called by the British social investigator Seebohm Rowntree at the end of the nineteenth century but already familiar much earlier. Single workers could earn well above subsistence level, and newly married wage earners with two full incomes could do better still. But the arrival of children triggered both an increase in expenditures and, as women left their jobs to undertake child care, a catastrophic drop in earnings. This "critical life situation" persisted until the oldest children were able to enter the labor market. Because of the trade-off between employment and domestic duties, the loss for any reason of the male earner could make the critical life situation fatal. Nor did the critical life situation necessarily end when the eldest child was able to earn. Because of the financial advantages of single earners, older children had an immediate incentive to break away from the family. Their departure put strains on the family, which could set up another critical life situation as elderly parents found themselves unable to earn their own living and became reliant on children who were increasingly independent.[5]

Adding to the burden of the poverty cycle and the decreasing reliability of close kin, urbanites were unable to rely on other support systems available in rural society: wider kin and neighbor networks were left behind and deferential relations with social superiors were broken. Of course, urban alternatives to these traditional support systems were developed in the early modern city—one thinks immediately of guilds and confraternities—but it is striking how persistently town dwellers looked to the country for relief.[6] Well into the nineteenth century, armies of seasonal migrants swept into cities to take temporary work when it was available but returned home when it slackened. Up to the 1850s, New England textile towns worked the "Waltham system" whereby unmarried young women were recruited from the countryside in times of high demand and returned to their rural house-holds when demand slackened.[7] As late as the 1880s, Milan registered at least half as many "emigrants" as "immigrants."[8] Up to the same period, Russian authorities were able to keep urban workers on a juridical umbilical cord to their estates of origin, thus fostering the illusion that "the factory worker is not a native inhabitant of the city, as he is abroad."[9] Even highly urbanized Britain did not grant "settlement"—the legal right to poor relief—to urban immigrants until midcentury.

But the legal fictions of conservative governments could not long resist the great urbanizing tide of the nineteenth century, which progressively made reliance on the rural refuge impossible and swamped the fledgling charitable institutions of the premodern period. Both "push" and "pull" factors sent unmanageable waves of immigrants fleeing into the cities. First, in the industrializing countries of the West, the rural demand for labor went into a state of terminal decline and agricultural laborers went on the march. By midcentury, St. Petersburg had become predominantly a city of peas-ants, Paris a city of non-Parisians, and only London, the oldest of the great cities, could claim that the majority of its citizens had been born within its limits.[10] Then steam transport made mass emigration from peripheral areas to the center possible for the first time, triggering a wave of emigrants even from stable rural economies. As early as 1845, a third of New York's popula-tion and a majority of its work force were foreign-born, largely Irish and German.[11] The Italians, Poles, and Jews who were to make most American cities mostly immigrant were still to come.[12]

As a consequence of these push factors, although the whole world was urbanizing, Europe, North America, and Australasia were urbanizing more rapidly than South America, Asia, and Africa and accounted for two-thirds of the world's urban population by the end of the century. Although only Britain and the Netherlands could be fairly described as fully urban societies by then, the United States, Australasia, and eight European states were well on their way to modern levels.[13] Traditional rural society was no more; was what had taken its place any improvement?

One way *not* to answer this question is to focus too narrowly on pro-letarianization, the collapse of the old urban trades, their deskilling and casualization. Proletarianization was experienced as a loss only by the old urban population, a diminishingly small proportion of the total.[14] For instance, although the proportion of masters versus journeymen and la-borers in the Lyons silk trade dropped from 70 to 20 percent in the course of the eighteenth century, the vast majority of deskilled laborers were new to the city and to the trade, and indeed the actual number of masters doubled.[15] Considering the miseries from which most of them were fleeing, urban immigrants may well have experienced employment even in casual dock work or clothing sweatshops as a fair trade as regards status and possibly earnings as well.[16]

The proletarianization of the old urban trades did, however, ensure that those few existing urban institutions which aimed to plug the holes in the family wage economy were to be swept away at just the time when unprecedented numbers of people were flooding into that economy. In other words, the perennial problems of urban employment were now to be experienced by a much higher proportion of the Western population, without the old safety nets either of the countryside or of the city to succor them.[17]

Worse still, urbanization and industrialization made those safety nets more necessary than ever by exacerbating the impact of the poverty cycle. For one thing, the development of mass production in textiles, coal, iron, and steel resulted in a new kind of city, one totally reliant on a single industry. Contemporaries were quick to appreciate the threat posed by the single-industry city, in which a very large number of people packed into a very small space could be simultaneously deprived of their livelihoods by a trade disruption in just one sector. But the threat of mass unemployment was only the tip of the iceberg. What contemporaries failed to appreciate, on the whole, was the effect the single-industry city often had in aggravating the poverty cycle by reducing further the opportunities for child and female labor, thus rendering the family even more precariously reliant on a single male wage. In textile towns, where both women and children might get work, family income could be kept up, though only at the cost of farming out infant care and thus boosting infant mortality levels.[18] Even so, the later entry of children into productive labor extended the critical period when at most two earners had to support many dependents, and the loss of one earner could be disastrous. In iron and steel towns or port towns, where neither child nor female labor was in demand, it was nearly impossible to keep the family wage above subsistence level even in the best of times.[19]

Single-industry cities, which arose through the development of new and growing sectors, might at least afford male earners relatively high wages. The greatest cities—the metropolises with which this volume is primarily concerned—did not. Whereas single-industry cities tended to attract only as many fleeing rural migrants as their economies could bear, the metropolises exerted a much greater pull. They were their nation's historical centers, already well known to ruralites as places of possible refuge, and they offered the age-old urban attractions of diversity, masterlessness, mobility, and "bright lights," what Emile Durkheim called the city's greater "moral density."[20] These cultural attractions continued to suck in migrants long after tales of appalling overcrowding, high mortality, and thin employment offerings had filtered back to the hinterlands. By the end of the nineteenth century, nine such metropolises had topped the million population mark, eight of them—London, New York, Paris, Berlin, Vienna, Chicago, Philadelphia, and St. Petersburg—in the West.[21]

In metropolitan conditions of labor surplus, male wages were invariably low and driven lower by progressive casualization. In late nineteenth-century London, four hundred thousand people—10 percent of the population—were supported solely by casual labor. Offsetting this situation was the greater diversity of employment opportunities in the larger centers, giving women and children chances to augment the family wage. Female and child labor was particularly in demand in capital cities, where the relatively large upper classes needed domestic servants and finished luxury goods, traditionally women's work, and where opportunities for scavenging and delivery work were greater.[22] Still, even in metropolitan conditions, a declining proportion of married women went out to work.

To sum up, in cities where female and child labor was not in demand, the family was dangerously dependent on a single male wage; that wage rarely left margins for savings and was itself at the mercy of the trade cycle. In cities where female and child labor was still in demand, wages were low and casual and the family wage was rarely adequate to provide subsistence. In all cities, families with many small children, families deprived of the male earner by disease or desertion or death, and older people without coresident earners were prey to the poverty cycle. The support systems of the countryside had been left behind, and the existing support systems of the city had been swamped or swept away entirely. How, then, did urban families of the nineteenth century survive?

Surviving the Nineteenth-Century Metropolis

One answer to this question could be that urban families did not survive. Just as anthropologists once considered the position of Third World slum dwellers to be hopeless, mired in the "culture of poverty," so historians used to take the despairing observations of middle-class contemporaries as factual: the new urban population lived like animals, overcrowded, disorganized, fatalistic, without prospect of improvement.[23] Most contemporaries, who believed that the poor were capable of supporting themselves, blamed poverty on ignorance and improvidence and prescribed a dose of middle-class self-help values. A few, like Pierre-Joseph Proudhon and Karl Marx, better aware of the structural inadequacies of the early industrial economy, were rightly skeptical about this prescription but in their own way accepted the description of a chaotic and undisciplined urban mass; thus Proudhon:

> When the worker has been stupefied by the fragmentary division of labor, by serving machines, by obscurantist education; when he has been discouraged by low wages, demoralized by unemployment and starved by monopoly; when he finally has neither bread nor cake, neither farthing nor groat, neither hearth nor home, then he begs, he filches, he cheats, he robs, he murders.[24]

In this view, which served as the model for much modern social and labor history, conditions could not improve until the new urban masses developed powerful institutions to redistribute wealth to working-class men. The rise of the working class could thus be traced through the rise of the friendly society, the trade union, the cooperative, the labor party, and the welfare state.[25]

In recent years, anthropologists have abandoned the culture of poverty thesis. They have reassessed the supposed marginality of the urban poor, showing how traditional practices were imported from rural society to cope with the anonymity and disorganization of the metropolis and revealing the rational calculations underlying apparently "antisocial" behaviors.[26] Historians are now following suit, often employing anthropological methods, able even to interview the last survivors of the nineteenth-century city. Beneath the written evidence left by the better-known working-class institutions, they have found a history of urban living. It is an oral, anecdotal, and autobiographical history, told more by men who did *not* join trade unions and political parties than by men who did and, crucially, told more by women and children than by men.

The history of urban living, particularly before the development of those working-class institutions, is primarily about the failure of working-class families to live up to middle-class norms. It is a story about the inadequacy of the single male wage and the means by which men, women, and children compensated for that inadequacy: in other words, the survival strategies of urban families. Cast by middle-class observers in this light of failure and inadequacy, it has taken a long time to reconstruct, for it is a story which working-class men were unlikely to tell each other, less likely still to tell to their social superiors, and about which the best potential narrators—women and children—were not until recently asked.

Men in work were peculiarly badly placed to begin reconstructing the economic safety nets of rural society. They worked long hours, often in small units, frequently far from home, with little leisure and not much opportunity for mutuality, especially in the metropolis, where their labor was particularly fragmented and casualized.[27] In late nineteenth-century Moscow, workers' independence was so limited that they referred to the lavatories at work as "our club."[28] Elsewhere, many of those who had leisure time devoted it to drink, and although drinking networks provided one basis for interdependence and the drinking place one fledgling working-class institution, not too much significance should be assigned to an activity that was in the end personally demoralizing and a net drain on family resources.[29] We might speculate, further, that opportunities for sociability and solidarity among un- or underemployed men were more limited still.[30] About men out of work, however—indeed, men out of the workplace—we know remarkably little.

We will see later what contributions men out of work might make to family survival. Most of these contributions must have been made outside the residential community, and yet that was where the principal building blocks of new urban support systems would be found. Places of employment might be scattered all over the nineteenth-century city, but residence was strongly class-segregated and in many cities grew more so as the century progressed. The residential community was literally transplanted from the country, early arrivals providing temporary lodging for late-comers, who would then seek permanent homes in the near vicinity. Ethnic immigrants, even more reliant on familiar faces because of language barriers and racial discrimination, formed particularly tight knots. Irish immigrants stepping off the ferries in London and New York would be met at the dock by lodging-house keepers, who would shepherd them to the Irish slums, where they would later make contacts for jobs and housing with old friends from the village of origin.[31]

Once settled in a neighborhood, the new urbanite was unlikely to move out of it. Although working-class families changed residence frequently, one step ahead of the rent collector, they rarely moved far. Working-class migration, noted Charles Booth of the London poor in 1892, "rarely proceeds outside the little charmed circle of alleys where 'old pals' reside: it is rather of the nature of a circular movement, so that at the end of ten years a man is as near his birthplace as at the beginning, having perhaps lived in each of the neighbouring streets in the meantime."[32] Moreover, grown children establishing new residences did not move far from their parents, nor did marriage take children out of the community, for the urban slums were marked by extraordinarily high rates of neighborhood endogamy. Ellen Ross has sampled three inner London parishes in the 1880s and 1890s and found that parish endogamy was virtually universal—over 90 percent in all three samples—and, furthermore, that street endogamy was the general rule. Michael Anderson found that over two-fifths of his Preston sample lived within a hundred yards of kin. With this clustering, astonishing concentrations of kin could build up. A Mrs. Spooner of Willis Street, Poplar, died in 1902 with thirty-four grandchildren and forty-two great-grandchildren resident on her street.[33]

The sheer physical pressure of overcrowding compounded this clustering of covillagers and kin and forced intimacies upon total strangers. Overcrowding seems to have been a problem in every nineteenth-century city, whatever its bricks-and-mortar endowment. London slums were mainly old middle-class neighborhoods come down in the world and thus composed largely of intensely subdivided town houses. This pattern of residence kept down the concentration of persons per acre but encouraged higher concentrations of persons per room. Even so, some notorious rookeries, like South St. Giles in the heart of the city, could have densities of over three hundred persons per acre. In Paris, the average building size was larger, and so average population per acre was higher: over two hundred in most central districts.[34] The new cities of America had room to sprawl so their average densities were not high. But they also had no existing housing stock and so had the freedom to develop new means of cramming the poor together. When the older town houses of New York were fully subdivided, the purpose-built tenement was devised to reduce working-class housing costs to a minimum. By the end of the century, the "dumbbell" tenement— the high-rise equivalent of the back-to-back—was testing the limits of human tolerance. The Lower East Side was packed to a density of 250,000 persons per square mile, peaks in certain precincts of 750,000 per square mile probably setting world records for population density not even matched by present-day Bombay.[35]

For the women and children who were the only twenty-four-hour residents of these urban slums, there was no such thing as a strictly private life.[36] They spilled out onto the street, the stoop, the staircase or corridor, any public refuge from the stifling conditions indoors. Domestic work also became public because the slum or tenement apartment was too small and ill-equipped for self-sufficiency. Women congregated around the public taps, which were, as in the modern shantytown, the sole sources of water; in communal laundries and washhouses; and in the shops upon which they were now reliant for food, clothing, and small domestic necessaries. Except for pubs and places of work, most of the nonresidential buildings in the urban slums were primarily places for women and children. The London Irish rookery of South St. Giles, for instance, contained within its sixty-eight acres a post office, public baths, a washhouse, an almshouse, a hospital, a boys' refuge, six schools, eight churches and chapels, and many lodging houses and shops, all institutions run by or for women and children, while for the men there were a hotel, a foundry, a cooperage, and forty-three pubs.[37]

These highly sophisticated urban communities and institutions must not be seen simply as the locus of domestic labor. They were, rather, an integral part of the working-class economy, virtual factories for the extension and augmentation of inadequate male wages. Domestic labor was part of this business: "good housekeeping," in the sense of stretching the budget, was an invaluable contribution to family income. But it was only a small part.

If few married women were able to go out to work, many contrived to do a good deal of earning at home. Elizabeth Roberts's sample of three provincial English cities reveals that a majority of women did full- or part-time work at some point in their marriage. Although there would never be as much sustaining homework in the city as in the country, industrialization did provide new outlets for women's work at home. Traditional women's skills at sewing and dressmaking provided ready entry into the clothing industry, which relied heavily on homeworkers until the invention of the sewing machine made the sweatshop possible. Mechanization could increase the total amount of homework available. The clothing industry continued to use homeworkers for finishing processes and delicate work such as embroidery, and the match industry farmed out boxmaking to homeworkers. Then the urban slum generated its own "penny capitalism." Women who went out to work paid others to do their domestic work—laundry, sewing, and child care. New arrivals required lodging. Any woman could—for the price of a daily trip to a wholesale market and a sign in the window or on the door—become a petty shopkeeper.[38]

Women were also able to recreate, after a fashion, the extended household of traditional rural society and to make use of kin resources to supplement wage work. Children, especially daughters, often lived at home until marriage. As the age of marriage rose, the number of adult earners in the average household also rose. In France in the years immediately before World War I, the contribution made by working children to family income doubled to almost 20 percent.[39] Though nearly all children now left their parents' household at marriage, daughters tended to remain near their mothers; sons, if need be, relocated to be nearer their wives' families. As a consequence, the kin networks created were women's networks.[40] These connections, persisting after the household's physical breakup, meant that daughters were often available to help their mothers in future crises. For instance, both widows and widowers were likely to end up lodging with their children, but widows more so than widowers.[41] This ability to rely on children for lodging and other assistance was no small benefit. Loss of the male earner through death or desertion was one of the most critical of critical life situations, and it was the nearly universal fate of married women who lived long enough.[42]

Women also formed networks with other women in their neighborhood who were not kin. Domestic labor was reduced by pooling or taken over altogether by neighbors in cases of disease or injury. Women neighbors put pressure on men who were not pulling their weight, slacking off on the job, for instance, or abusing their wives. Neighborhood networks ran savings schemes such as clothing clubs or lotteries on strict rotation so that every week one woman would benefit from a lump sum to go toward a major household purchase. Other forms of reciprocity were more subtle but also the stuff of everyday life: the sharing of staples, the circulation of children's clothing, the friendly offering to the temporarily needy.[43]

These connections were not as close as those between kin, and there was a reluctance to contrast relationships that might conflict with familial ones, but neighbors could be relied upon to step in when kin failed. Neighbors could also become a kind of kin via godparenthood, and this relationship perhaps accounts for the continuing importance that working-class families accorded to christenings long after other forms of religious observance had been discarded. Where religious observance persisted, as in many Catholic communities, opportunities for godparenthood multiplied: not only at birth but at confirmation, marriage, and even in full adulthood.[44]

Finally, huge numbers of women took in boarders, perhaps the single most important source of family income outside of paid work. In some communities, such as that of the Jews of New York City at the turn of the twentieth century, almost half of all households had nonkin boarders under their roofs.[45] Boarding neatly ties together the disparate functions that "nonworking" women played in family survival strategies, for taking in a boarder might at the same time add to family income and further cement kin, neighborhood, and ethnic networks.

In sum, we might recast Proudhon's dictum:

> When the worker has been stupefied by the fragmentary division of labor, by serving machines, by obscurantist education; when he has been discouraged by low wages, demoralized by unemployment and starved by monopoly; when he finally has neither bread nor cake, neither farthing nor groat,

he turns to hearth and home, where his wife feeds him, clothes him, shelters him, and provides for his family all the necessaries which his wage alone cannot. Wives and mothers had rebuilt the support systems of the rural community in the new urban slums, drawing on their own labor as well as reconstructed kin and neighborhood networks to fill the holes in the family wage economy. The tightly knit and tightly packed urban slum made for extremely efficient use of limited resources to augment or substitute for the outside earnings of men.

But this was not all. Both men and women who worked without pay were able to draw in resources from outside the working-class community, to coax from social superiors the voluntary donation that had been one of the linchpins of rural society and had by no means vanished in the nineteenth-century city. On the contrary, although more elusive, charitable resources were more plentiful than ever before and to working-class women especially represented a tempting alternative to squeezing the last sou out of neighbors and kin.

The Uses of Charity

Historians have not generally accorded charity much importance in the working-class survival strategy. In comparison to its role as a vital social and economic cement in premodern communities, charity is considered to have had a primarily symbolic value in the nineteenth-century city. As a statement of the intentions of the givers, this view has something to recommend it. The new urban patriciates—bourgeois patriciates—certainly cleaved to a robust individualism that left the working-class family to its own resources, and these patriciates did their best to embed this individualism not only in state policy but also in the hearts and minds of the people.

Although in some countries statutory provisions for the poor had been fortified during the economic transition of the eighteenth century, they were now scaled back or repealed altogether.[46] Even if municipal authorities had wanted to pursue the eighteenth-century fashion for institutionalization, relieving the poor "indoors" in return for productive labor, they would not have been able to cope with the numbers now involved. Instead, the normative assumption was established that the able-bodied male should be able to support his family and that relief would be extended only to a narrow category of "deserving" poor. In many places, orphans, widows, and the aged and infirm were judged to be deserving prima facie and thus eligible for limited doles "outdoors" (that is, without confinement). In Britain, all but orphans were deemed to be victims of their own improvidence and in theory entitled only to the most meager dole administered in a penal workhouse.

In certain circumstances, able-bodied men and their families could be considered deserving, too, but to uphold the normative assumption these cases had to be approached carefully. The general rule was to exclude the able-bodied from statutory provision so as to preclude any claim that such relief was a "right" and to assign the task of able-bodied relief to voluntary charity (including the churches). Plenty of middle-class volunteers were available to penetrate into the homes of relief candidates—not only the able-bodied but often the prima facie deserving as well—and make face-to-face judgments about the advisability of granting aid.

These "friendly visits" were more concerned with morals than with money. Middle-class charity rested firmly on the view that only the exercise of individual prudence and industry could guarantee the continued sustenance of the urban population. Aid in cash or in kind would tend to undermine prudence and industry, save in those exceptional cases in which the need resulted from unaccountable catastrophe. Friendly visitors could detect and relieve those few cases, but in the vast bulk of their visits their mission would have to be educational and hortatory. This is why subsequent observers have considered nineteenth-century charity to be basically symbolic. Like premodern charity, it broadcast a message of community and connection between the classes, but now the community was a moral one alone, the connection looser and less organic, unsecured by material or political dependence. Social superiors continued to demonstrate their concern for natural dependents—orphans, lunatics, perhaps also the crippled, the widowed, and the aged—but for others the aim (in charity as elsewhere in society) was independence.

Reinforcing the belief in the supposed material irrelevance of nineteenth-century charity is the supposition that the poor shared this aim of the rich. The poor themselves, it has often been argued, came to feel that the male wage earner had a duty to support his family single-handed. As a result, recourse to aid from social superiors—in earlier days natural and inevitable—now seemed humiliating and dishonorable. Working-class families vied with each other in a race for "respectability," the absorption or mimicking of middle-class mores, and in this race the acceptance of charity was an immediate disqualifier. The stigma which dependence on charity is said to have conveyed was not branded on the poor from without but was, rather, a central feature of working-class morality.

It was precisely to maintain their independence from outside aid that "respectable" workingmen developed the characteristic institutions of working-class self-help: the friendly society, the trade union, the cooperative. These institutions are said to have been built up almost as bulwarks against state intervention, preserving not only the independence of the class but also the independence of the individual.[47] Even their mutual aid functions might be draped in mystery and ritual to disguise their true import, not only from the outside world but also from one's own women and children. In general, it is often assumed, the more organized the working-class community got, the more respectable its members were and the less dependent.[48]

There are good reasons for questioning this view of charity's place in the nineteenth-century metropolis. For one thing, it accords too neatly with the middle-class view of the situation. Because of the quantity and articulateness of the evidence they supply, middle-class prescriptions are too easily read as descriptions. It is no coincidence, for instance, that the evidence for the "stigma of pauperism" is most extensive in Britain, the country whose government labored hardest to impose a stigma. Relief (in theory, at least) was available only in a workhouse designed purposefully to deter applicants and in the most degrading circumstances, involving the separation of spouses, the incarceration of children, and the deprivation of all worldly goods. Rather than concluding that "the town poor shunned the poor law," we might say that the poor law shunned the town poor.[49] In systems like those of late eighteenth-century Antwerp or early nineteenth-century Florence—or, for that matter, some twentieth-century welfare states—where relief is openly acknowledged to be an essential part of the working family's life cycle, the question of a stigma hardly arises.[50]

Middle-class interpretations of working-class intentions must be viewed with the greatest suspicion. Not only did middle-class observers have an interest in recording mostly what they wanted to hear, but working-class supplicants had an interest in saying what their masters wanted to hear. It is reasonable to suspect that there was more than a small element of theatricality in some of the eloquent testimonies (proudly transcribed by middle-class auditors) to the "independent spirit" of the laboring poor.[51] Applicants for relief had naturally to make themselves appear deserving according to middle-class norms, whatever the facts of the case. Donors were not often prepared to accept that a man could not find work, even less prepared to accept that he could not support his family on his full-time wage, and so some emergency or mitigating circumstance had to be manufactured, the applicant all the while swearing allegiance to the ideals of respectability.[52]

The historic want of communication between the classes left enormous scope for misunderstanding. Middle-class contemporaries in both Britain and France observed the absolute horror with which mortally ill poor people viewed the prospect of entering the workhouse or hospital and concluded that pride made them prefer independent death to dependent life. An alternative explanation—more prosaic but also more compelling— never occurred to them. Workhouse or hospital corpses could be withheld from the grieving families, denied a Christian burial, and handed over instead to the anatomy schools for dissection: to many people a fate *worse* than death.[53]

That was a fairly mild case of misunderstanding compared to cases in which there was no basis for communication between donor and recipient. Neither side can play its role in the theater of charity if the cultural or linguistic gulf is too wide. The first great outburst of urban philanthropy in Russia—the "Sunday school movement" of 1859–62—failed because the patrons were repelled by their clients' strangeness and passivity and the clients were paralyzed by their patrons' withholding of warmth and intimacy.[54] In the case of ethnic immigrants, smooth philanthropic transactions were practically impossible. One Chicago charity told of giving an immigrant family a turkey, only to find on a follow-up visit that the bird had been "dressed up in one of the children's dresses and put in the only bed in the place to keep it warm. . . . Being foreigners, [they] did not understand the eatableness of the bird, and therefore, used it as plaything."[55] The Associated Charities of Boston made a more perceptive assessment in its 1892 report:

> Until the Italians became numerous, we had at least intelligent means of communication with most of the families we know. We not only spoke the same language, but they knew what we were talking about when we urged the advantages of temperance, industry, or economical living. Though their acquiescence in our standards might be feigned and though they might never live up to them, we seldom failed to agree in theory. . . . [But the Italians] are truly foreigners to us. We do not speak a common language; our standards have no meaning to them, and we may well doubt whether they have any applicability.[56]

Even within ethnic groups miscommunication remained a problem, as Nancy Green's essay on Jewish philanthropy in this volume suggests.

Given these evidentiary and analytical difficulties, we must put aside the assumption that charity played only a minor role in the working-class economy and even scrutinize the assumption that dependence on charity carried a stigma for the poor, looking with more discrimination at how working-class families used and viewed charitable offerings in specific settings. The essays in this volume do precisely that. Here we can undertake only the most cursory survey and hazard the most tentative generalizations.

Let us begin with the case of working-class men (for it is primarily they to whom the alleged stigma has been attached). As we have seen, wage-earning work was the alpha and the omega of their waking lives. But it is not likely that they were as blind to the inadequacies of the urban economy as were their middle-class contemporaries. New arrivals from the country, in particular, must have keenly appreciated the pitfalls of the family wage economy. No amount of middle-class propaganda could convince them overnight of the joys of supporting large numbers of dependents on a single small and irregular wage. Nor would the importance of finding work blind them to the need for alternative sources of income when, as was often the case, work was not to be found.

Did working-class men view charitable "earnings" as much less desirable than other income supplements? It is hard to say. If we know that working-men valued wages before mutual aid, and mutual aid before charity, we still know little about how workingmen viewed charity. Especially early in the century, no strict line seems to have been drawn between these categories. In New York and London, workingmen organized charities of their own to visit and assist families in need, a formal version of routine neighborhood sharing.[57] Ethnic immigrants formed elaborate mutual aid societies, which testify eloquently to the tightly knit networks formed by men as well as women but tell us nothing about attitudes toward charity. Once linguistic and cultural barriers were surmounted and adequate familiarity with the host culture and class system acquired, might not charity be seen as an acceptable supplement when mutual aid failed? In Buffalo's Little Italy, for instance, the existence of both thirty-two mutual aid societies and a strong "familist" bias against outside assistance did not prevent a tenth or more of families from accepting aid from the Charity Organization Society.[58]

If the appeal to middle-class charity was more difficult and more demeaning than self-help or mutual aid, the rewards to be reaped were greater, and workingmen seemed quite capable of making this calculation and acting accordingly. This was axiomatic to at least one shrewd observer, Eugène Buret, whose *De la misère des classes laborieuses en Angleterre et en France* appeared in 1840:

> People easily grow seasoned to dangers that they foresee and have already experienced; the soul very quickly grows hardened against the feeling of a shame that is inevitable. The intelligent poor do not long harbor prejudices which wound their self-respect, and this is why the sentiment which keeps all those who are able to do without it away from charity, so pronounced elsewhere, is not so strong in Paris.[59]

When unemployed, men were generally quite ready to accept outdoor relief. In early nineteenth-century Antwerp, where employment levels were very low, between one-fifth and two-fifths of the population received some form of assistance from the municipal Charity Bureau, and a fairly consistent 10 percent was on permanent relief.[60] The Congregation of San Giovanni Battista, Florence's principal channel for outdoor relief, assisted 8,600 people in an average year in the 1810s and employed another 2,700, thus accounting for half the city's poor.[61] Paris routinely relieved one-twelfth of its population, some 60 to 75,000 people and in trade or harvest crises could support almost a third (that is, the bulk of the working population). Most cities launched massive distributions of food and fuel in such emergencies. Fifteen thousand people—one-fifth of the population—received public or private doles in New York during the crisis winter of 1817, and 20,000 people were on the dole in Brooklyn alone in 1860.[62] When in 1897 the occasion of Queen Victoria's Diamond Jubilee provided an opportunity for the distribution of relief in kind to the metropolitan poor without the pretext of emergency, the Melbourne Charity Organization Society was able to find 15,000 people in "absolute necessity" in their supposedly dispauperized city.[63] Clearly, huge numbers of "independent family men" were able—and willing?—to depend on the public purse.

It is hard to find any evidence for a stigma effectively attaching to outdoor relief for men out of work, even when the relievers did their best to impose one. In the winter of 1892–93, for instance, London's Mansion House Conference undertook a rare experiment in outdoor relief. Unemployed dockworkers who applied for assistance were first carefully screened. Only men with families, locally resident for over a year, and lodged in proper premises were considered. Only 700 of these men could be found for interview. Of those interviewed, hardly a third were judged deserving of aid. These worthy 253 were then administered a labor test, unskilled manual labor to be paid at dockers' rates. Over 80 percent accepted these terms. These men were then interviewed again, by a committee, with a view toward finding permanent situations for them. Hardly a third passed this second scrutiny. Most of this handful then rejected the committee's proposed solution—emigration. The committee regretted that so few had been "effectually assisted." But what might strike us more forcibly today is that so many were willing to run this obstacle course of interviews and tests so that a few could qualify for derisory assistance.[64]

If unemployed men readily accepted outdoor relief, it cannot be that dependence alone conferred a stigma. If they shunned indoor relief, it may have been circumstances rather than the fact of relief that interfered. Understandably, men with families hated workhouses and almshouses. In Britain, the family was supposed to enter with the household head, abandoning hard-won housing and handing over all disposable assets. Everywhere, institutionalization spelled an end to the search for work, an end to self-help, an end to assistance from kin and neighbors; it was, in short, not an income supplement but an all-or-nothing proposition attractive only to the absolutely starving.

Single men without the same constraints could put institutions to better (or more cynical) use. Whereas formerly single men without work might drift back to the country to exploit the safety nets available there, by the late nineteenth century the city offered more off-season resources to the mobile man. As the chief constable of Manchester complained in 1906, "In the winter season, tramps flock to large towns such as Manchester, where they can obtain warm sleeping-quarters in the various brick-yards, boiler-houses, and different buildings connected with factories and workshops;

also they can generally obtain free meals, which are provided by the various philanthropic societies in Manchester during the cold season." Local authorities in Boston provided a Wayfarer's Lodge—known more prosaically as the Hawkins Street Woodyard—with the unprecedented luxury of cots (albeit fifty to a room) if the alternative of the police station tramp room or "Bughouse Mary's" shanty near the South End did not appeal.[65] London's attractions in the same period included several night refuges (free accommodation on easy terms, good company, and cheery communal facilities), the famous Salvation Army "elevators" (providing food as well as lodging but extracting eight hours' work), and a string of facilities along the Thames Embankment: the Salvation Army's "Penny Sit-Up" at Blackfriars, Eustace Miles's Food Barrow at Cleopatra's Needle, the *Morning Post*'s Embankment Home at Millbank, and the relief ticket distribution point at Craven Street arches (sometimes two thousand were handed out on one night).[66] There were, in addition, the unpleasant casual wards of the workhouses and the permanent wards as a last resort when there seemed no point in seeking work for a time; a substantial proportion of Britain's paupers were "ins and outs," admitted more than once a year.[67]

Men without work resorted easily enough to charity; so did men unable to work. Since middle-class doctrine looked more favorably on men patently unable to work than on men who said they were unable to find it, charitable assistance for the former was easier to obtain. Even in Britain, with its obsessive policy of institutionalization, sick or injured men could get outdoor relief, though they still had to jump through the bureaucratic hoop of a referral from their local medical officer.[68] Old men had to enter the workhouse, and their reluctance to do so is responsible for much of the stigma folklore.[69] Again, the stigma was certainly imposed from without, but how thoroughly was it internalized by the poor? The risk of body-snatching, both in Britain and France, was a factor. The British workhouse also separated old couples in single-sex wards. Nevertheless, many old people accepted these terms, and they accounted for three-fifths of the workhouse population. In France, rather than carrying a stigma, admission to a home for the aged poor might be claimed as a right, as the *Annales d'Hygiène* alleged in 1832: "The working class population in Paris has been accustomed from time immemorial to regard the Bicêtre, Salpetrière and Incurables homes as its own domain. It is a retirement to which they are entitled in their old age and they take full advantage of it."[70] This may overstate the case. Old people everywhere naturally preferred to live with or near kin, if the alternative was open to them, and we have seen how kin networks were constructed to make this possible. But for old people without kin able to take them in, institutional care was essential and widely accepted.[71]

Despite the best efforts of the authorities to impose a stigma, therefore, men who were unable to work readily accepted charitable assistance, and such assistance made the difference between life and death for large numbers of the unemployed, the sick, and the aged. Assistance was usually shunned only when it was offered on terms that made it useless: indoor relief that reduced family income by precluding other sources, aid offered in a form that was not wanted (such as emigration assistance), or aid with highly unacceptable strings attached (such as family breakup, total dispossession, or the threat of dissection). Single men, especially old single men, might accept relief on almost any terms, including institutionalization.

So far I have dealt only with households headed by men unable to work. The vast majority of poor families were headed, most of the time, by men who worked. This increasingly became the case as the century progressed, and it may have been that as men's role as wage earners stabilized, their openness to outside assistance diminished; I will return to this point later. But as we have seen, even the fully employed man was not always able to support his family, especially if he had many small children. Thus just as men increasingly specialized as wage earners, women increasingly became wage supplementers. Working-class women developed elaborate survival strategies to supplement their wage earner's income, milking all possible sources—their own and their children's labor, penny capitalism, kin, and neighbors. Strangers, too, fell into their net.

In the nineteenth-century city, charity was if anything a more important resource for women than for men. This was a matter both of demand and supply. On the demand side, as men's work grew more reliable and women spent more time at home, men's opportunities to reap charitable gains declined and women's opportunities increased. On the supply side, charity was increasingly restricted on ideological grounds to "natural" dependents: mothers, children, widows, and servants. Not only the receiving but also the giving of charity was recast as a domestic function. Early in the century, men and women of the middle classes collaborated in charitable activity, and public relief schemes were run by men only. In the latter half of the century, when most premodern public relief facilities had been extinguished, the organization (and, increasingly, the funding) of charity was largely a private and female function.[72]

The targeting of charitable resources by women on women did not entail a diminution but, on the contrary, a vast extension of the sphere of charity. Shifting the focus from the ideologically difficult case of able-bodied men gave a freer vent to the rapidly accumulating funds and energies of the urban middle classes. Toward the end of the century, Frank Prochaska has calculated, perhaps half a million English women devoted nearly all their leisure time to charitable work, and another twenty thousand did full-time professional work for charities. Total charitable receipts per annum in London alone exceeded the public expenditure for poor relief for the whole of England and Wales; in 1899, a thousand London charities took in over £6 million, more than many European governments took in for all purposes.[73]

Although women (being natural dependents) were not subject to as harsh an ideological screening as able-bodied men, their access to these vast funds was still limited by the theoretical responsibility of men to maintain them. Women who had lost their husbands therefore found it easiest to procure assistance. Even the highly restrictive British system in practice extended outdoor relief to women with children but without spouses, although they, too, were herded into the workhouse in periods of clampdown.[74] In France, private charity shunned women with children born out of wedlock, but even they could find succor from secularist and natalist public authorities. In Britain, schemes to help young girls, unmarried mothers, spinsters, and widows alike mushroomed dramatically. Seebohm Rowntree's study of York at the end of the century found that a third of all women who had lost their husbands were dependent on public or private charity.[75]

Women with husbands were on the whole the province of private charities, whose friendly visitors were able to make the delicate assessment of deserts. In Anglo-American cities in the latter half of the century, the relief of families was almost totally handed over to "scientific" charities, such as the various Charity Organization Societies, in an attempt to stamp out outdoor relief, which caused pauperism. The hope was that the good moral influence of friendly visitors would make material assistance unnecessary.[76] Probably the bulk of charities' labor resources went into friendly visiting. In London, two hundred churches and chapels mobilized twenty-two hundred visitors, supplemented by a wide array of specialized visiting societies, the largest of which (the London City Mission) claimed to make 2 million visits a year.[77]

Although visiting understandably loomed large in the middle-class vision of charity, it was the most problematic form of charity for the poor themselves. Visitors were simply unable to supply the things their clients needed. Middle-class women clearly could not get jobs for working-class men.[78] They were not permitted to help women whose husbands were not fulfilling their maintenance responsibilities (the "undeserving"), except by breaking up the family and taking women and children into institutions. The advice they offered was in many cases counterproductive—urging women who needed to forage for extra income to devote themselves fully to domestic labor.[79] In short, this vast enterprise of middle-class labor produced only paltry amounts in the way of direct income supplement, which was what most of their clients probably wanted and needed most.

To tap the huge sums theoretically available in charitable coffers, working-class women had to contort their needs and behaviors to suit middle-class prejudices. The best way to do this was to hide behind the ultimate natural dependent, the child. All national cultures in this period worried about the fate of poor children, each in its distinctive way. Paternalist Russia accepted unwanted children at urban foundling hospitals and distributed them to wet nurses in the country (where most of them died). Republican France, anxious about its birth rate, rewarded large families and warred against child mortality. Catholic Italy, which was concerned with sexual purity, offered dowries for poor girls and provided beds to ensure gender segregation in overcrowded homes. Victorian England held the parents responsible but still admitted children to workhouses and pauper schools.

Working-class families naturally partook of these national peculiarities, but everywhere material considerations remained paramount for them. They were most in need when burdened with small children; charitable aid was widely available for small children, albeit in odd forms, and so recipients worked themselves into the positions desired by donors. Three of the essays below deal specifically with such negotiations: Rachel Fuchs discusses the resources available to Parisian women in childbirth; Ellen Ross scrutinizes the charitable provision of meals to children in London; and Bruce Bellingham shows how poor New Yorkers accepted charitable fostering to secure maintenance and job training for their adolescent children. In all these cases, resources offered by charitable authorities to protect children from their families were accepted by parents largely as supplements to family income.

Women, like men, would enter institutions only as a last resort. This preference had little or nothing to do with pride or independence, and much to do with practicality. Just as for men institutionalization meant an end to employment and other earning opportunities, it severed women from their safety nets in home and neighborhood. But as two of the essays below show, even the most forbiddingly deterrent institutions could be put to practical use. The workhouse could serve as a refuge from bill collectors or abusive husbands. Children could be deposited so their mothers could go out to work, simultaneously reducing expenses and augmenting income until the family budget had been balanced.[80] Lynn Lees shows how a policy of institutionalization consciously designed by London poor law authorities to break up pauper families was manipulated by the poor in the short term to keep families together in the long term. Catharina Lis and Hugo Soly deal with an even more extreme case of the use of theoretically disciplinary institutions—houses of correction—for last-ditch family maintenance in early nineteenth-century Antwerp. Although authorities frowned on these temporary usages, conceiving their own role as protective and rehabilitative at best, deterrent at worst, nevertheless (as Bellingham also shows) resourceful parents could get a good deal of what they needed by thus manipulating institutions.[81]

The relief poor families most needed—a straightforward income supplement—was only rarely available. When it was, in the form of unconditional outdoor doles, it was taken up readily. Other forms of relief were subject to negotiation between donors and recipients. Aid that interfered with survival strategies was shunned. When aid was offered in peculiar but still useful forms, recipients did their best to conform to the donors' expectations. This ritual conformity began with the theatrical assumption of "deserving" traits and could go as far as the temporary surrender of children or the acceptance of incarceration. But the meeting of minds was usually superficial and temporary. The gap between the motives and the uses of charity could be bridged, but it was rarely closed.

Toward Welfare

Some progress was made, however, in closing the gap toward the end of the nineteenth and in the early years of the twentieth centuries. Changes took place on both sides. The working-class economy gradually began to approximate middle-class norms. Whether in cultural emulation of bourgeois norms or as yet another family survival strategy, working-class fertility dropped everywhere after 1870, precipitously in most places after 1900.[82]

Especially after the great price deflation at the end of the nineteenth century, the real value of male wages crept upward, and real income improved as a result of industrial expansion and decasualization. Furthermore, whether or not family income was increasing to compensate, fewer women were working for pay in or out of the home.[83]

Now, indeed, work not only consumed a man's time but might also provide a source of pride and identity. It was at least possible to expect to support a family on the proceeds of work alone without having to scavenge and supplicate. This did not mean that working-class men accepted their work as they found it; on the contrary, they were now better able to seek improvement through the workplace. This new sense of purpose expressed itself most clearly in strikes, unionization, and other direct efforts to secure higher wages. But it also made possible for the first time a self-assertive (rather than deferential or deceptive) relationship to the state. Having proved his moral strength as a toiler and an earner, the male worker could—through trade unions and working-class political organizations—claim from the state an acknowledgment that occasional lapses did not necessarily stem from moral weakness. Even before World War I, most Western nations had begun to move toward unemployment insurance and pension schemes to cover male workers unable to work through no fault of their own. For their part, whatever the actual facts of the case (whether more men actually *were* able to maintain their families), states were probably more amenable to the welfare claims of men who at least attempted to establish their family maintenance bona fides.[84]

Almost certainly, those men who constructed a new work-centered identity with its own independent welfare institutions, now construed as mutual aid, became more hostile to old-fashioned charity. Their former instrumentalism yielded to a haughty disdain. Having been admitted to the ranks of the deserving, they were more ready to distance themselves from those who were still excluded—casuals, migrants, and the hard-core unemployed. States that extended workers' rights in this period often at the same time repressed and institutionalized the nonworking, and workers collaborated in this process, sometimes to their own detriment.[85] When working-class parties won local political control, for instance, they were not necessarily better able to help the unemployed than were bourgeois parties.[86]

Work-centered men also grew more distant from the struggles of women to keep up family income. Considerations of pride aside, full-time workers increasingly lost touch with the world outside the workplace. Charles Booth, surveying the London poor in the 1890s, noted the growing reluctance of men to interact with charity workers: "[I]f the man answered to the knock, he will very likely say, 'ah you're from the church; you want to see the missus' and will then clear out."[87] Women had become "the family's public representative." Not only did men collaborate less in the survival strategies of the urban family, but their insistence on greater self-reliance might actually impair those strategies. The single-earner family, with all its vulnerabilities, was becoming an article of faith.[88] Women were pressured to cut back on their outside earning and to focus instead on domestic labor. Children were excluded from the workplace by child labor laws and compulsory education. The ideal of man as earner and woman as spender was in many places institutionalized in an "internal wage" system, whereby the male earner handed over his pay packet to his wife, who was thereafter solely responsible for the family budget, including her husband's pocket money and even his trade-union dues. This division of labor gave women greater power over the family income and greater opportunities for the organization of saving but fewer opportunities to add to family income.[89]

As alternative survival strategies dropped away, charitable assistance probably became more important to the family budget. This put intense pressure on existing charitable resources, resulting in a "charity bust" in many Western cities in the 1890s and a subsequent relaxation of restrictions on the disbursement of aid. Again, changes occurred on both sides. Both private and public agencies at the turn of the century came better to recognize the real need of working-class families for assistance, while at the same time they could portray their new liberality as a just reward for working-class women's greater commitment to conventional domesticity. Charities were more likely now to start from the assumption that women *wanted* to meet their domestic responsibilities, that their difficulties arose as much from temporary circumstance as from immorality, and therefore that charity might play a constructive role in helping them toward the consensual end. Instead of "aiding" natural dependents by separating them from their parents, charities were readier to help keep families together, even if this meant more liberal outdoor relief in the form of fuel allocations, grocery orders, even cash. The proportion of American charities dispensing material aid climbed from one-half to two-thirds in the course of the 1890s.[90]

As overt moralizing gave way to sympathy, the friendly visitor saw herself not as a missionary but as a neighbor, and this metaphor was literalized in the settlement movement. Of course, settlement workers were a superior kind of neighbor. In place of the overtly moralizing tract or lecture, they dispensed professional services and scientific expertise to help their clients make the final leap into bourgeois domesticity. The new professionalism manifested itself not only in the settlement movement but throughout the friendly visiting world, metamorphosing into the modern social work profession. In their early phases, settlement and social work were peculiarly metropolitan phenomena. The great cities had not only the greatest social problems—the vast urban sinks, submerged by overcrowding and casualization—but also the richest supply both of female visitors and of male professionals and civil servants, who served as role models. In Chicago and New York, nurses visited the homes of the poor with cut-price medicines; "baby tents," "Pasteur Stations," or "milk depots" were erected in areas with high child mortality to provide counseling and uncontaminated milk, and playgroups and social centers were organized for the idle young.[91] Elsewhere, these professional services were drawn within the ambit of local and national government. In France, the maternal societies, crèches, kindergartens, and playgroups of midcentury charity were municipalized by republican administrations and converted into universal public services.[92] Even the deterrent workhouse of the English city could be renamed "poor law institution" and turned over to more specialized, social-work functions such as outpatient infirmary care.[93] Again, metropolitan—particularly capital city—experiments served as models for the provinces and for legislators' attempts to formulate national policies.

Settlement workers and social-work professionals prided themselves on their close, intimate, "neighborly" understanding of their clients, and they could now agree that scientific charity might be of positive use to the poor.[94] But were the uses of charity hypothesized by the donors the same as those perceived by the recipients? Here there are grounds for skepticism. If donors no longer labored to ensure that their gift carried a stigma, they considered it all the more important that it carry the positive message they wished to convey, and this might still be quite different from the message recipients wanted to hear. As Michael Katz's case study in Chapter 8 indicates clearly, the theatrical element in the charity business had by no means been reduced by the new assumption of a common cause between donor and recipient.[95]

On the most basic level, the donor's fundamental aim—recasting the working-class family in a middle-class mold—could still conflict directly with the recipient's fundamental aim of income augmentation. The familist bias of pre–World War I welfare severely disrupted women's survival strategies. The authorities insisted on withdrawing women and children from the work force but could not guarantee benefits that would compensate for the loss of wages. Well before World War I, the London School Board was reducing its kindergarten facilities, and municipal authorities in France were closing crèches so as to keep women at home, though cash incentives in the form of family allowances were largely a postwar phenomenon.[96] The milk depot, deemed to encourage bottle-feeding and thus surrogate care, was superseded in London and Manchester by health-visitor programs preaching maternalism and domesticity, a more comprehensive approach to the problem of child mortality but one that deliberately narrowed women's earning opportunities.[97] And although compulsory education for older children was welcomed by many parents on social grounds, others remained uneasy about both the loss of income and the scope for intra-familial meddling it entailed.[98]

Professionalization gave social workers a new authority—both among themselves and in the eyes of the state—which could as easily translate into arrogance and *dirigisme* as into genuine sympathy and understanding. The "scientific" case notes of social workers in Chicago read to one observer as "little more than a systematic listing of middle case platitudes about the 'vices' of the poor."[99] Social workers also had a wide range of powers with which to act upon their diagnoses. Charity, at least, had been a purely voluntary engagement. But the state was now giving social workers the power to compel clients to conform. Though the prevailing ideology accepted most working-class families as deserving of sympathetic treatment, it also consigned undeserving deviants to harsh courses of treatment in labor camps, prisons, hospitals, and asylums.[100]

Even when assistance was not actually damaging, it could be alienating or annoying. Ethnic immigrants, who had always been more self-reliant than the native poor, now found themselves subject to cultural bombardment aimed at assimilating them into the dominant culture. Gone was the simple playacting required to extract cash from a friendly visitor; coping with the settlement worker meant a full-scale confrontation between cultures, for the settlement worker wanted not only to relieve the poor but to give them an entirely new set of values. Herbert Gans documented such a confrontation between caretakers and clients in Boston's Italian West End as late as the 1950s. The caretakers believed that education, youth clubs, community centers, and other neighborhood activities were designed to break up existing neighborhood networks based on gangs and extended families and to orient the Italians toward the outside world of career, status, and consumption. The clients, however, wanted to use the facilities offered to reinforce existing networks, which to the caretakers was no use at all. The difference could be resolved only by razing the West End neighborhood and dispersing its inhabitants.[101]

Elsewhere, these persistent and deep-rooted differences over the uses of welfare would be settled more peacefully with the emergence of the notion of entitlement, of welfare not as a boon but as a right. We cannot settle here the complicated question of the origins of the modern welfare state. Undoubtedly, both donors and recipients played their roles. The professionalization of giving led inevitably to more bureaucratic and less personalized mechanisms. More powerful working-class political organizations were able to press for more benefits with less interference. Those who still felt the stigma of dependence could view tax-based schemes as self-help or even as benefits from a kind of national mutual aid society; those who had never feared a stigma simply called it justice. Other interests hopped on the bandwagon, and redistribution of income by the state became an accepted way of settling or sublimating dangerous political conflicts.

But for whatever reasons, automatic entitlement to cash assistance on the basis of some objective criterion such as age, income, or number of dependents gradually replaced the testing and personalized (that is, screened) administration of benefits characteristic of the early welfare state. Entitlement drew adult and able-bodied males into the welfare system en masse and reduced the gender differentiation that had for so long dogged charity and welfare alike. This gradual withdrawal of the stigma culminated in the institution of universal programs that added middle-class clients to the welfare rolls and in so doing consolidated their political base. The donors became recipients, and the gap between them closed accordingly.

Or did it? Over the last decade, in both Europe and America, this gap has begun to reopen, as middle-class taxpayers have proved unwilling to pay into redistributive schemes and have even uncoupled themselves from some universal programs from which they benefited the most. Charitable giving is back in vogue, and with it some of the nineteenth-century vocabulary, for the movement from welfare to charity must entail both a separation of donors from recipients and a reassertion of the values and morals of the former. This might be a good moment to remind ourselves—as the essays that follow do—that the aims of charity are not the same as its uses.

Notes

1. Because early modern social history has not been so dominated by the study of labor, it has found more room for charity. See, e.g., Brian S. Pullan, *Rich and Poor in Renaissance Venice* (Cambridge, Mass.: Harvard University Press, 1971); Paul Slack, "Poverty and Politics in Salisbury, 1557–1666," in Peter Clark and Paul Slack, eds., *Crisis and Order in English Towns, 1500–1700* (London: Routledge & Kegan Paul, 1972), 164–203; Natalie Zemon Davis, *Society and Culture in Early Modern France* (Stanford: Stanford University Press, 1975); Cissie C. Fairchilds, *Poverty and Charity in Aix-en-Provence, 1670–1789* (Baltimore: Johns Hopkins University Press, 1976); Colin Jones, *Charity and Bienfaisance: The Treatment of the Poor in the Montpellier Region, 1740–1815* (Cambridge: Cambridge University Press, 1982); Kathryn Norberg, *Rich and Poor in Grenoble, 1600–1814* (Berkeley: University of California Press, 1985).

2. Stuart Woolf, *The Poor in Western Europe in the Eighteenth and Nineteenth Centuries* (London: Methuen, 1986), 5–6, 11–13.

3. A satisfying account of these rural support systems and their breakdown from the end of the eighteenth century is given by K. D. M. Snell, *Annals of the Labouring Poor: Social Change and Agrarian England, 1660–1900* (Cambridge: Cambridge University Press, 1985).

4. See, e.g., ibid.; Woolf, *Poor in Western Europe*; and Olwen H. Hufton, *The Poor of Eighteenth-Century France, 1680–1789* (Oxford: Clarendon Press, 1974). In England, assistance from social superiors (in the form of legal poor relief) was most important because the poor were more mobile and less able to depend upon kin.

5. Louise A. Tilly and Joan W. Scott, *Women, Work, and Family* (New York: Holt, Rinehart and Winston, 1978), 104–6, 116–23; Michael Anderson, *Family Structure in Nineteenth Century Lancashire* (Cambridge: Cambridge University Press, 1971), 137–38.

6. For an interesting general analysis of poverty which emphasizes this "refuge in a subsistence economy" and the dire consequences that result when refuge is no longer available, see Kenneth H. Parsons, "Poverty as an Issue in Development Policy: A Comparison of United States and Underdeveloped Countries," *Land Economics* 45 (1969), 25–65, a reference I owe to Michael Katz.

7. Alexander Keyssar, *Out of Work: The First Century of Unemployment in Massachusetts* (Cambridge: Cambridge University Press, 1986), 23–24.

8. Woolf, *Poor in Western Europe*, 69–70.

9. Reginald E. Zelnik, *Labor and Society in Tsarist Russia* (Stanford: Stanford University Press, 1971), 20–28.

10. Ibid., 49; Lynn Lees, "Metropolitan Types," in H. J. Dyos and Michael Wolff, eds., *The Victorian City: Images and Realities* (London: Routledge & Kegan Paul, 1973), 415–16.

11. Christine Stansell, *City of Women: Sex and Class in New York, 1789–1869* (New York: Knopf, 1986), 44. By 1880, over three-quarters of the populations of San

Francisco, St. Louis, New York, Cleveland, Detroit, Milwaukee, and Chicago were immigrants or the children of immigrants.

12. See Ewa Morawska, *For Bread with Butter: The Life-Worlds of East Central Europeans in Johnstown, Pennsylvania, 1890–1940* (Cambridge: Cambridge University Press, 1985), esp. ch. 1 on the combination of "push" and "pull" forces behind migration.

13. H. J. Dyos, "The Victorian Slum," in David Cannadine and David Reeder, eds., *Exploring the Urban Past: Essays in Urban History by H. J. Dyos* (Cambridge: Cambridge University Press, 1982), 23–25; Eric E. Lampard, "The Urbanizing World," in Dyos and Wolff, eds., *Victorian City*, 4–5, 8, 32.

14. Thus it is not really pertinent, from the social-historical point of view, to compare the eighteenth-century and nineteenth-century urbanite, as has been the practice of most students of proletarianization: e.g., Gareth Stedman Jones, "Working-Class Culture and Working-Class Politics in London, 1870–1900," *Journal of Social History* 7 (1974), 463–65; Catharina Lis and Hugo Soly, *Poverty and Capitalism in Pre-Industrial Europe* (Hassocks, England: Harvester Press, 1979), 171–94. For a treatment that emphasizes rural proletarianization, see Charles Tilly, "Demographic Origins of the European Proletariat," in David Levine, ed., *Proletarianization and Family History* (Orlando: Academic Press, 1984), 1–85.

15. Lis and Soly, *Poverty and Capitalism*, 166–67.

16. Again, standard-of-living calculations often compare preindustrial urbanites with their industrial-era counterparts, which is comparing different populations.

17. In many places in the late eighteenth century, governments tried to replace the old safety nets before the desirability of poor relief was completely rethought in the nineteenth century. Obvious illustrations are the liberal relief schedules in Napoleonic-era Britain and the peaks of government intervention in immediate prerevolutionary France. Catharina Lis, *Social Change and the Labouring Poor: Antwerp, 1770–1860* (New Haven: Yale University Press, 1986), 12–16, describes an interesting urban experiment in Antwerp, where the New Poor Law Administration attempted to substitute for guild relief funds. And, of course, some premodern mutual aid institutions were able to adapt to urbanization and industrialization; for instance, the French confraternities that reemerged as mutual aid societies in the early nineteenth century discussed in William H. Sewell, Jr., *Work and Revolution in France: The Language of Labor from the Old Regime to 1848* (Cambridge: Cambridge University Press, 1980), ch. 8.

18. Tilly and Scott, *Women, Work, and Family*, 129–32, surveying the textile towns of Stockport, Roubaix, and Preston; for Roubaix, see also Louise A. Tilly, "Individual Lives and Family Strategies in the French Proletariat," *Journal of Family History* 4 (1979), 137–52; for Preston, see also Anderson, *Family Structure*; for Manchester, New Hampshire, Tamara K. Hareven, *Family Time and Industrial Time: The Relationship between the Family and Work in a New England Industrial Community* (Cambridge: Cambridge University Press, 1982). Elizabeth A. M. Roberts, " 'Women's Strategies', 1890–1940," in Jane Lewis, ed.,

Labour and Love: Women's Experience of Home and Family, 1850–1940 (Oxford: Basil Blackwell, 1986), 227, comparing Preston to Barrow and Lancaster, argues that paid women's work in all kinds of cities has generally been underestimated. In *A Woman's Place: An Oral History of Working-Class Women, 1890–1940* (Oxford: Basil Blackwell, 1984), 164–68, Roberts also discusses the ambiguous correlations between women in paid employment and child mortality rates.

19. See the studies of Bochum in David F. Crew, *Town in the Ruhr: A Social History of Bochum, 1860–1914* (New York: Columbia University Press, 1979), esp. 48–55, and Antwerp in Lis, *Social Change*, esp. 32–38. Even in textile towns like Roubaix, most of the women at work were single. See Tilly and Scott, *Women, Work, and Family*, 87.

20. J. A. Banks, "The Contagion of Numbers," in Dyos and Wolff, eds., *Victorian City*, 105–22.

21. The ninth was Tokyo-Yokohama. Of the twenty-eight cities with over half a million population, twenty were European and American, five Asian, two South American, and one Australian (Lampard, "Urbanizing World," 9).

22. Gareth Stedman Jones, *Outcast London: A Study in the Relationship between Classes in Victorian Society* (Oxford: Clarendon Press, 1971), 19–36, 56, 64. See also the comparison of London and Paris in Lees, "Metropolitan Types," 413–28.

23. See, e.g., Oscar Handlin, *Boston's Immigrants, 1790–1865* (Cambridge, Mass.: Harvard University Press, 1941) and *The Uprooted* (Boston: Little, 1953), on the "loneliness," "helplessness," and "disorganization" of the American urban slum; for Paris, Louis Chevalier, *Labouring Classes and Dangerous Classes in Paris during the First Half of the Nineteenth Century* (London: Routledge & Kegan Paul, 1973; first published in French in 1958), 440, on "the brutalities of the street, the workshop and the barricade." The "culture of poverty" argument was developed for Third World slums in the work of Oscar Lewis.

24. Quoted by Chevalier, *Labouring Classes*, 269.

25. This view persists even in some recent studies of the working-class economy, such as Paul Johnson, *Saving and Spending: The Working-Class Economy in Britain, 1870–1939* (Oxford: Clarendon Press, 1985), or Herbert G. Gutman and Donald H. Bell, eds., *The New England Working Class and the New Labour History* (Urbana: University of Illinois Press, 1987), which devote perhaps disproportionate attention to men's resources and institutions. Stedman Jones, "Working-Class Culture," also infers that the failure of working-class men to develop these characteristic institutions is evidence of a defeated and demoralized community.

26. See the discussion in Bryan Roberts, *Cities of Peasants: The Political Economy of Urbanization in the Third World* (London: Edward Arnold, 1978), 139–53, and, for a particularly interesting case study, Larissa Adler Lomnitz, *Networks and Marginality: Life in a Mexican Shantytown* (New York: Academic Press, 1977). Just as anthropologists discarded the culture of poverty framework, however, sociologists picked it up again in their analyses of the American "underclass" of the 1980s. See, e.g., Erol R. Ricketts and Isabel Sawhill, "Defining and Mea-

suring the Underclass," *Journal of Policy Analysis and Management* 7 (1987), 316–25.

27. For a stimulating discussion of the peculiar character of metropolitan labor, see Eric Hobsbawm, "Labour in the Great City," *New Left Review* 166 (November–December 1987), 39–51.

28. Robert Eugene Johnson, *Peasant and Proletarian: The Working Class of Moscow in the Late Nineteenth Century* (Leicester: Leicester University Press, 1979), 93–94.

29. Trade unions and friendly societies frequently began life in the back rooms of pubs and taverns. Lomnitz, *Networks and Marginality*, 176–78, discusses drinking networks in the modern shantytown, noting, however, that the stronger the network the greater the drain on individual resources.

30. The instability—both geographical and psychological—engendered by male unemployment in this period is sensitively discussed in Keyssar, *Out of Work*, chs. 5 and 6.

31. Anderson, *Family Structure*, 101–4. Judith E. Smith, "The Transformation of Family and Community Culture in Immigrant Neighborhoods, 1900–1940," in Gutman and Bell, eds., *New England Working Class*, esp. 167–73, suggests that because of tight job networking and exclusion from other working-class organizations (such as trade unions and benefit societies) male as well as female immigrants formed strong community networks.

32. Quoted by Anderson, *Family Structure*, 104. This high persistence rate was characteristic of metropolitan areas, with greater diversity of employment and better transport, but not of smaller industrial cities. See Keyssar, *Out of Work*, 123–30.

33. Ellen Ross, "Survival Networks: Women's Neighborhood Sharing in London before World War I," *History Workshop Journal* 15 (Spring 1983), 9, 27; Anderson, *Family Structure*, 56–58, 104. Lynn Hollen Lees, *Exiles of Erin: Irish Migrants in Victorian London* (Manchester: Manchester University Press, 1979), 153–54, found not only that the London Irish married within their community, but that they tended to marry into families from their regions of origin.

34. Lees, "Metropolitan Types," 417, and *Exiles of Erin*, 84. Lis, *Social Change*, 78–79, compares overcrowding in Brussels, Berlin, London, Paris, and Amsterdam.

35. Stansell, *City of Women*, 46–47; Kenneth T. Jackson, "The Capital of Capitalism: The New York Metropolitan Region, 1890–1940," in Anthony Sutcliffe ed., *Metropolis, 1890–1940* (London: Mansell, 1984), 324–26.

36. For the portrait of the urban slum which follows, I am indebted to Stansell, *City of Women*, and Ross, "Survival Networks."

37. Lees, *Exiles of Erin*, 84. I have exaggerated gender segregation here, for of course women drank in pubs and men made use of hospitals and almshouses; still, primary use was made by the sexes as I have divided them. Even in immigrant communities, men and women gravitated to separate institutions (e.g., mutual aid societies for the men, churches for the women).

38. Roberts, "'Women's Strategies,'" 227, 231–38.

39. Tilly and Scott, *Women, Work, and Family*, 185.

40. Anderson, *Family Structure*, 56; Woolf, *Poor in Western Europe*, 171–72; Roberts, *Woman's Place*, 177–78. Ross, "Survival Networks," 9, found that women in one sampled tenement were twice as likely to have kin in the same building as men.

41. This may in part be because widows were more useful as domestic laborers. See Lis, *Social Change*, 152–53; Anderson, *Family Structure*, 139, 143.

42. James H. Treble, *Urban Poverty in Britain, 1830–1914* (London: Batsford Academic, 1979), 96, makes the point that desertion rates could be very high: 20 percent of the 2,240 new female applicants for parochial aid in Glasgow in 1905–6 cited desertion as a cause.

43. Stansell, *City of Women*, 55–62; Ross, "Survival Networks"; Keyssar, *Out of Work*, 164–65; Roberts, *Woman's Place*, 187–94.

44. Virginia Yans-McLaughlin, *Family and Community: Italian Immigrants in Buffalo, 1880–1930* (Ithaca: Cornell University Press, 1977), 61, 64–66, on the importance of godparenthood (*comparraggio*) in the Italian community of Buffalo. See also Lomnitz, *Networks and Reciprocity*, 164–72, for the varieties of *compadrazgo* in the modern Mexican shantytown.

45. Herbert G. Gutman, *Work, Culture, and Society in Industrializing America* (Oxford: Oxford University Press, 1977), 77. For lower but still considerable proportions, see Hareven, *Family Time*, 160; Yans-McLaughlin, *Family and Community*, 64–66. Roberts, *Woman's Place*, 141, finds low rates of boarding in English provincial towns where the housing stock was very cramped.

46. For this and what follows, I am indebted to the survey in Woolf, *Poor in Western Europe*, ch. 1.

47. Henry Pelling, "The Working Class and the Origins of the Welfare State," in *Popular Politics and Society in Late Victorian Britain* (London: Macmillan, 1968), 1–18.

48. Trygve R. Tholfsen, "The Transition to Democracy in Victorian England," *International Review of Social History* 6 (1961), 226–48.

49. Michael E. Rose, ed., *The Poor and the City: The English Poor Law in its Urban Context, 1834–1914* (Leicester: Leicester University Press, 1983), 3. For an early acknowledgment of government's role in conveying the stigma—far more effectively than private charity ever could or did—see Edwin Cannan, "The Stigma of Pauperism," *Economic Review* 5 (1895), 380–91.

50. Lis, *Social Change*, 16; Woolf, *Poor in Western Europe*, 161.

51. Peter Bailey, "'Will the Real Bill Banks Please Stand Up?': Towards a Role Analysis of Mid-Victorian Working-Class Respectability," *Journal of Social History* 12 (1978–9), 336–53.

52. This element of theater has had an infinite capacity to confuse historians, who invariably assert that the poor hated relief and sought it only in desperation. All we can say for certain is that, since relief was available only to the desperate, all applicants appeared desperate. See, e.g., Treble, *Urban Poverty*, 143–44; Chevalier, *Labouring Classes*, 351–52; Johnson, *Saving and Spending*, 81–83; Anderson, *Family Structure*, 137–38; Hareven, *Family Time*, 109, 360.

53. Ruth Richardson, *Death, Dissection and the Destitute* (London: Routledge,

1987), 266–80. Chevalier, *Labouring Classes*, 351–52, sees no inconsistency between the evidence he cites from Balzac's *Cousin Pons* and Sue's *Les Mystères de Paris*, the one testifying to the poor's obstinacy and pride, the other to their horror of the anatomists.

54. Zelnik, *Labor and Society*, 180–82.

55. Kathleen D. McCarthy, *Noblesse Oblige: Charity and Cultural Philanthropy in Chicago, 1849–1929* (Chicago: University of Chicago Press, 1982), 28–29.

56. Roy Lubove, *The Professional Altruist: The Emergence of Social Work as a Career, 1880–1930* (Cambridge, Mass.: Harvard University Press, 1965), 17. It is little wonder that ethnic immigrants organized their own philanthropy. See, e.g., Nancy L. Green's chapter in this volume.

57. Frank K. Prochaska, *Women and Philanthropy in Nineteenth-Century England* (Oxford: Clarendon Press, 1980), 100, on the West Street Chapel Benevolent Society in Seven Dials; Raymond A. Mohl, *Poverty in New York, 1783–1825* (New York: Oxford University Press, 1971), 140–42, on the New York Assistance Society.

58. Yans-McLaughlin, *Family and Community*, 64, 151–52. Historians have told us little about benefit societies; for instance, Yans-McLaughlin, ibid., 130–31, devotes only a single paragraph to the thirty-two benefit societies in Buffalo's Little Italy, though acknowledging that they were "Little Italy's most successful organizations." In contrast, trade unions and political organizations, because better documented, warrant an entire chapter. For unusually full discussion of benefit societies see Sewell, *Work and Revolution*, ch. 8, and Gary Mormino and George Pozzetta, *The Immigrant World of Ybor City: Italians and their Latin Neighbors in Tampa, 1885–1985* (Urbana: University of Illinois Press, 1985), ch. 6.

59. Quoted by Chevalier, *Labouring Classes*, 151–52.

60. Lis, *Social Change*, 113.

61. Woolf, *Poor in Western Europe*, 163–64.

62. Chevalier, *Labouring Classes*, 354–55; Mohl, *Poverty in New York*, 20; Michael B. Katz, *Poverty and Policy in American History* (New York: Academic Press, 1983), 190.

63. Richard Kennedy, *Charity Warfare: The Charity Organization Society in Colonial Melbourne* (Melbourne: Hyland House, 1985), 215.

64. H. V. Toynbee, "A Winter's Experiment," *Macmillan's Magazine* 69 (1893–94), 54–58.

65. Keyssar, *Out of Work*, 134–35.

66. Raphael Samuel, "Comers and Goers," in Dyos and Wolff, eds., *Victorian City*, 129, 141–43; José Harris, *Unemployment and Politics: A Study in English Social Policy, 1886–1914* (Oxford: Clarendon Press, 1972), 126, 373, 376. See Mohl, *Poverty in New York*, 86–99, on New York's institutional offerings.

67. M. A. Crowther, *The Workhouse System, 1834–1929* (London, 1981), 229–31.

68. Treble, *Urban Poverty*, 94.

69. Crowther, *Workhouse System*, 223–25, citing fears of separation and a preference for outdoor relief: it was clearly the workhouse that was shunned, not relief per se. Treble, *Urban Poverty*, 105–6, does not make this distinction.

70. Chevalier, *Labouring Classes*, 351–52.

71. See, e.g., Lis, *Social Change*, 156–57. Peter Townsend, "The Effects of Family Structure on the Likelihood of Admission to an Institution in Old Age," in Ethel Shanas and Gordon Streib, eds., *Social Structure and the Family: Generational Relationships* (Englewood Cliffs, N.J.: Prentice-Hall, 1965), shows that old people in institutions today are also disproportionately unmarried, childless, or widowed.

72. Prochaska, *Women and Philanthropy*, 29, found that only 10 to 15 percent of charitable funds were provided by women at the beginning of the century and perhaps over half by the end. See also, for early nineteenth-century England, Leonore Davidoff and Catherine Hall, *Family Fortunes: Men and Women of the English Middle Class, 1780–1850* (London: Hutchinson, 1987), 429–36; for Chicago, McCarthy, *Noblesse Oblige*, 30; for Boston, Nathan I. Huggins, *Protestants against Poverty: Boston's Charities, 1870–1900* (Westport, Conn.: Greenwood, 1971), ch. 3; for Lille, in France's industrial Nord, Bonnie G. Smith, *Ladies of the Leisure Class: The Bourgeoises of Northern France in the Nineteenth Century* (Princeton: Princeton University Press, 1981), 137; for Melbourne, Kennedy, *Charity Warfare*, esp. ch. 4. In England and America, the feminization of giving can be attributed in part to married women's property acts. The process was slower in Germany.

73. Prochaska, *Woman and Philanthropy*, 21; Brian Harrison, "Philanthropy and the Victorians," in *Peaceable Kingdom: Stability and Change in Modern Britain* (Oxford: Clarendon Press, 1982), 217, 249, pointing out, however, that much of this charitable budget went to animals. The predominance of private over public expenditures on poor relief may, moreover, be a British peculiarity.

74. Pat Thane, "Women and the Poor Law in Victorian and Edwardian England," *History Workshop Journal* 6 (Autumn 1978), 29–36; Treble, *Urban Poverty*, 96–98; Karel Williams, *From Pauperism to Poverty* (London: Routledge & Kegan Paul, 1981), 102–4.

75. These amounted to over 10 percent of all households sampled. B. Seebohm Rowntree, *Poverty: A Study of Town Life* (London: Macmillan, 1901), 123–24.

76. There was, of course, much more to scientific charity than this: see, e.g., Stedman Jones, *Outcast London*, 257–70.

77. Prochaska, *Women and Philanthropy*, 105–6. In Melbourne, the Charity Organization Society acted as a central coordinating body and left visiting to the separate Ladies' Benevolent Society (Kennedy, *Charity Warfare*, chs. 3, 4).

78. On the London Charity Organization Society's failure to grasp the problem of unemployment, see Harris, *Unemployment and Politics*, 107–10; and for the uselessness of Boston's Associated Charities in the unemployment crisis of 1893–94, Huggins, *Protestants against Poverty*, 147–52; on the "charity bust" in Melbourne in 1892, Kennedy, *Charity Warfare*, ch. 5.

79. Stansell, *City of Women*, 72–73.

80. Crowther, *Workhouse System*, 228–29, found that three-quarters of the inmates of the Holborn workhouse in 1866–68 had resorted to it as a temporary expedient.

81. See also Julie V. Brown, "Peasant Survival Strategies in Late Imperial Russia: The Social Uses of the Mental Hospital," *Social Problems* 34 (1987), 311–29.

82. For an analysis of survival strategies that challenges the prevailing cultural interpretations in the British case, see David Levine, "Industrialization and the Proletarian Family in England," *Past and Present* 107 (May 1985), 168–203, esp. 188–200; also, for France, Tilly, "Individual Lives," 148–50. For a startling case of family limitation as a response to the transition from the family wage to the single-earner economy, see Karl Ittmann, "Family Economy and Family Limitation in Bradford, West Yorkshire, 1851–1881," *Journal of Social History*, forthcoming.

83. Tilly and Scott, *Women, Work, and Family*, 196–98.

84. Pat Thane, "The Working Class and State 'Welfare' in Britain, 1880–1914," *Historical Journal* 27 (1984), 877–900, shows how the individualism of family maintenance and the collectivism of mutual aid were combined both in private and public welfare schemes before World War I.

85. Stedman Jones, *Outcast London*, 300–307; Harris, *Unemployment and Politics*, 43–47; Keyssar, *Out of Work*, ch. 7.

86. See P. A. Ryan, " 'Poplarism,' 1894–1930," in Pat Thane, ed., *The Origins of British Social Policy* (London: Croom Helm, 1978), esp. 62–69, on the struggles of Labour politicians in the London Borough of Poplar during the unemployment crisis of 1903–5. Similarly, the strength of the Australian labor movement (with extensive self-help resources) retarded the development of welfare programs for the low-paid and unemployed.

87. Quoted by Stedman Jones, "Working-Class Culture," 472.

88. Wally Seccombe, "Patriarchy Stabilized: The Construction of the Male Breadwinner Norm in Nineteenth-Century Britain," *Social History* 11 (1986), 53–76, considers the ideological construction of the single-earner norm to be a "general trend" throughout western Europe, but consolidated first in mid-nineteenth-century Britain.

89. Tilly and Scott, *Women, Work, and Family*, 196–204, 208; Ellen Ross, "Labour and Love: Rediscovering London's Working-Class Mothers, 1870–1918," in Lewis, ed., *Labour and Love*, 74–88.

90. Lubove, *Professional Altruist*, 7–15; McCarthy, *Noblesse Oblige*, 130.

91. McCarthy, *Noblesse Oblige*, 129–35; Roy Lubove, *The Progressives and the Slums: Tenement House Reform in New York City, 1890–1917* (Pittsburgh: University of Pittsburgh Press, 1962), 188–95.

92. Smith, *Ladies of the Leisure Class*, 149–61.

93. Crowther, *Workhouse System*, 42–48.

94. This view has been endorsed by those historians who diagnose a "culture of poverty" and offer middle-class aid as its antidote. See, e.g., Lubove, *Progressives and the Slums*, 193; McCarthy, *Noblesse Oblige*, 135.

95. See also the case study of a woman's dealings with the Philadelphia Society for Organizing Charity in 1909, in Katz, *Poverty and Policy*, 18–56.

96. Jane Lewis, "The Working-Class Wife and Mother and State Intervention, 1870–1914," in Lewis, ed., *Labour and Love*, 110–14; Ross, Chapter 6 below; Smith, *Ladies of the Leisure Class*, 156–61.

97. Deborah Dwork, *War Is Good for Babies and Other Young Children: A History of the Infant and Child Welfare Movement in England, 1898–1918* (London: Tavistock Publications, 1987), chs. 4 and 5. Note also Dwork's comments, pp. 226–30, regarding her disagreement with Jane Lewis and others over the motives behind child welfare programs. But Dwork does not delve very deeply into the question of recipients' attitudes; see pp. 164–65.

98. Ross, Chapter 6 below, and "Labour and Love," 74–75, 88–90.

99. Kenneth L. Kusmer, "The Functions of Organized Charity in the Progressive Era: Chicago as a Case Study," *Journal of American History* 60 (1973–74), 668.

100. For England, see Harris, *Unemployment and Politics*, 43–47; Crowther, *Workhouse System*, 42–43; Stedman Jones, *Outcast London*, 300–306.

101. Herbert J. Gans, *The Urban Villagers: Group and Class in the Life of Italian-Americans* (New York: Free Press of Glencoe, 1962), 89–97, 129–31, 142–44, 148–54.

Catharina Lis and Hugo Soly

2. "Total Institutions" and the Survival Strategies of the Laboring Poor in Antwerp, 1770–1860

MANY STUDIES OF SOCIAL POLICY tend to describe the laboring poor as passive agents. Although authors generally admit that not all interventions by elite groups have been successful, they usually attribute these failures to the contradictory interests and goals of the elite groups that make the development of efficient control mechanisms impossible. Hardly any attention is paid to the responses of the people being controlled. Historians may indicate perfunctorily that resistance existed only to return their attention to the strategies of the ruling classes.

The purpose of this essay is to demonstrate that the functions of discipline-wielding institutions are not predetermined but can be transformed by the active involvement of the laboring poor. In particular, we will argue that the coercive measures instituted by the Antwerp bourgeoisie at the end of the *ancien régime* and during the first half of the nineteenth century were not wholly effective, at least in part because the laboring poor were able to incorporate these measures into their survival strategies. The workers added a new and, for the policy makers, unexpected dimension to these social interventions by subverting the instruments of labor regulation and social control into means toward their own ends, thereby trying to prevent or retard the process of impoverishment. The nature and direction of these new coercive measures became increasingly determined by initiatives from below, progressively serving purposes that substantially deviated from the original intentions of the elite groups. These transformations were part of a continually shifting dynamic between resistance and subordination whereby the laboring poor adjusted their survival strategies to the new forces and relations of production that were shaping their daily lives.

To understand the attitudes toward social control of the laboring poor during the century after 1750, it is necessary to describe briefly the processes and consequences of Antwerp's economic transformation. The second half of the eighteenth century was a time of industrial expansion. Some branches of the textile industry were crippled and others failed, but the production of mixed fabrics and cotton spinning thrived. By the end of the *ancien régime* Antwerp had become a manufacturing center of the first order. Although industrial expansion was accompanied by the proletarianization of many small craftsmen and the impoverishment of most wage laborers, the lower orders escaped utter destitution because, in most cases, not only men but women and children contributed to the income of the family. During the first half of the nineteenth century, however, pauperization occurred on a massive scale because of rapid deindustrialization and the creation of a labor market in which steady work was scarce. From the 1800s onward, commercial circles in Antwerp pursued a policy of industrial disinvestment and were thus responsible for the collapse of the town's flourishing textile industry. The metropolis turned into an international port, where manufacturing played only a minor role. The social costs of this structural shift were immense. The expansion of shipping and commerce did not compensate for the unemployment caused by the decay of the textile industry. As a result, the vast majority of the male population became dependent on casual labor opportunities and, lacking alternatives, competed fiercely for the same jobs. At the same time, the breakup of the textile industry rendered the labor of women, children, and the elderly largely redundant. Increasing pressure on the wages of able-bodied men was thus coupled with growing underemployment and even unemployment of other members of the household. These adverse effects of deindustrialization, moreover, were aggravated by the continuous flow of uprooted country dwellers into the city, swelling the ranks of Antwerp's proletariat and sending rents soaring. The cumulative effect of all these changes was that the proportion of the needy in the total population almost doubled in the years between 1770 and 1860, from 22 to 40 percent.[1]

Both the industrial expansion of the second half of the eighteenth century and the rapid growth of port-associated activities after 1800 spurred the Antwerp bourgeoisie to develop more efficient methods of social control. During both periods, the fundamental objective was to use public charity as an instrument to regulate the labor market, but whereas the eighteenth-century entrepreneurs directed their efforts at the mobilization of very young workers and the large-scale employment of women, in the nineteenth century their strategy was systematically to lower adult male wages. To realize those aims mere restriction of charity did not suffice.

Coercive measures were necessary. In this essay we will explore the question of how the laboring poor responded to the various interventions by local authorities and, in particular, we will examine their attitudes toward the institutions that were designed to embody the new imperatives of discipline.

Changing Levels of Intolerance

During the 1760s and 1770s urban entrepreneurs increasingly advocated an economic approach to poverty. The reasons are self-evident. The production of mixed cotton-linen fabrics had assumed enormous proportions in the Austrian Netherlands and invigorated the cotton mills, Antwerp's in particular, increasing the number of workers employed in this trade to four thousand in 1789. This increased demand for labor put upward pressure on wages in the spinning sector, which already accounted for a greater percentage of labor costs than any other phase in the cotton-linen manufacturing process. The new poor relief system, devised by François-Joseph Taintenier, a textile entrepreneur and an alderman in the town of Ath (Hainaut), was designed to meet these pressures. The new system provided for strict prohibition of begging, centralization of all existing relief funds into an *aumône générale*, registration of all people in need, and restricting support to the "truly indigent," whose allowances were not to exceed the subsistence level. Such a social policy was intended to drive all able-bodied poor, men as well as women and children, into the labor market and thus to reduce wages.[2]

Taintenier's program was introduced only in those Brabant and Flemish towns where the new social policy would serve entrepreneurs' interests, such as Kortrijk (1774), Bruges (1776), Ghent (1777), Antwerp (1779), and Lier (1787). The story of Antwerp shows the importance of the economic motives underlying the institution of this new social policy. Hardly two weeks after the creation of the New Poor Law Administration (Nieuwe Bestiering van de Armen), eighteen manufacturers of mixed fabrics petitioned the directors for some five hundred cotton spinners. Two years later, the almoners stipulated that all children eight years or older whose parents were on relief should learn a trade, under the threat of their parents' removal from the charity lists. In 1782, the municipal government went so far as to set up a spinning workshop that compelled unemployed paupers to work for the textile manufacturers.[3]

The evidence shows, however, that enforcement of the new social policy did not go smoothly. The extremely formal and restrictive criteria for relief provoked many protests. Since only 10 percent of the Antwerp population turned out to be eligible for routine help, even though the relieving officers admitted that in actuality twice as many were in need, such protests are not surprising.[4] Families who were turned down for public assistance maintained that anyone who lived in misery should be entitled to support and insisted that the new rules were arbitrary. Some did not hesitate to use verbal violence to underscore their points. The refusal of the New Poor Law Administration to support able-bodied people provoked the most resentment and anger. When the widow Wautier was struck off the paupers list because her oldest son had been unemployed for eight months, she cursed the overseer, calling him "a baiter, rogue, killer of the poor, ass, pest."[5] At the end of the *ancien régime*, such scenes were the order of the day, as indicated by the many sentences passed down for offending almoners.[6]

The severe restriction of allowances was another source of conflict, particularly when in 1781 the board of the New Poor Law Administration decided to cut them back even further. Henceforth, single persons had to make do with the equivalent of less than 2.5 kilograms of rye bread per day, and large families were to survive on about 4 kilograms.[7] The cotton spinner Petrus Peeters immediately demanded an increase of his allowance to the maximum 2.5 kilograms when his wife fell sick and he had to care for her and their small child. When the almoners refused his request, he went to visit one of the responsible men at home, threatening and cursing him, whereupon he was jailed for six weeks.[8] The complaints lodged against large numbers of "troublesome" and "aggressive" dole-drawers attest to the embitterment of the poor, who, no longer trying to induce sympathy, faced their overseers aggressively.[9]

The New Poor Law Administration was not indifferent to all the needy families it turned down. Some families received aid in kind: mixed loaves, clothes, and blankets. Bread was eagerly accepted, but other goods were often sold to buy food or liquor. As the criminal proceedings indicate, in such cases the poor law administration charged people with fraud. The testimonies show that most of the accused were unaware of any wrongdoing. Why could they not dispose of charitable contributions freely? Were they not entitled to extra cash? And was one a criminal just for wanting to drink a few pitchers of beer? The judges, however, subscribed to the almoners' view that, in selling the goods under false pretext, the accused had defrauded the poor law administration. Widow Anna De Clopper was sentenced to jail for three months for selling socks and linens the almoners had given her. In 1783 a more severe sentence was meted out to Johannes Claessens for committing a comparable "crime": he was condemned to forced labor in the town's workhouse until he had repaid the sum in question, which meant a sentence of five months' imprisonment.[10]

Neither could the poor bring the donated goods to the Berg van Barmhartigheid, the municipal pawnshop and sole outlet for pawns in the city. No doubt most ignored the prohibition, though the almoners left no measure untried to track down and subpoena offenders, an action that resulted in automatic detention: two weeks for Maria Catharina Fleger, a cotton spinner who brought her skirt to the pawnbroker; six weeks for Maria Barbara Vanopbergen, even though she could prove she earned too little to support herself and her young daughter; two months for nineteen-year-old Helena Okkaert, who had given a new shirt and a new apron in security.[11] But it was very difficult to track down such cases of fraud, and the almoners themselves admitted that these penalties had little effect.

The public pawnbroker was a thorn in the side of the merchant-entrepreneurs because the textile workers increasingly pledged raw materials and tools, intended for production, to meet their immediate needs. In the course of the 1770s this evil practice spread so quickly that manufacturers pressured the authorities to intervene. On July 29, 1779, one week before the establishment of the New Poor Law Administration, Charles of Lorraine, governor of the Austrian Netherlands, stipulated that the director of the Antwerp pawnshop was no longer allowed to accept bales of cotton, linen, and wool of less than fifty pounds or packs of silk under twenty-five pounds. The central government was forced to modify this ruling after strong protests from smaller merchants and artisans, who themselves frequently pledged raw materials, and in 1782 the minimum amount was reduced to six pounds.[12] For this reason, the campaign against embezzlement was foredoomed to failure. Two or three textile workers, for example, would combine their individual wares and hand them to a middleman, who would bring their goods to the public pawnshop for a small cut. The Berg van Barmhartigheid thus continued to play an important role in the survival strategies of the laboring poor. It is not possible to determine exactly how many of the proletariat turned to this institution, but figures on the total value of the securities suggest that their number must have been considerable, increasing dramatically during the last quarter of the eighteenth century.[13]

The law against begging was one of the cornerstones of the new social policy. The Antwerp magistracy issued a proclamation on August 9, 1779, ruling that beggars were to be placed under arrest in the municipal workhouse on water and bread for eight days, six weeks in cases of recidivism, and at least one month imprisonment in the Vilvoorde provincial house of correction for each subsequent transgression.[14] This proclamation was no empty gesture. Between 1780 and 1794 no less than 115 people—among them 80 textile workers—were found guilty of begging, compared to only six between 1765 and 1779.[15]

Despite these measures, the authorities and the almoners were not able to win the struggle against begging, as can be deduced from testimonies by contemporaries. This is hardly surprising since the unemployed who were no longer eligible for public support had no alternative but to beg. Moreover, they did not understand why traditional remedies were suddenly deemed criminal offenses. "The almoners consider me employable, I therefore do not receive any allowance," declared widower Adriaen Wuyts, "but at seventy-seven I'm only able to get odd jobs that earn me no money whatsoever, so I'm forced to ask for alms."[16] For many of the assisted poor the situation was not substantially different. The Blaevier family, for example, received six *stuivers* in food stamps from the poor law administration every week. The husband, crippled in the right arm, was unable to work, and the wife earned three *stuivers* a day in cotton spinning. How could they and their young child possibly survive without begging, they asked, when the price of a kilo of rye bread fluctuated between 1.3 and 1.9 *stuivers*?[17] Some members of the middling class, with no immediate interest in the regulation of the labor market, appeared to be sensitive to such appeals. Although Bishop Jacob Wellens subscribed to the new social policy in a pastoral letter, his congregants continued to give charity to people on an individual basis. Available evidence shows that the well-to-do rarely turned beggars over to the police and that when they did feel threatened, the beggars were always strangers, never neighbors.[18] Furthermore, the prohibition on begging was only in force within the city of Antwerp. As a consequence, many of the destitute went to beg in the surrounding hamlets and villages, especially on Sunday, when urban dwellers visited the country inns, where liquor was much cheaper than in the city.[19]

Central government strongly supported the many efforts of the Antwerp administration and city councils in Brabant and Flanders to eradicate begging, not so much to assist regulation of the labor market as because government considered the growing numbers of beggars and tramps a threat to public order. In 1766 representatives of central government had tried to persuade the Estates of Brabant to establish a house of correction to discipline incorrigible tramps, but the cities of Antwerp, Brussels, and Leuven had balked at the high financial burden.[20] Again, in the 1770s, Charles of Lorraine urged the creation of such an institution. He pointed out that the Estates of Flanders had accepted their president's proposal to build a provincial house of correction (*tuchthuis*) and that, if Brabant did not follow their example, it would be flooded with beggars and tramps from Flanders. The Estates of Brabant made objections but eventually agreed to erect a house of correction at Vilvoorde, near Brussels, at their own expense. The delegates of Antwerp laid down two preconditions, however: the institution was not to manufacture any goods that would compete with private entrepreneurs, and it should accept not only criminals but also "unruly and debauched persons who have committed no breach of law."[21] The underlying motive of the first requirement seems clear enough, but how are we to interpret the second? The question calls for an overview of the population imprisoned at Vilvoorde.

From its opening in February 1779 until the end of December 1784, a total of 623 people were detained in the provincial house of correction. Although a minority of the delinquents (107 internees or 17.2 percent) was convicted either by the Court of Brabant, the high bailiff of the Duchy, or the clerical courts, the majority had been sent by the sponsors of the house of correction, the authorities of the three "capitals" (Brussels, Antwerp, and Leuven), the small towns, and the rural municipalities. The inmates sent by the sponsoring authorities can be divided into two groups, criminals sentenced to prison and detainees confined at the initiative of their relatives. No less than 211 people belonged to the latter category. Thus, to a large degree, the Brabant house of correction served as a correctional institution for people who had not violated a law but who were deemed a nuisance by their own families. In seven out of ten cases "misconduct" or "irregular lifestyle" was the only reason given for detention. Almost all of the families concerned were financially unable to care for the members detained.[22]

Why did the laboring poor turn to the authorities to discipline their own people? Were they acting on values conveyed to them by their social superiors, or were they trying to realize their own ends by using the apparatus of repression? Systematic analysis of the Antwerp petition registers (*rekestboeken*) provides answers to these questions.

The petition registers record all private requests for legal commitments, with a summary of the aldermen's decision.[23] Between 1710 and 1789 no less than 863 applications were submitted to the authorities, of which 852, or 98.6 percent, were granted. Available information suggests that the aldermen put very little effort into investigating the appropriateness of such petitions. It was quite the exception for authorities to interrogate neighbors, to have the accused examined by a physician, or to consult the parish priest. The authorities appear generally to have been willing to accept the arguments of the plaintiffs without further questioning.

Some families requested the magistrate to extend a detention or to imprison a recidivist for a second time. If we exclude those cases, it appears that 604 individuals ended up at an institution at the initiative of relatives. These confinements were not evenly spread over the period; more people were imprisoned for the first time between 1770 and 1789 than in the previous sixty years. This increase cannot be ascribed to the opening of the provincial house of correction at Vilvoorde in 1779 because the number of first-time confinements increased from 86 in 1760–69 to 156 in 1770–79, after which it remained at this high level. By the end of the *ancien régime*, commitment on request had become a common phenomenon. In any one year, one in every two hundred households was seeking commitment of a family member, and in the last decades one in every thirty-nine Antwerp households had turned to the state to discipline one of its own.[24]

The petition registers do not provide straightforward information on the social backgrounds of the families listed. Sometimes occupations are mentioned, but such data are difficult to interpret. The assessment lists, which would have enabled us positively to identify the petitioners, have been lost. Fortunately, the location of confinement was usually mentioned so that it is possible to distinguish the lower orders from the other social groups. This point requires further explanation.

In principle, a family had the choice of placing an "unruly" member in either a religious establishment or a public institution. In reality, the laboring poor had no alternative because incarceration in a hospital (which in the Austrian Netherlands was always governed by the clergy), in a monastery, or in a nunnery had to be paid for by the family. Although precise figures on boarding are scarce, those that exist indicate that neither the Alexian Brothers, who specialized in the care of "insane" men, nor the other religious orders admitted an unruly individual for less than 200 Brabant guilders a year, a sum that no wage laborer could possibly muster. Nor could the lower orders cover the expenses of confinement in the town's workhouse, its lunatic asylum, or the provincial house of correction, where the cost of board amounted to about 120 Brabant guilders a year.[25] Detention in a public institution, however, was free if the plaintiffs could prove that their income was insufficient to cover these expenses. Some lower-middle-class families preferred these cheaper public institutions to religious societies, but they were in the minority.[26] We may, therefore, infer the social status of the family from the location of the confinement.

In the 1710–69 period the plaintiffs belonged to the propertied classes. About 82 percent of men and 54 percent of women incarcerated by petition were confined in religious institutions. Between 1770 and 1789, respectable families continued to call upon the authorities to discipline their own, but by this time the laboring poor were in the majority, as indicated by the growing proportions of males and females placed in public institutions, about 59 and 67 percent, respectively. The early 1770s were the turning point in this new trend. The number of unruly persons who were incarcerated for the first time in a workhouse or a lunatic asylum increased from 32 between 1750 and 1769 to 194 in the twenty years following. This sixfold increase occurred while the number of people who were placed in religious institutions remained static.

To explain this remarkable trend, we need to turn our attention to the relationship between the plaintiffs and the accused, as well as to the text of the complaints filed by the former against the latter. To this end five categories of confined persons can be distinguished:

(1) children confined by parents or guardians;
(2) bachelors or spinsters confined by relatives;
(3) spouses confined by wives or husbands;
(4) married persons confined by relatives;
(5) divorced or widowed persons confined by relatives.

Notably more men than women were detained. Although the proportion of men declined somewhat after 1750, men still made up 62 percent of the total at the end of the *ancien régime*. This proportion is all the more remarkable because there was a great excess of women in Antwerp. Men over the age of twelve represented only 40.5 and 42.4 percent in 1755 and 1796, respectively, of all inhabitants in that age group.[27]

Most of the males were sons confined by parents or husbands confined by wives, rather than more distant relations. The proportion of males in these categories rose from around 73 percent in 1710–69 to about 80 percent in 1770–89, mostly children and adolescents but including a rising number of husbands. For females, the pattern was somewhat different. Fewer girls than boys were locked up at the instigation of their parents or guardians, both in absolute numbers and proportionally, and the percentage of married women placed in an institution at the request of their husbands remained unchanged.

Various factors make it difficult to classify the complaints. Some requests are not specific enough. For instance, without further description or explanation, the accused is said to have led an "irregular life" or "behaved badly." The plaintiffs may have chosen to elaborate on the request in person to prevent local clerks from compromising the honor of the family. We may assume that relatively well-to-do families were involved because almost all those confined on these vague grounds were sent to religious institutions. In any case, their share decreased from about 14 percent from 1710 to 1796 to less than 4 percent thereafter. But the many petitions that contain an abundance of descriptive details are no less problematic. A close analysis of such petitions, which takes into account all the separate elements and their various combinations, allows us to trace the principal motives.

Within the scope of this essay it is not feasible to discuss in great detail all complaints. Because they were in the overwhelming majority, we will focus on the men accused, and in particular on those who had been charged either by their parents or by their wives.

As we indicated earlier, the largest percentage of males committed to an institution by members of their family were children and adolescents. In absolute terms, these numbers grew even more considerably. In the twenty years between 1770 and 1789 almost as many were confined as during all of the previous sixty years. In addition, different arguments were presented at the end of the *ancien régime*. In this period most parents complained about their sons' laziness and spendthrift ways. For example, fifteen-year-old Benedictus Claukens had been dismissed by at least twenty different employers and spent most of his days in the tavern. Seventeen-year-old Herman De Smet abandoned one boss after the other and hung out with other bad boys. Sixteen-year-old Albert Valck refused to work and stole his parents' hard-earned money to play dice.[28] Such were the stories told, and almost always they turned around the fact that the "degenerate" son did nothing to contribute to the income of the family. This was the new and crucial element in the complaints. Up to 1770 only three out of ten parents who petitioned for their sons' imprisonment had used the argument of extravagance.[29] This explains the shift we observed earlier in the location of detention. Before 1770, as many as 80 percent of the children and adolescents ended up in a private institution compared to only 15 percent in the later period.

In the 1770s and 1780s increasing numbers of women committed their husbands, presenting substantially different arguments than in the earlier period. In the 1710–69 period the principal theme had been "insanity" (53 percent of the cases), but now the story centered on the husband's neglect of his economic responsibilities, leaving all the work to his wife and children. The calico-printer Jacob Lauwers, nicknamed "Loaded Lauwie" ("*zat Lauwken*"), had not lifted a finger for months, sold the furniture, and gave himself over to liquor. Engelbert Bal, weaver and slater, also lived off his wife and children and beat them whenever they failed to turn their wages over to him. Petrus van Dyck ruined his family not only because he refused to work but also because he sold the very raw cotton the merchant-entrepreneurs had provided his wife for spinning.[30] In the 1770s and 1780s no less than 84 percent of the women requesting their husbands' detention presented similar accusations, whereas in the 1710–69 period only a third had made such charges. Beyond doubt, all families under discussion belonged to the proletariat. Almost without exception, the accused ended up in public institutions, obliging the authorities to pay the costs for incarceration because their wives had no financial resources.

It would be a mistake to attribute this change in attitude toward the apparatus of repression simply to a successful strategy of social control on the part of the authorities. Rather, proletarianization and impoverishment were responsible for the change in attitude, raising the level of intolerance among the laboring poor toward unruly members of their own families. The industrial transformation that took place during the third quarter of the eighteenth century had severe social consequences. The decline of the traditional textile industries was amply compensated for by the development of new industrial sectors, but many artisans, reduced to the status of wage earner and paid miserably for jobs that required little skill, now competed with women and young workers. The accusations that women leveled against their husbands or parents lodged against their sons must be considered against this background.

As a consequence of the industrial restructuring, the income of many adult men fell, while progressively more women earning a wage were responsible for an increasing share of the family income. As the wives had more cash at their disposal, they could act more independently toward their husbands and felt more justified in calling them to order if they failed to contribute their share, that is, if they were not regularly employed or if they squandered their money. This is not to say that the wife would easily turn to the authorities. The petitions show that she took such steps only when her

spouse's misbehavior had rendered everyday life unbearable, both financially and emotionally. Many of the accused men were indeed so bewildered
as a result of their social degradation and the changed balance of power
within their families that they not only gave themselves over to liquor but
also brutalized and terrorized their wives and children. On the basis of such
accusations, some women filed for divorce, yet some preferred to seek their
husband's detention, hoping he might mend his ways.[31] That is the reason
why they generally asked for a short term of detention; 86 percent of the
men concerned were freed within two years, half within one.

Furthermore, textile workers, both men and women, were confronted
with the paradox that while the spread of child labor led to lower wages,
they were in dire need of the wages of their offspring. Financial need
compelled more parents to force their daughters and sons to bring grist to
the mill. They had little trouble with their daughters because girls six years
or older had been accustomed since the early part of the eighteenth century
to employment for wages, in particular in the lace industry. But employment of young boys on a large scale was a new phenomenon, and sons were
less willing to go to work. From the 1760s on, countless children were
forced to spin under the supervision of "cellarmen" (*kelderboeren*) in base-
ment rooms; these rooms were deliberately selected for their dampness to
keep the threads moist.

It is hardly surprising that the boys repeatedly ran away from such jobs,
which forced them to work from morning till evening for miserable wages
under harsh supervision. Fifteen-year-old cotton spinner Leonard Hoore-
mans, whose parents were supported by the New Poor Law Administration, was unable to hold a job for more than one week, incapable, according
to the almoners, of accepting any discipline.[32] Some children begged on the
streets without the knowledge of their parents as a way to escape wage
labor. Others attempted to counterfeit the stamps entitling them to public
allowances. Still others formed gangs that committed small thefts at the
instructions of professional receivers.[33] That this was by no means a trivial
phenomenon is suggested by the terms of the punitive measures taken by
magistrates against various forms of juvenile delinquency in the 1770s and
1780s. Teenagers were singled out in special prohibitions against smashing
windows or plastering walls, playing on the streets during working hours,
passing through the town in groups, organizing boxing matches, provok-
ing almoners, begging under the pretext of birthday celebrations or parties,
and so on.[34] In this context it is understandable that so many proletarian
families turned to the authorities to discipline their sons. Under the threat

of losing income and even of being crossed off the charity list, parents were held responsible for their sons' "misbehavior" and had to bear the brunt of the consequences of their "idleness." Parents argued that three to six months of forced labor in a house of correction would make these boys mend their ways, but they did consider a longer term of imprisonment undesirable. "Free him," implored a widow, "because he has repented, and now that my husband has died, I cannot do without my son's wages."[35] Her reasoning summarizes our argument: proletarian families did not seek to punish their unruly members but rather to make them contribute their share to the family income. To them a request for detention was simply a strategy of survival.

New Strategies of Survival

In the late eighteenth and early nineteenth centuries, important poor relief reforms were carried through in Antwerp, the underlying principles of which remained effective until 1925. These institutional reforms did not, however, signify any break with the social policy of the 1770s and 1780s, giving the laboring poor ample opportunity to continue their traditional survival strategies.

The New Poor Law Administration was superseded, and in its place two new secular institutions were created under the supervision of the munici-pal authorities: the Commission for the Civil Hospices, entrusted with the administration of all charitable foundations and hospitals, and the Charity Bureau, controlling outdoor relief. The overseers of the Charity Bureau were instructed to support all persons unable to provide for their own subsistence, but because the subsidies granted by the town council lagged far behind the growth in the numbers applying for relief, the Charity Bureau was obliged to employ ever stricter criteria of selection and to lower the allowances of the families satisfying these formal requirements. By midcentury, poor relief had become a farce. In the overseers' own words, "The aid provided by the Charity Bureau is in most cases absolutely inade-quate; it suffices not even to pay for a part of the rent . . . it is an inexplicable mystery to us how most of these families manage to stay alive."[36] And these recipients were the lucky ones because half of the people in need did not receive any aid at all.

The correspondence of the Charity Bureau indicates that this retrench-ment policy pursued in the early nineteenth century provoked many protests. The destitute continued to consider public assistance a right and made terrible scenes when excluded from it, not hesitating to abuse the overseers physically. According to the director, those deemed eligible to draw a dole were no less belligerent. They did not cease to condemn and threaten the overseers for the levels at which they set the allowances. Although he treated "troublemakers" harshly, the bureau director had to admit that people in need were rightfully disgruntled because relief funds at his disposal were utterly inadequate.[37]

From the second decade of the nineteenth century, however, the poor's attitude toward the poor relief administration began to change. The poor still continued to apply for relief and to press for higher allowances, but they now put their requests "properly," that is, subserviently. This change is not only indicated by the overseers' reports, which no longer mention "unpleasant" incidents, but also and especially by the form of the requests. Even those people who clearly had great difficulty putting anything on paper were profuse in their use of deferential formulae.[38] It was not necessarily that the laboring poor had come to think of relief as a privilege rather than as a right. Rather, they had learned through bitter experience that protests only resulted in elimination from the charity list. Moreover, because living conditions continued to deteriorate, their need for aid under any terms had become more pressing. The combination of declining family income and rising rents forced them to swallow their pride and submit themselves obediently to the overseers. This is not to argue that they unconditionally accepted the Charity Bureau's rules and decisions. On the contrary, the almoners now reported more frequently that applicants had provided false information on their health or family size or ages of children.[39]

Furthermore, the laboring poor now made greater use of some of the remaining loopholes in the poor relief system, particularly by selective employment of foundations under the control of the Commission for the Civil Hospices. To take one example, until 1884 Saint Elisabeth's Hospital was the only institution in Antwerp that provided medical care for the poor. Admission to the hospital was granted on production of a medical certificate obtained from one of the doctors employed by the Charity Bureau. These doctors were to grant certificates only to the seriously wounded, carriers of a contagious disease, or those in a "critical condition" requiring immediate intensive care. The notion of "critical condition" was, of course, subject to interpretation. People in need contended that one had to be half dead to be considered for admittance to the hospital. For example, widow De Pooter, who was sick and in bed, testified with great bitterness that she was being treated like a dog, apparently condemned to die a miserable death at home.[40] Some doctors, on the other hand, were so sensitive to the needs of the poor that they would issue certificates to the merely "famished." If patients were not exactly pampered at Saint Elisabeth's—and rations there were decreased in the first half of the nineteenth century—they were at least better fed than most other people in need.[41] Ever-growing numbers of people tried therefore to acquire a medical certificate so they could pass a couple of weeks at the hospital.

Appalled by the intensifying misery on one hand and by the Charity Bureau's cheapness on the other, doctors increasingly assented to requests, as is illustrated by the spectacular growth in admissions. While the total population of Antwerp only doubled, the average number of admissions rose from about thirteen hundred per annum at the end of the *ancien régime* to over six thousand in the 1850s. Almost all patients lived in Antwerp and were destitute. The majority consisted of adolescents and young adults: in 1853, 27 percent were between the ages of sixteen and twenty-five, a further 24 percent between twenty-six and thirty-five.[42]

The director of the Commission for the Civil Hospices, who had to pay the costs, frequently protested against the "irresponsible" attitude of the doctors. Did they not realize that "a great many people took advantage of the hospital" and that many so-called patients "are in fact troublemakers, and, pretending to be sick, form a true plague on our services that seems to take root everywhere?" The director was supported in his allegation by the hospital's medical superintendent, Corneille Broeckx, who thought 60 percent of admissions were completely without justification. Doctors, however, were confronted daily with social reality. They recognized that numerous patients were in need of material assistance rather than medical care in the proper sense, but they believed that undernourished people should at least be diagnosed as potentially sick.[43]

Saint Elisabeth's housed its largest contingent of patients during the months of December, January, and February. In a town such as Antwerp, where more and more people depended directly on the port for their livelihood, the slow season in the harbor left hundreds of wage laborers unemployed every winter. The problem was that the hospital could not accommodate more than seven hundred people simultaneously and so most patients had to content themselves with only a short stay. Three-quarters of the patients were dismissed within a month and 30 percent within ten days.[44] As a result, many who were in need turned to the workhouses, the *ateliers de charité*, even though the treatment there was far harsher.

The workhouses, established in 1802, were administered by the Charity Bureau and had two departments: the workhouse proper, in which the unemployed had to pass the day under penalty of being struck from the charity list, and the *atelier de force*, a house of correction for incorrigibles and beggars. Although the latter department was phased out after the establishment in 1810 of the *dépôt de mendicité* in Hoogstraten (discussed below), the workhouse function substantially expanded during the following decades. The expansion occurred not because the Charity Bureau implemented a more repressive policy but because many people in need offered themselves voluntarily, even though the poor relief administration tried every means to make the workhouse as unappealing as possible.

It had never been the authorities' intention to employ large numbers of paupers. The purpose of the iron discipline of the workhouse was to discourage the unemployed so that poor relief could be cut back and the supply of cheap labor in the private sector would increase. This did not mean that no interest was taken in the profitable employment of the needy in workhouses. Twice the Charity Bureau tried deliberately to increase the proceeds of pauper industry, but such efforts had to be dropped because of the resistance of local entrepreneurs and because most paupers were unskilled laborers, whose low-quality work was difficult to market.[45]

The Charity Bureau saw to it that the people in need did not go to the workhouses too readily. They had to toil twelve to fifteen hours a day to get a simple meal; it was forbidden to speak, to sing, or to whistle in the workshops as well as in the halls and the refectory; making obscene gestures was prohibited; nor could an inmate go to the toilet without the approval of an overseer.[46] Nevertheless, more and more people lined up to secure admission to the workhouse. In the 1820s and 1830s, the rush became so great that the authorities started to use dismissal from the workhouse as a punitive measure, even though originally admission had been intended as a punitive resort for those denied outdoor relief.

The laboring poor used the workhouse purposefully and selectively. This behavior can be deduced from seasonal fluctuations in applications. About two hundred signed up during the summer and at least twice that number during the winter months in normal years, one to two thousand in difficult periods, and over three thousand in times of crisis.[47] The laboring poor entered the workhouse only when they were caught in the most dire circumstances, and in particular when confronted with a combination of adversities, such as structural unemployment and high food prices. They increasingly resorted to the workhouse as a temporary shelter, as ever-growing numbers became unemployed during the first half of the nineteenth century, as the cost of living rose, and as the Charity Bureau was forced to exclude progressively more families from the outdoor lists. By 1844 the authorities had acquiesced in the effective transformation of the workhouses into shelters. They established a special department to provide free meals for those who were completely unsuited for employment: 125 grams of rye bread, one and a half liters of soup, and a cup of watered milk.[48] During the coincidence of famine and mass unemployment three years later, such overwhelming numbers turned to the agency that the Charity Bureau was obliged to waive the last vestige of the old workhouse system: paupers were no longer required to pass the entire day at the institution to be eligible for the food ration.[49]

To appreciate why the workhouse played such a crucial role in the survival strategies of the laboring poor, we have to turn our attention to the demographic characteristics of the applicants. The board distinguished three categories:

(1) able-bodied adults, whose labor would be sufficient to provide for the cost of their support;

(2) children and adolescents who could only partially provide for their food ration; and

(3) the elderly, disabled, and children, who were not fit to work.

The registration records show not only that the second and third categories grew the fastest, but also that their numbers increased more rapidly in times of adversity and dropped more sharply in more prosperous periods than those in the first category. The overwhelming majority of the able-bodied adults who applied were women, in normal times mostly widows and unmarried women but in times of crisis predominantly married mothers.[50] In short, the workhouse sheltered the most vulnerable members of the proletariat: the elderly, women, and young children, the three groups hit hardest by the decline of the textile industry.

According to the Charity Bureau, the transformation of workhouses into shelters reflected the growing immorality of the proletariat. Only heartlessness and egotism could bring someone to commit an aged mother or wife to an institution. Nevertheless, the director had to admit that the families involved usually acted out of dire need because their income was inadequate and public assistance unavailable.[51] He might have added that these survival strategies actually contributed to the preservation of family ties. By temporarily depositing a parent, a wife, or a young child in the workhouse many proletarian families were able to care for their dependents during the remainder of the year.

As we mentioned earlier, from 1810 beggars were sent to the *dépôt de mendicité* in Hoogstraten for "reeducation." Even though the establishment served as a penal colony for the entire province, it primarily housed beggars from the city of Antwerp. At first glance, that seems hardly surprising. The metropolis had more inhabitants than all other urban centers together, and its administrators did everything within their power to eradicate begging. They had good reasons. Keeping labor costs low was one of Antwerp's most important weapons in the war against its Dutch competitors in Rotterdam and Amsterdam. Social policy had now more than ever to be aimed at strict control of the reserve army and smooth regulation of the labor market. This meant not only that the poor lists had to be purged and the allowances reduced as far as possible, but also that incorrigible beggars needed to be stigmatized and penalized. The police were instructed to abide strictly by the law and to arrest anyone who was caught begging. They were to pay special attention to those areas where the poor were likely to encounter their social superiors: church porches, especially on Sundays, public squares and markets, in particular at fair time, and public thoroughfares. The police dutifully carried out their instructions. During the second quarter of the nineteenth century, they made an average of 122 arrests for vagrancy per year.[52]

Despite these measures, the apparatus of repression did not function smoothly, according to the municipal authorities. Ironically, they were little concerned about their inability to eradicate begging. They were fully aware that the beggars arrested were merely the tip of the iceberg and that very little could be done about the bulk. Too few police officers and overseers were available to track down all the beggars. In addition, the police could not count on unconditional support from the well-to-do, who continued to distribute alms, provided of course that they were addressed with the proper deference and subservience. The authorities did not mind this generosity because they felt that these donations tended to be limited to the deserving poor—young children, the elderly, and the disabled.[53] What did bother them was that, like the workhouse, the *dépôt de mendicité* was gradually transformed from a disciplinary institution into a shelter for paupers who had committed no crime.

In the early nineteenth century, the number of voluntary admissions to

Hoogstraten—mostly from the laboring poor of Antwerp—rose steadily. At first, no action was taken to stem this tide because the settlement laws required each town council to support its own beggars, whether or not convicted as such. But by 1826 the yearly expenses had soared so high that the authorities decided to curb the flood of voluntary admissions. From then on, no one could be admitted without the written permission of the council of the town of residence. But this act had barely any effect. Likewise, a royal decree of August 28, 1833, stipulating a maximum stay of a few weeks for voluntary entrants, failed to stem the tide. Throughout the 1830s, the share of voluntary admissions to Hoogstraten continued to fluctuate between 70 and 80 percent of the total. The 1833 decree's only discernible effect was to shorten the detention terms, resulting in a greater turnover of inmates. When by the 1840s the average number of voluntary admissions to Hoogstraten rose to almost five hundred, the Antwerp town council had finally had enough. From June 1843, it refused to pay for paupers who came to Hoogstraten on their own accord. But this decision, too, was neutralized by the terrible crisis of 1845–47, during which the poor law administration felt obliged to respond positively to so many requests that Hoogstraten served once again as a shelter. Only on April 3, 1848, did a statute finally put an end to the voluntary influx into the *dépôts*.[54]

The question remains why so many paupers went on their own accord to an institution infamous for its iron discipline. According to the very able investigator Edouard Ducpétiaux, even prison regime was less strenuous than the *dépôts de mendicité*, and his judgment was supported by a member of the Council of Inspection who wrote to the minister of justice that the so-called reeducation program at Hoogstraten rested exclusively on intimidation and cruelty.[55] The answer must be that paupers simply did not have any alternatives. What other choices remained to the thirty-nine-year-old unmarried day laborer who had been unemployed for months and was not eligible for public assistance, or the fifty-four-year-old bachelor, once a spinner, now only able to find odd jobs that barely yielded any income? What opportunities were left to the embroiderer who at twenty was unable to earn an adequate living to feed herself and her illegitimate child, or to the forty-nine-year-old hawker who was idle during the winter months and had been deserted by her lover of many years, or to the fifty-two-year-old day laborer and childless widow who, unable to pay her rent, found herself evicted?[56]

We could add many more examples. All show that paupers who asked to be imprisoned at Hoogstraten were in such extremely dire circumstances that detention in a penal colony appeared more desirable than freedom. Some were old and disabled, yet most were able-bodied wage laborers in the prime of life. Six out of ten fell in the twenty-to-fifty-four age group and were healthy. Available data suggest that their misery was a result of an interplay of three forces: structural unemployment, exclusion from public assistance, and lack of an informal support network.[57]

Apparently the latter factor was of decisive importance because 74 percent of adult men and women who came voluntarily to the *dépôt de mendicité* were single.[58] Not able to resort to partners or children in times of crisis, bachelors and spinsters were a particularly vulnerable—and growing—group.[59] Lower-class celibacy increased substantially in the first half of the nineteenth century because potential brides could contribute little or nothing financially and the founding of a new family required a large expenditure owing to the extraordinary rise in rents.[60] Although, in general, the Charity Bureau was willing to support the elderly left without any form of support from relatives, able-bodied persons in need of assistance who were under sixty and childless were not eligible for any official aid unless they were sick or disabled. Single persons were allowed to register with the workhouse but could do so only as long as they paid for their room. At Hoogstraten, on the other hand, the destitutes were not only fed but also enjoyed free housing and medical care.

For the overwhelming majority of the able-bodied people who asked for voluntary detention, Hoogstraten was a brief and singular interlude in their struggle for survival. They went to the *dépôt* out of despair, stayed for some months, usually six, and left the institution as soon as they had saved up some money, for they were entitled to a small reward if they worked overtime. Most of them never returned: only 16 percent of the needy who voluntarily entered the *dépôts* of Hoogstraten, Terkameren (Brabant), and Rekem (Limburg) in 1840–42 had been there before. Even during the economic crisis that followed shortly thereafter, newcomers remained the majority.[61]

Financial problems also explain why some children ended up in a *dépôt de mendicité* at their parents' initiative, just as under the *ancien régime* they had been committed to the house of correction. The court records are succinct, yet there can be no doubt about the plaintiffs' economic circumstances or motives. In 1836, for example, the Antwerp town council granted a widower permission to send his thirteen-year-old-son to Hoogstraten "because the father's wage is insufficient for both to live on and the son refuses to work, so that it is feared he will end up a vagabond." The same applied to another thirteen-year-old, "whose behavior is incorrigible and whose parents have the greatest difficulty in making ends meet," and to a fourteen-year-old girl, "who passes the time idle, even though her parents need her help desperately."[62]

It is no coincidence that these and other boys and girls deposited in the *dépôt* by relatives were all younger than fifteen years old; new laws governing commitment to correctional institutions had been introduced since 1795. The French revolutionaries had forbidden all forms of arbitrary arrest and commitment because such practices were in conflict with the principles of human and civil rights. The new statute became effective when the Southern Netherlands was annexed by France and remained in force during the Dutch and Belgian regimes that followed. The statute declared that with the exception of children under the age of fifteen, who could be detained at the request of the head of the family and with the permission of local authorities, no one could be deprived of his or her liberty who had not committed a crime or had not lost all intellectual faculties.[63]

But the definition of "intellectual faculties" still left an opening for the commitment of adults. Town councils were held responsible for all damage caused by "frenzied people and untamed animals," and families could be penalized with heavy fines for letting loose "dangerous lunatics." According to the *code civil*, a person could be declared insane only after a medical examination and a verdict by a court of first instance, which had to place the person under guardianship. But this expensive and time-consuming legal procedure was rarely followed, and at the beginning of Dutch rule the barriers to arbitrary commitment were removed. By a decree of February 23, 1815, courts of first instance could imprison and give provisional custody, with the possibility of one-year extensions if no improvement was shown, to anyone who had been accused by close relatives of "insanity, serious licentiousness or any other kind of misbehavior," without any further investigation. After the Belgian Revolution this loose provision was deleted, yet the equally vague French laws with regard to insanity remained effective until the 1850s. In daily practice the police had the authority to arrest anyone deemed insane by his or her family and to place such persons in an institution after a medical examination.[64]

Thus in the first half of the nineteenth century, commitment for insanity went virtually unchecked. Ducpétiaux and other reformers repeatedly alerted the authorities to the serious abuses stemming from the absence of an efficient and enlightened policy. People were declared insane on the basis of vague accusations and faulty medical reports, locked up in all kinds of institutions from regular hospitals to prisons, and often treated in a degrading fashion.[65] Here we must confine ourselves to the question of who were the people declared insane and to what extent such a resort remained part of the survival strategy of the very poor. Our investigation thus far does not allow us to pursue the question in great detail. There is no lack of primary source material. A very great deal of quantitative material and innumerable medical dossiers of the period have been saved, but even the most modest and elementary analysis of these sources would be extraordinarily time-consuming. It is possible, however, to formulate some provisional conclusions on the basis of published material and some random samples of the Antwerp records.

There was a steady increase in the Belgian asylum population from 4.6 persons per 10,000 inhabitants in 1824 to 9.75 per 10,000 in 1858. The phenomenon must be primarily ascribed to the spectacular increase in the number of patients in need, who made up 74 percent of the total asylum population in the middle of the century.[66] These impressive figures underestimate the real numbers because institutions for the insane were too few and their capacity too limited to absorb all lunatic paupers so that some of them (the question is how many) ended up in institutions intended for very different purposes.[67] It is tempting to follow Michel Foucault's reasoning that "madness was perceived through the condemnation of idleness" and that incarceration for madness was a means employed by the powerful to police the poor, but such an interpretation is not justified by our data.[68]

Successive central governments made no concerted attempts to institutionalize the insane, preferring care at home or, if impossible, admission to a private asylum. A proposal submitted by a committee instructed to investigate the treatment of the insane, which sought to establish a network of specialized public institutions, was resolutely rejected.[69] Numerous official reports show, moreover, that local authorities were astonished by the sheer numbers of pauper lunatics. A partial explanation for their reaction is that they were financially responsible for maintenance costs of all residents in need who were certified insane. As expenditures rose, they started to question the foundation of the complaints and the validity of the medical certificates.[70]

More thorough research is needed to assess the precise motivation of the petitioners and the doctors' diagnoses. In any case, fragmentary data in Antwerp records suggest that mentally disturbed paupers were committed at their families' initiative and that alcohol addiction, coupled with excessive aggressiveness, was the most common charge.[71] This is remarkable because alcohol consumption in the metropolis decreased substantially during the first half of the nineteenth century. Illicit distillation of liquor, gin in particular, might have played a role because many doctors make reference to the consumption of noxious concoctions containing sulfuric acid, vitriol, ammonia, and the like.[72] Yet alcoholism alone cannot explain why the requests for commitment increased dramatically each time the laboring poor were confronted with a major economic crisis or why the great majority of the insane in such periods were women.[73]

Given these factors, it seems plausible to assume that in times of adversity the laboring poor tended to get their relatives certified insane to relieve themselves of an economic burden. This should not lead to the conclusion that they took such a decision lightly or that the accused were simply inconvenient to their families. Records of the Charity Bureau and contemporary reports show that the laboring poor left few means untried to keep the insane at home, and the medical certificates, even if they are difficult to assess, justify the conclusion that relatives who charged family members with insanity genuinely believed in the justice of their charges.[74] We can only conclude that progressive pauperization was gradually undermining the effectiveness of informal bonds and compelled desperate families to lock up their unruly members in lunatic asylums.

Total Institutions?

During the last quarter of the eighteenth century and the first half of the nineteenth century, the Antwerp bourgeoisie carried out a social policy intended to regulate the labor market and to control the growing reserve army of labor. By excluding many of the laboring poor from public assistance and by developing new modes of discipline, they attempted to keep wages to a minimum and to put a premium on respectability. The punitive measures taken by Antwerp's local authorities also met the interests of the central government, which felt that political order was threatened by the city's surplus population.

Yet the repressive institutions established by local and central authorities were ambiguous instruments. Oversimplified social control theories of institutionalization inspired by Foucault must be rejected out of hand. As Michael Ignatieff has remarked, what is missing in such interpretations "is the idea that public order strategies were defined within limits marked out not only by the holders of power but also by those they were trying, often vainly, to persuade, subdue, cajole or repress."[75] The example of Antwerp shows that the laboring poor were active participants in the process of institutionalization. To be sure, they offered little open resistance against the ongoing cutbacks of poor relief funds and against new forms of surveillance that curbed their freedom, but they succeeded in finding covert and effective ways to circumvent legal restrictions and to absorb the instruments of social control of the ruling classes into their strategies of survival, giving an unexpected and novel dimension to "the carrot and the stick."

In the earlier period, when the textile industry thrived, many families escaped complete destitution, provided that all members of the family worked to contribute to the family income. But the very fact that all members of the family had to make a financial contribution, and were indeed able to do so, raised the levels of intolerance of the laboring poor toward unruliness within their own families. Husbands and children who were unwilling to work or who squandered their wages were locked away in houses of correction. The purpose of such commitments was not to ostracize the accused. Request for detention was a strategy to obtain temporary relief from a family member who threatened the survival of the household as a whole and it was a way to teach him or her a lesson.

Against the background of mass-scale pauperization and redundancy, this strategy became obsolete. Antwerp's transition from a textile center to a port town resulted in underemployment and unemployment for a majority of women, children, and old people and dramatically reduced the wages of those who could still find jobs. Consequently, it became increasingly difficult to maintain relations of reciprocity with both immediate family and more distant kin. Growing numbers of people took refuge at Saint Elisabeth's Hospital or voluntarily signed up for the workhouses or even the *dépôts de mendicité* to bridge the times of adversity. However degrading the workhouses and the penal colony were, they were used by the laboring poor as shelters, to the dismay and resentment of the authorities. The intensification of economic problems also explains why so many people in need were certified insane on their own families' initiative. The insane asylum became the last resort when all other means had failed.[76] This is not to argue that the measures were essentially not coercive or that the institutions created by the authorities were in fact meeting the needs of the laboring poor or that the latter subscribed to these disciplinary methods. The relations between state and civil society cannot be defined in terms either of coercion or consensus. Social reality is more complex than that. Even though the workhouses and the *dépôts de mendicité* were transformed into shelters by the active intervention of the laboring poor, they continued to function as vehicles of repression. But if the lower classes increasingly did turn to these institutions of repression, that does not mean that they accepted or internalized the dominant ideology.

It is possible and indeed likely that the rapid growth of the number of requests for detention in the 1760s and 1770s induced representatives of Antwerp and the other capitals of Brabant to give up their resistance to the establishment of a provincial house of correction. The capacity of existing institutions was too limited to meet the swelling stream of debauched people. This does not mean, however, that the ruling classes were simply ratifying a line of demarcation between the deviant and the respectable already indigenous to the poor. The mere fact that many proletarian families requested detention for their own people and that the authorities granted such requests is not evidence of consensus. It only shows that the immediate interests of both groups were more or less parallel. To be sure, the laboring poor presented arguments the authorities would be sensitive to, such as extravagance, alcoholism, and idleness, but that does not mean that their objectives or understandings were identical. The families concerned tried foremost to maximize their opportunities for survival, while the authorities wanted to place sanctions upon behavior in conflict with the work ethos. Representatives of the state and local authorities used the new institution at Vilvoorde as an instrument to curb begging, in short, as a powerful weapon to impose *their* moral imperatives.

Although in the last decades of the *ancien régime* a convergence of interests occurred, radical changes took place during the first half of the nineteenth century, when all social programs were overwhelmed by a torrent of misery. Every institution of social control was largely stripped of its original function and ideological content. As the various avenues of repression became ever more integrated into the complex of survival strategies, it became more difficult for the ruling classes to distinguish between the deserving and the undeserving poor. But it would be overstating the case to conclude that the laboring poor realized their own objectives by transforming the workhouses and the *dépôts de mendicité* into shelters. They were not able to persuade the bourgeoisie to extend relief and to provide adequate allowances, to establish a system of public assistance that would meet their material needs and would respect their human dignity. To some degree they were forced to conform to the avenues and categories left open to them, offering themselves "voluntarily" to penal institutions or seeking to have their relatives certified as insane.

These strategies, born from need, in turn obliged the authorities once again to reform welfare institutions. By the middle of the nineteenth century, most institutions were serving indiscriminately as shelters, not only creating financial burdens but also threatening social stability. Therefore, various attempts were made to redefine the social problem, and the result was a new law on the care of the insane, the creation of reform institutions for teenagers, the abolition of the workhouses, and the establishment of new hospitals. Whether these reforms met the needs of the working classes is yet another question.

Notes

The authors and editor would like to thank Ruth Oldenziel of Yale University for her translation of this essay from the original Dutch and for substantive suggestions that helped to clarify the argument.

ABBREVIATIONS

ARAB	Algemeen Rijksarchief, Brussels
BG	Burgerlijke Godshuizen
BW	Bureel van Weldadigheid
EG	Elisabethgasthuis
KK	Kerken en Kloosters
MA	Modern Archief
OCMWA	Openbaar Centrum voor Maatschappelijk Welzijn, Antwerp
PA	Provinciaal Archief
PK	Privilegekamer
RAA	Rijksarchief, Antwerp
SAA	Stadsarchief, Antwerp
SB	Staten van Brabant
V	Vierschaar

1. For a detailed analysis see Catharina Lis, *Social Change and the Labouring Poor: Antwerp, 1770–1860* (New Haven: Yale University Press, 1986). In 1770 Antwerp had about 46,000 inhabitants. By 1860 the number had increased to 112,000.
2. Catharina Lis and Hugo Soly, *Poverty and Capitalism in Pre-Industrial Europe* (Atlantic Highlands, N.J.: Humanities Press, 1979), 203–5. See also Paul Bonenfant, *Le problème du paupérisme en Belgique à la fin de l'ancien régime* (Brussels: Académie royale de Belgique, 1934), 307–20, 326–28.
3. Catharina Lis, "Sociale politiek in Antwerpen, 1779," *Tijdschrift voor Sociale Geschiedenis* 2 (1976), 146–66; and *Social Change*, 12–24.
4. SAA, KK 2112.
5. SAA, V 1822.
6. Lieve Van Damme, "Misdadigheid te Antwerpen, 1765–1794" (Licentiate thesis, Ghent University, 1973), 72–74.

7. OCMWA, Library, Collection factice, no. 27.

8. SAA, V 282 (March 14, 1781).

9. Only some sources have survived. See SAA, V 282–83, and V 1822.

10. SAA, V 282 (July 8, 1782, and January 10, 1783).

11. SAA, V 283 (September 30 and October 13, 1784), and V 1822 (January 18, 1788).

12. SAA, PK 451, no. 116; *Recueil des Ordonnances des Pays-Bas autrichiens*, vol. 12 (Brussels: Académie royale de Belgique, 1910), 158–59; J. F. and J. B. van der Straelen, *De kronijk van Antwerpen, 1770–1817*, vol. 1 (Antwerp: Voor God en't Volk, 1929), 78.

13. Paul Soetaert, "Consumptief krediet te Antwerpen (14de–18de eeuw)," *Drie-maandelijks Tijdschrift van het Gemeentekrediet van België* 31 (1977), 272–74, and his *De Bergen van Barmhartigheid in de Spaanse, de Oostenrijkse en de Franse Nederlanden, 1618–1795* (Brussels: Gemeentekrediet van België, 1986), 228, 231, 234–37, 258, 266–68, 286–87.

14. SAA, PK 927, f° 256 and 263v[o].

15. Van Damme, "Misdadigheid," 93–94.

16. SAA, V 1822 (June 7, 1793).

17. SAA, V 124 (December 12, 1791).

18. See SAA, V 282–83.

19. Bonenfant, *Problème*, 391–92.

20. SAA, PK 455, f° 316–20.

21. ARAB, SB, Boxes 505–6; SAA, PK 1798, f° 285[o]–291; Bonenfant, *Problème*, 293–95.

22. SAA, PK 455, f° 330–36; Stadsarchief, Brussels, file 447.

23. SAA, PK 794–895. Examination of the requests for extension of detention and a comparison of the petition records registers with the list of the Vilvoorde prisoners show that there are no gaps in the series, with the exception of 1700–1709 and 1790–95, periods of political turmoil and military operations.

24. Calculations based on population figures from P. M. M. Klep, *Bevolking en arbeid in transformatie. Een onderzoek in Brabant, 1700–1900* (Nijmegen: SUN, 1981), 432.

25. ARAB, SB, Registers, no. 292; SAA, PK 869, f[o] 151v[o]; Jozef Geldhof, "Pelgrims, dulle lieden en vondelingen te Brugge in de 18de eeuw, 1740–1789" (Licentiate thesis, Ghent University, 1988), 178 and 191. Around 1780 weavers of mixed fabrics in Antwerp received on average 8 *stuivers* a day, or 5.4 kilos of rye bread. Assuming that they were employed 270 days a year, a high estimate, their annual income would have been 108 Brabant guilders.

26. During the period under examination only twenty-nine people were confined in a public institution at relatives' expense: twenty in the town's workhouse, five in its lunatic asylum, and four in the provincial house of correction.

27. Calculation compiled from Claude Bruneel, "La population du duché de Brabant en 1755," *Bijdragen tot de Geschiedenis* 58 (1975), 240, and Jas De Belder, "Elementen van sociale identificatie van de Antwerpse bevolking op het einde van de XVIIIde eeuw. Een kwantitatieve studie," 2 vols. (Ph.D. thesis, Ghent University, 1974), 2:77 and 132.

28. SAA, PK 878 f° 162 and 180, PK 880, f[o] 145v[o].

29. After 1770 the number of rich parents who had their sons committed also increased, but their share was rather small. See Karell Degryses, "De Antwerpse fortuinen" (Ph.D. thesis, Ghent University, 1986), 640ff.

30. SAA, PK 873, f[o] 12v[o] and 39v[o], PK 884, f[o] 49.

31. SAA, PK 868, f[o] 81, and PK 873, f[o] 37v[o]; Jozef De Brouwer, *De kerkelijke rechtspraak en haar evolutie in de bisdommen Antwerpen, Gent en Mechelen tussen 1570 en 1795*, 2 vols. (Tielt: Uitgeverij E. Veys, 1972), 1:138–40, 2:512–14, 521–22, 524–28, 542.

32. SAA, V 282.

33. SAA, V 118.

34. SAA, PK 927–28, passim.

35. SAA, PK 873, f[o] 34.

36. Lis, *Social Change*, 102–12, 184–86.

37. OCMWA, BW, Cop. I, 4–5.

38. Numerous examples in OCMWA, BW, Rep. I, 1–2.

39. SAA, MA 187.

40. OCMWA, BW, Rep. I, 1, no. 123.

41. Lis, *Social Change*, 89–90, 182. See also OCMWA, BG, Comptes moraux, 1815–20, and BG, EG, D 8 (October 6, 1856).

42. Luc Vermeiren, "De negentiende eeuw (tot 1925). Van Gasthuis naar ziekenhuis," in *Het Sint-Elisabethziekenhuis te Antwerpen: 750 jaar Gasthuis op 't Elzenveld, 1238–1988* (Brussels: Gemeentekrediet van België, 1988), 173–74, 182–88.

43. SAA, MA 168; Antoine Kums, "Nos piliers d'hôpital," *Annales de la Société de Médecine d'Anvers* 41 (1880), 13 and 52.

44. Vermeiren, "Negentiende eeuw," 185.

45. Catharina Lis, "Verarmingsprocessen te Antwerpen, 1750–1850," 4 vols. (Ph.D. thesis, Brussels University, 1975), 4:68–77.

46. Lis, *Social Change*, 155. See also Marleen Abelshausen, "De Antwerpse werkuizen van liefdadigheid, 1802–1870: Weldadigheidsinstelling of fabriek?" *Annalen van de Belgische Vereniging voor Hospitaalgeschiedenis* 20 (1982), 79–87.

47. OCMWA, Ateliers de charité, Boxes 1–4, and "Rapport décennal, 1846 à 1855."

48. Odile Vorlat-Raeymaeckers, "De sociale toestand in Antwerpen, 1845–1850," *Noordgouw* 9 (1969), 177.

49. OCMWA, "Rapport décennal, 1846 à 1855."

50. Ibid., and SAA, MA 18, MA 190, MA 3532/0–52.

51. SAA, MA 187.

52. RAA, PA, J 46–47, J 70–77, and SAA, MA 140/9.

53. Lis, *Social Change*, 128–132.

54. Gerarda Gentjens, "Het bedelaarsgesticht van Hoogstraten, 1808–1848" (Licentiate thesis, Leuven University, 1972), 59 and 61. Before 1848 the majority of detainees in other Belgian *dépôts de mendicité* were also voluntary admissions. At Terkameren, near Brussels, they accounted for nearly 87 percent of the total in the period between 1840 and 1847. See E. M. Meuwissen, "Les dépôts de mendicité au tribunal de l'histoire," *Annalen van de Belgische Vereniging voor Hospitaalgeschiedenis* 19 (1981), 55–60.

55. ARAB, section IV, no. 163; Edouard Ducpétiaux, *Des moyens de soulager et de prévenir l'indigence et d'éteindre la mendicité* (Brussels: Laurent, 1832), 41–45.

56. SAA, MA 144/1.

57. Calculations based on SAA, MA 140/9, and *Exposé de la situation administrative de la province d'Anvers, 1837–42*.

58. Calculations based on SAA, MA 144/1–2.

59. Lis, *Social Change*, 151–54, 159–62.

60. This is not to argue that marriage offered a guarantee of support because relations of reciprocity were under great stress in the context of intensifying pauperization, but family ties were still the principal source of support (ibid., 140–42).

61. Edouard Ducpétiaux, *Institutions de bienfaisance de la Belgique. Résumé statistique* (Brussels: Commission centrale de statistique, 1852), 63.

62. SAA, MA 144/1.

63. Wim Van Waesberghe, "Het Belgische krankzinnigenbeleid in de XIXde eeuw," *Annalen van de Belgische Vereniging voor de Geschedenis van de Hospitalen en de Volksgezondheid* 22 (1984), 73–79; Carine Van Bruwaene, "Krankzinnigenzorg te Gent, Sint-Niklaas en Geel," in *Het openbaar initiatief van de gemeenten in België, 1795–1940. Handelingen van het 12de Internationaal Colloquium te Spa, 4–7 sept. 1984*, 2 vols. (Brussels: Gemeentekrediet van België, 1986), 1:450–51.

64. Charles De Brouckère and François Tielemans, *Répertoire de l'administration et du droit administratif*, 6 vols. (Brussels: Weissenbruch, 1836), 2:53–59; *Rapport de la Commission chargée par M. le Ministre de la Justice de proposer un plan pour l'amélioration de la condition des aliénés en Belgique* (Brussels: Imprimerie de Mortier, 1842), 37–39; Hector Willemaers, *La loi sur le régime des aliénés* (Brussels: Larcier, 1899), 8–11.

65. Edouard Ducpétiaux, *De l'état des aliénés en Belgique et des moyens d'améliorer leur sort* (Brussels: Laurent, 1832); Joseph Guislain, *Exposé sur l'état actuel des aliénés en Belgique et notamment dans la Flandre Orientale, avec l'indication des moyens propres à améliorer leur sort* (Ghent: F. and E. Gyselinck, 1838).

66. Calculated from Van Waesberghe, "Belgische krankzinnigenbeleid," 83–85.

67. Ducpétiaux, *Institutions*, 40.

68. Michel Foucault, *Madness and Civilization: A History of Insanity in the Age of Reason*, trans. Richard Howard (New York: Random House, 1965), 58. See also Klaus Doerner, *Madmen and the Bourgeoisie*, trans. J. Neugroscher and J. Steinberg (Oxford: Basil Blackwell, 1981), 14.

69. Van Bruwaene, "Krankzinnigenzorg," 451.

70. See, for example, *Admission des aliénés indigents dans les hospices de la ville de Gand* (Ghent: C. Annoot-Braeckman, 1866), 3–6.

71. SAA, MA 173/1–2, MA 174/1–7, and MA 1618.

72. Lis, *Social Change*, 94.

73. *Rapport de la commission permanente d'inspection des établissements d'aliénés, instituée par arrêté royal du 18 novembre 1851* (Brussels: Hayez, 1853); *Rapport de la commission permanente d'inspection des établissements d'aliénés, instituée par arrêté royal du 17 mars 1853* (Brussels: E. Devroye and F. Gobbaerts, 1854–84), vols. 1–

12; Fritz Sano, *La statistique des aliénés à Anvers* (Ghent: Vander Haeghen, 1899); and Sano, *Du régime des aliénés à Anvers* (Antwerp: Buschmann, 1899), 18–21.

74. Numerous examples in OCMWA, BW, Rep. I, 1–2.

75. Michael Ignatieff, "State, Civil Society and Total Institutions: A Critique of Recent Social Histories of Punishment," in Stanley Cohen and Andrew Scull, eds., *Social Control and the State: Historical and Comparative Essays* (Oxford: Basil Blackwell, 1983), 86. See also the pertinent remarks by Ignatieff in his review article "Total Institutions and Working Classes," *History Workshop* 15 (1983), 167–73.

76. This is also the conclusion of J. K. Walton, who examined a small sample from the medical registers of the Lancaster Asylum for 1842 and 1843: "Casting Out and Bringing Back in Victorian England: Pauper Lunatics, 1840–1870," in W. F. Bynum, Roy Porter and Michael Shepherd, eds., *The Anatomy of Madness: Essays in the History of Psychiatry*, vol. 2, *Institutions and Society* (London: Tavistock, 1985), 141.

Lynn Hollen Lees

3. The Survival of the Unfit: Welfare Policies and Family Maintenance in Nineteenth-Century London

WHEN THE AUTHORS of the 1834 English Poor Law *Report* made their aim the "dispauperizing of the able-bodied," they envisaged a process by which the poor would be returned to sturdy independence through the disciplinary effects of the workhouse.[1] The typical applicant, in their eyes, was a healthy adult male, who could easily get a job if he desired. People of other ages and conditions, or women, were assumed to be nonproblematic categories. When confronted by the threat of harsh discipline, meager meals, and institutional confinement for himself or his kin, the rational male would immediately decide to work and to support his wife, children, and parents. The combination of a well-run poor law and the ties of kinship would therefore help solve the poverty problem, augmenting the number of independent, male-headed nuclear families and leaving only a few residual cases to be supported by the state. This image of the interaction between the pauper and the state presupposed a world of male-headed nuclear families and an economy that provided full employment.

Although the inadequacy of this analysis has generally been recognized, many historians have moved from the fact that welfare was *meant* to carry a stigma to the belief that workers *felt* this stigma and rejected all contact with public institutions. Those studying the Victorian poor laws usually stress the distrust and avoidance of public support by the English population. Edward Thompson calls "parish relief or the hated workhouse (after 1834) . . . the last resort of despair." Michael Rose asserts that "the town poor shunned the poor law," and Derek Fraser accepts a common mid-nineteenth-century judgment that "the best of the working class will rather starve—and often do rather starve—than apply for the [workhouse]."[2] Dislike of the workhouse has generally been interpreted to entail avoidance of all poor law services, particularly by workers with claims to "respectabil-ity." Yet these arguments neglect evidence both of the poor's regular in-volvement with local welfare administrators and of the conviction by many workers that they had a right to relief. Low-skilled urban workers in the nineteenth century regularly needed to tap resources beyond those of their immediate household, and the state was one of the available sources of help. Since poor law aid came in several forms, potential clients could discrimi-nate and shape demands to what was available. Applying for relief was an active, negotiated process between administrators and the poor in which official policies set parameters but did not impose either outlooks or out-comes. Rather than stressing workers' dislike of this negotiated process, it is more illuminating to examine their involvement with it in order to understand the contributions made by public funds and institutions to the survival of the urban poor.

Philip Summers, a black ship's steward in London's East End, normally supported his family. But he had seven children, his wife drank, and in the mid-1880s he became unemployed because of illness. Parish officials consid-ered him "steady and respectable." Yet instead of rejecting the poor law, he or his wife applied for aid at least seven times during the 1880s, and they sent two of their sons into the workhouse while the father was ill.[3] The behavior of William Turner, a fifty-six-year-old street trader, who was married and had six children, one of whom was mentally retarded, is also illustrative. This family was self-supporting and lived in a "comfortable and clean home." In 1885, Turner brought his eighty-one-year-old father into the household, where he remained until he became bedridden. But at that point, Turner contacted poor law authorities, who took the father into the sick asylum, where he later died. Then in 1887, the family and the local Anglican curate spoke to poor law officials about their feeble-minded son, who was soon shipped off to the parish lunatic asylum. Family obligation to maintain both the very old and the very young was waived in cases of illness and permanent debility.[4]

Households without employed adult males had even stronger incentives to seek help from parishes and poor law unions.[5] Even when kin were ready and willing to support dependent relatives, workers sometimes needed extra resources. Harriet Clough, a thirty-eight-year-old widow, fell ill a few months after her husband's death. In 1885, she sent one daughter to live with a grandmother, a second child into a fever hospital and later to a workhouse school, and she entered the poor law infirmary in Stepney. An effort to support herself as a servant failed, and she soon moved in with her mother and a widowed brother, relying on the poor law to supply her with medicines.[6]

Case histories of the London poor demonstrate their periodic recourse to parish or poor law union officials for aid. They came in times of illness or unemployment and after childbirth, accidents, or a death in the family. Economic hardship and life cycle crises brought them to the doors of the relieving officer. In fact, I calculate that 30 percent of the London population, the proportion that Charles Booth calculated lived in poverty during the late nineteenth century, may have applied for relief over a four-year period at 1870 levels of aid incidence and over a six-and-a-half-year period at the rates of 1900.[7] For the average London worker's family, the poor law, despite its reputation for nastiness and inhumanity, was a familiar and accepted donor of services.

Poor London workers regularly sought welfare aid for their kin. Although solitary paupers certainly dragged themselves to the workhouse door, the ordinary applicant was a relative seeking help for someone else in the household. Parents asked for schooling for children, wives sought medicine for husbands, daughters petitioned for the elderly. Family ties among the poor regularly led the stronger members of a household not to avoid poor law authorities but to apply for state aid. This use of welfare to support kin was at variance with administrators' aims for the poor laws and with official theory of their deterrent effects. Welfare officials expected families to do more, and when they failed to meet the state's high standards, they became part of the "undeserving poor."

English poor law administrators were therefore bound by a legal obligation to support people whose moral entitlement to aid they doubted. In contrast, many of the English poor felt themselves to be legally as well as morally entitled to state support. These disparate images of a rudimentary social security system came into conflict daily in the workhouses and meeting rooms where the needy came to make their claims. The dual obligations of state and kin, their forms and their extent, were the battleground of this conflict. Who was to pay? In what form was aid to be given? What were the limits of family accountability? What aid, if any, should be given by the state to maintain family units? These were some of the questions regularly faced by poor law administrators and their charges that will be explored in this essay, first by an examination of the way families and the state shared legal responsibility for maintenance and then by a look at the supply of and demands for welfare services. Applications for relief took place in a context defined by law, policy, and preference. Welfare clients as well as administrators shaped the system as contending visions of need were articulated.

Entitlement and Responsibility

Historically in England, families and communities shared legal responsibility for helping the poor. Parliament enacted in the 1570s, and again in 1601, statutes that assigned to parishes the duty of providing for the destitute, irrespective of their age and physical condition, who had acquired a legal settlement within parish boundaries.[8] Despite much hesitation, the legislature reaffirmed in 1834 this commitment to offer "compulsory provision for the relief of the indigent."[9] In addition, the law of 1834 left in place statutes requiring that the children, parents, and grandchildren of the poor provide support as long as they were able. Therefore, the community was to act as the almsgiver of last resort, stepping in only when families could not provide for their members.

Law and practice often diverge, however, and both the common law and administrative practices narrowed the financial obligations of kin toward the dependent poor. During the eighteenth century, judges in support cases specified a small circle of relatives who could be forced to provide aid for the elderly; married daughters and in-laws as well as grandchildren were released from financial liability, and the courts reaffirmed the exemptions of siblings, aunts, and uncles. A destitute old person had rights to a small allowance only from sons and in limited cases from unmarried daughters, and he or she had to prove indigence, as well as consanguinity, to the satisfaction of the magistrates to get legal support for financial claims. Moreover, an Englishman's home was his castle, and he could not be forced to take into it a needy relative, even if that person were his mother or father.[10]

Younger paupers had greater rights to family support. Children under sixteen, whether legitimate or illegitimate, were entitled to maintenance from their parents, and husbands were liable under certain conditions for the support of wives. Legal depositions from children and married female paupers in St. Martin in the Fields, London, during the 1850s and 1860s were commonly taken in a local police court, where magistrates' orders for support payments from, or in some cases for the arrest of, absent husbands and fathers could be obtained.[11] London poor law administrators tried to ensure that kin contributed resources to dependent paupers. Despite the difficulties of enforcing compliance, the Local Government Board re-affirmed in 1878 the need of local officials to investigate relatives' incomes and to bring suit when necessary to recover relief costs.[12] Even if these efforts were ineffective, they produced an expectation among officials that relatives were obligated to support close kin.

Although the indigent were clearly entitled to relief, the division of legal responsibility for them between the state and a pauper's nuclear family led to contention. Relieving officers expected relatives to do more than they offered, and paupers and their kin made claims on poor law administrators that local officials were not willing to accept. The poor law inspector of St. Luke, Chelsea, sometimes noted what he regarded as family sins of omis-sion. When investigating the case of a frail, sixty-year-old widow, he dis-covered that she had a brother-in-law with some resources. In his view, the brother-in-law ought to have provided support, for "relations have a greater right to provide for each other where they possess the means of doing so, rather than [to] call upon their neighbors." He also felt aggrieved when a laundress permitted her blind, elderly father to apply for aid.[13]

The inspector's ideas of the responsibilities of kinship were not identical to those of his charges, however. A claim for the support of stepchildren was advanced on the grounds that if the mother had not remarried, "the parish *must* have kept the mother and children, and therefore it ought to assist in supporting them now."[14] The inspector usually wanted to shrink the state's field of responsibility, while the clients wanted to enlarge it. The Chelsea relieving officer made sense of disputes by dividing applicants into two categories—those who accepted his judgments with thanks and the ungrateful, whom he saw as the "least necessitous," the "least worthy" of the applicants.[15] Expecting to find shame and deference, he often encoun-tered pride and resistance. Discussions of entitlement led some applicants to challenge official rulings and to offer their own claims for types and amounts of aid. Instead of shunning the poor law administration, they did battle with it.

Changing Forms of Relief

Popular attitudes to relief were conditioned by the form in which it came; several alternatives were possible and, to some extent, negotiable. Although people equated going into a workhouse with being "bastilled," this was not

TABLE 3.1   Persons Given Poor Relief in the Metropolis on Sample Days in January, 1850–1900

Year	Indoor	Outdoor	Total	Rate/1,000 Population
1850*	9,806	44,330	54,136	23
1860	25,430	63,349	88,779	32
1871	36,868	98,711	135,579	41
1880	46,663	50,330	96,993	27
1890	61,533	41,500	103,033	25
1900	68,178	37,183	105,361	23

Sources:
Poor Law Board, Second Annual Report, 1849–1850 (London: HMSO, 1850), 122–25.
Poor Law Board, Twelfth Annual Report, 1859–1860 (London: HMSO, 1860), 188.
Local Government Board, "Statements for 1911 of the Numbers of Paupers Relieved," Pauperism in England and Wales (London: HMSO, 1911), 4.
*Middlesex County only.

the sure result of asking a relieving officer for help. Before the 1870s, most London paupers received cash or bread weekly according to local officials' scale of what constituted fair or equitable relief. Many elderly and some widows had, in effect, permanent pensions; others received temporary aid during times of illness or unemployment. The second alternative, public maintenance in a workhouse, was much less common until the second half of the century. In Middlesex County in 1803, only 24 percent of all paupers had entered workhouses, and in 1815, when the number of people given temporary help skyrocketed, the proportion of the "indoor poor" declined to 14 percent.[16] When investigated in 1834, most London parishes housed very few paupers in a workhouse, and only five metropolitan parishes had poorhouses with more than five hundred residents.[17]

The use of the workhouse rose slowly after 1834, however, and became increasingly popular in the second half of the nineteenth century. The proportion of London paupers living in state institutions—workhouses, hospitals, asylums, and district schools—stood at 18 percent in 1850, 29 percent in 1860, and approximately 60 percent in the 1890s.

During the later decades of the nineteenth century, metropolitan poor law officials aggressively offered institutional remedies to the poor (see Table 3.1). Since virtually every London parish (apart from City parishes) had a workhouse or house of industry in 1834, the emphasis of the New Poor Law on indoor relief could be implemented immediately, and by 1840 most unions had planned extensive construction to bring their buildings in line with Poor Law Commission standards.[18] Only Bethnal Green, White-chapel, Kensington, and the city of London initially refused to change their facilities.[19] Although the cost of model workhouses helped to repress the edifice complexes of many officials, after 1867 the charges for indoor pau-pers were shared by the entire city. Building strategies then became more elaborate. New wards, district schools for children, separate infirmaries, and fever hospitals multiplied. Also in 1867, the Metropolitan Asylums Board took over the care of lunatics and the sick, creating a medical constituency to agitate for a range of institutions separate from the work-houses. By the time the Royal Commission of 1909 called for the creation of old age homes, orphanages, asylums, and hospitals, this plan had long since been implemented in London, which then had fifty-one workhouses and ninety-four other poor law institutions.[20] Only 43 percent of all indoor paupers remained in the capital's general workhouse units in 1915.[21] By the late nineteenth century, metropolitan guardians of the poor dispensed aid largely through the medium of specialized asylums. Over time, the alterna-tives offered to relief applicants had narrowed in some ways and expanded in others. Relatively few could get outdoor relief on more than a temporary basis, yet if they were willing to enter a state institution, they received care designed for their particular age, family status, and malady. Orphans went to boarding schools, the sick entered hospitals or visited dispensaries, pregnant women gave birth in lying-in wards, the mentally ill were sent to asylums, and the elderly moved into the workhouses, now increasingly run as old age homes.

The Recipients of State Aid

Although the mandate of the poor laws was to relieve the destitute, officials treated people differently according to their gender, age, and family status. The Royal Commission of 1834 singled out the male able-bodied laborer as a target of hostility. He was assumed to be undeserving and in need of rehabilitation. Workhouse residence and scanty aid were to return him to the labor force. In practice, this attitude meant limited rights to relief for adult males in London during most of the period between 1835 and 1880 (see Table 3.2).

A majority of London's paupers were women and children, who were assumed to be dependent and therefore deserving of help (see Table 3.3). Deserted wives, widows, and single, unemployed females regularly ac-

TABLE 3.2   Sex and Age Distribution of People Receiving Outdoor Relief in London, 1841 and 1850 (in percent)

Year	Male Adults	Female Adults	Children
1841	13	34	53
1850	15	38	47

Sources:
Poor Law Commission, *Eighth Annual Report, 1840–1841* (London: HMSO, 1841), 350–61.
Poor Law Board, *Third Annual Report, 1850–1851* (London: HMSO, 1851), 125.

counted for a major share of those on relief—over 40 percent in the later nineteenth century—and the proportion did not vary much over time. Their children formed the other large group on welfare. Support for children, however, declined substantially after 1850. Over 50 percent of those given outdoor relief in 1840 were under age sixteen, but in 1860 the proportion of children among the outdoor poor sank to 45 percent and by 1900 to 32 percent. In addition, children formed only a small part of the population in London's workhouses (see Figure 3.1). By 1870, children made up only 37 percent of the entire group relieved in London, and in 1900 they made up only 30 percent (see Table 3.3).

This shift was greater than the decrease in the proportion of children in the overall population in the late nineteenth century. Although child mortality declined in the late nineteenth century, so did fertility rates. The net effect of these two trends upon the families of low-skilled workers is unclear, but they probably did not produce significant changes in average family size before 1900. In any case, large families were overrepresented in the ranks of the poor, and birth rates remained high among unskilled laborers until the twentieth century.[22] Therefore, the decline in aid to children probably indicates a substantial shift in welfare resources away from the young to the old during the late nineteenth and early twentieth centuries.[23]

In England as a whole, people over age sixty-five, who accounted for 3 percent of the total population in 1851 and only 5 percent in 1900, formed 20 percent and 37 percent of workhouse inmates in those two years.[24] Elderly males moved into London workhouses in increasing numbers after 1870. In parts of central London in 1906, well over a third of the residents over sixty-five were on poor relief.[25] If the paupers found in London workhouses and infirmaries on census days are tallied, the growing dominance of the elderly among the recipients of state support becomes even clearer (see Figure 3.1).

TABLE 3.3   Sex and Age Distribution of People on Relief in London, 1860–1906

Year	Male Adults		Female Adults		Children		Total
	I	O	I	O	I	O	
1860	7,167	8,773	10,345	25,907	7,734	28,612	88,538
1871–72 to* 1879–80	11,445	6,971	13,510	27,744	11,638	24,077	95,385
1880–81 to* 1887–88	15,721	4,758	16,337	19,386	15,252	15,581	87,035
1888–89 to* 1895–96	19,505	5,152	17,674	19,436	16,659	13,948	92,374
1896–97 to* 1905–6	23,122	6,062	19,870	22,284	18,170	13,425	102,933
	Percentage Distribution						
1860	8.1	9.9	11.7	29.3	8.7	32.3	100.0
1870–71 to 1879–80	12.0	7.3	14.2	29.1	12.2	25.2	100.0
1880–81 to 1887–88	18.1	5.5	18.8	22.3	17.5	17.9	100.1
1888–89 to 1895–96	21.1	5.6	19.1	21.0	18.0	15.1	99.9
1896–97 to 1905–6	22.5	5.9	19.3	21.6	17.7	13.0	100.0

Source: Great Britain, Parliament, Report of the Royal Commission on the Poor Laws and Relief of Distress. P.P. 1910, 53:14.
I = indoor relief; O = outdoor relief.
*Mean numbers relieved on sample days in each year.

In 1851, 51.5 percent of the inmates (N = 1,786) in a one-in-ten sample of metropolitan workhouses were over age sixty; this proportion had risen to 55.1 percent by 1880 as the share of older males increased.[26]

The New Poor Law directed administrators to discriminate between the able-bodied and the impotent poor. Yet these terms were largely defined in terms of age and gender. Consequently, welfare in the metropolis went primarily to women, children, and the elderly. After the passage of the New Poor Law in 1834, adult male Londoners who were neither sick nor of unsound mind received very little public aid. This decision by poor law officials had immediate implications for workers' families, who found it more difficult to get aid after the passage of the New Poor Law.

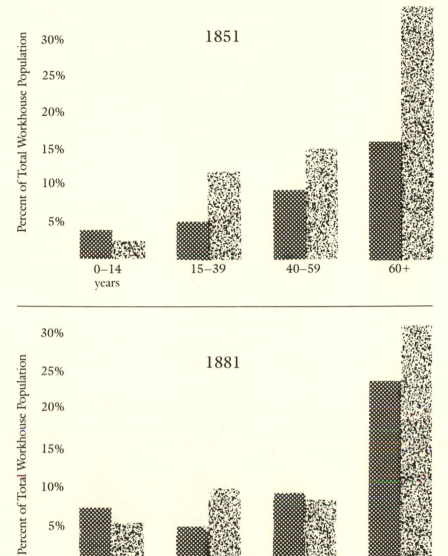

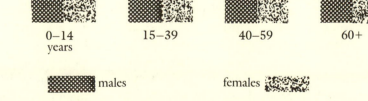

FIGURE 3.1. Age and sex distribution of inmates in London workhouses, 1851 and 1881.

The Decline of Family Maintenance

Under the old poor law, parish authorities in London gave substantial amounts of aid to adult males with children. Unemployed men with families in Poplar, Shadwell, and Bethnal Green regularly got temporary allowances, and both Spitalfields and Bethnal Green in the early 1830s gave weavers grants to supplement their wages.[27] In St. Luke, Chelsea, in 1833, 45 percent of the relief applicants investigated were male-headed nuclear families. When the inspector made his parish rounds, usually summoned by the wife, who had applied for aid, he often met unemployed or ill men in the family's rooms. Although suspicious of their character and energy, he usually recommended a weekly allowance in proportion to his judgment of their income and need. Some clearly had other income from pensions or wages. He offered the Spurning family of five, two of whom were ill, a grant of 4s. weekly, although the father, a "good workman" in "constant employment," earned about 12s., and one daughter had a job.[28] He chided several other families for not being as careful as they ought to be but still allotted 2s. per week to help them over a difficult time.

Although parish officials in 1834 denounced the practice of giving grants to supplement wages, most admitted that they gave relief to large families. In the words of the Limehouse vestry clerk, William Baker, "No doubt many families are relieved on the ground that their wages are insufficient to maintain their children. This is generally the case in the docks, where the wages paid are generally very small in amount to even constant laborers." The assistant overseer of St. James, Westminster, noted that able-bodied males with large families were given outdoor relief "to enable them to bring up their children, which they would hardly be able to do, even though constantly employed and the earnings well laid out."[29] Even Irish families, who clearly did not have the legal right to parish maintenance, were regularly relieved in central London. Married couples and their children made up 30 percent of the applicants for aid in St. Giles during 1830 and 1831, and most received small grants of money and food.[30] Family allowances and income supplements were therefore common forms of welfare in the metropolis before 1834.

Under the old poor laws, families received grants proportional to their size. Payments to the outdoor poor in Whitechapel, St. George in the East, and adjacent riverside districts averaged 1s. 6d. per individual pauper per week around 1830, assuming all the outdoor poor received grants during the entire year, which they did not.[31] Actual grants must have been at least double that figure. Parish records in St. George, Southwark, reported weekly allowances of 3*s.* per person under the old poor laws and scales of between 1*s.* 3*d.* and 3*s.* 6*d.* per person per week were claimed elsewhere in the metropolis.[32] Although relieving officers seem to have had much discretion in setting the amount of payments, they expressed fear of magistrates' interference if they set payments too low. Moreover, parish officials also gave money for fuel, shoes, spectacles, rent, and sometimes clothing or furniture. Keith Snell argues that grants to paupers in southern counties during the late eighteenth and early nineteenth centuries were "generous."[33] Even if, as Joanna Innes argues, metropolitan relief payments were lower than those of surrounding counties, the grants reported in London in 1834 were probably adequate to guarantee subsistence for families with several children.[34] An individual pauper would have had difficulty surviving on a London parish dole, but those with family grants could manage.

After 1834, London poor law administrators moved away from policies that permitted families to continue to live together as independent units to practices that treated each member individually. Although officials continued to insist that families were obligated to provide for dependent members, both the theory and the practice of relief in the metropolis after 1834 helped dissolve kinship bonds and coresidence.

The New Poor Law ordered officials to limit grants to adult males and their families outside the workhouse. One immediate result in the metropolis was a decrease in funds offered to certain categories of the London poor. As metropolitan unions cut back the number of people on relief during the late 1830s and early 1840s, adult males constituted only 13 percent of those aided in their homes, and the male proportion declined to under 6 percent during the second half of the century (see Tables 3.2 and 3.3). The reluctance to aid males soon produced a decline in the appearance before relief officials of men and their families. In St. Pancras in 1850 and 1851, adult males constituted only 28 percent of those who asked for aid, and most of these were single and over forty. Moreover, under 0.1 percent of all relief cases were nuclear families consisting of husband, wife, and children.[35] Since most Londoners lived in family units, and many local residents were casual laborers and underemployed tailors and shoemakers, applicants could hardly have been a random sample of the local poor. Destitute families became more reluctant to apply for aid when it became clear that they were unlikely to receive money grants to supplement other income.

Those people who did succeed in getting weekly pensions after the adoption of the New Poor Law discovered that the amounts were cut.

Average payments dropped in St. George, Southwark, to 1s. 3d. per head per week in 1843 and to 9 3/4d. per head per week in 1865.[36] Grants in St. Luke, Chelsea, during 1852 came to a maximum of 3s. per family per week, plus some meat and bread, and the nonsettled poor received less.[37] Bermondsey guardians gave Irish families during the late 1830s a maximum of 1s. per child per week, and most had to be content with weekly grants of under 3s. whatever their family size.[38] Not only were poor law officials reluctant to aid their large Irish population, but as need rose during 1848, payments dropped to an average of 3s. 9d. per head per year.[39] By the time J. H. Stallard investigated outdoor relief practices in the mid-1860s, East End parishes and poorer districts in central areas gave applicants less than 1s. per head per week; even in the more affluent West End, weekly grants did not exceed 2s. per head per week, with maximum amounts set for families.[40] At the end of the century, Bermondsey was giving outdoor relief in kind only.[41] By 1875 it had become common knowledge that outdoor relief only supplemented other resources; people who needed complete maintenance or a big grant had to enter the workhouse.[42] David Thomson has calculated that by the mid-1880s in London poor law payments to the elderly poor dropped to about 30 percent of an average worker's weekly income.[43] Relief policies after 1840 increasingly discriminated against male-headed households, large families, and the completely destitute. The welfare system offered them maintenance only in the workhouse.

The disinclination to support people outside welfare institutions grew after 1870, when the Local Government Board renewed its strong commitment to "deterrent" forms of relief.[44] Henry Longley, a poor law inspector for the metropolitan area, who strongly defended this change in policy, wanted indoor relief to become the rule and outdoor aid the exception. He argued that the community would benefit from "the inducement to a struggle for independence which the discipline, if not the disgrace, incident to residence in the Workhouse will offer to the pauper himself, in a far greater degree than does a mere weekly pittance, the receipt of which cannot but sap the independence and self-reliance of all but the most active and energetic, the very class who are conspicuous by their absence from the ranks of pauperism." Longley recommended not only that able-bodied males be denied outdoor relief, but that support for widows, deserted wives, single women, and the disabled be limited. Moreover, he urged that all outdoor aid end after three months and medical care after one, forcing the applicant either to resume self-support or enter the workhouse. To those who objected to breaking up the households of the poor, he replied that it was often erroneous to believe that the poor had a home, or "such a home that its loss will be otherwise than to the ultimate benefit of himself and his family."[45] Similar hostility to outdoor relief led most local guardians to tighten their administration of it and others virtually to abandon direct grants.

London welfare policies after 1850 were intended to be a destabilizing pressure on the household structures of the poor. Settlement officers, intent on repressing destitution and reforming behavior, increasingly recommended the workhouse for people formerly given money and largely ignored. Guardians of the poor put deserted wives in the workhouse and jailed their husbands for nonsupport, if they could be found.[46] Even if a family entered a workhouse together, separate wards for men and women, old and young, sick and well put them in different wards or buildings, and elaborate regulations kept them apart. Children soon left for district schools or cottage homes and had little possibility of contact with parents. Charlie Chaplin recounts in his autobiography how he and his brother were separated from his mother after her application for relief. When she left the workhouse to look for a job, the children were kept in a workhouse boarding school. Occasionally she asked for their release so that she could see them for a day or so; then they returned to the school.[47] The New Poor Law treated the indigent as individuals and meted out treatment according to age, sex, and physical condition, largely ignoring emotional or collective needs. Pauper families were not units that were valued and supported by welfare officials.

This policy followed directly from common attitudes to paupers, who were seen as threatening to the wider community. They had a contagious disease that could easily spread to others. Paupers were tainted in their "blood and bones," bred from an inferior stock, and a menace to the community around them, argued Norman Pearson in the magazine *Nineteenth Century and After*.[48] Even critics of the poor laws, such as Sidney and Beatrice Webb, believed in the communicability of the culture of poverty: "The neglected infant, the child abandoned to illiteracy and destitution, the overworked factory operative, injured coal-miner or half-starved labourer did not necessarily die, and thus remove their individual degeneracy from the continual stream of the nation's life; they persisted in living at the lower level down to which they were pressed, and by their mere existence in disease and squalor, vice, mendicancy and crime, infecting and contaminating the rest of the community."[49] The appropriate response to such moral contagion was isolation of paupers and restriction of their contact with the wider society. Children should be taken away from inadequate parents and loafers forced to work in labor colonies. Outdoor relief and the "promiscuous workhouse" both stood condemned for their openness to contact between old and young, male and female, parent and child. The ending of contagion required strict separation between the different categories of pauper, each of which might be redeemed if the pernicious effects of family and neighborhood example were removed. By the late nineteenth century, the categories of deserving and undeserving poor had been replaced by a view of all paupers as morally deficient. Since the "pauper family" spread moral pollution and perpetuated a culture of poverty, officials had an obligation to repress rather than maintain it. Policies were set accordingly.

Demands for Support

Thousands of poor Londoners, whose kin provided their main source of support, refused the poor law's scenario of sturdy independence from the state. For them, family and welfare were not alternative means to survival but complementary resources. Poor law aid was less a stigma than a necessity in times of need. Despite much well-documented dislike for the poor law, it was perceived by workers as offering insurance against the hazards of an unstable economy and the regular crises of the human life cycle. Some workers demanded their "rights" when confronting poor law officials and asked for more generous pensions. Others challenged attempts to end or lower allowances.[50] Guardians complained in the 1870s to parliamentary investigators that some of their poor parishioners claimed a right to relief because they had paid poor rates all their lives.[51] Stepney guardians noted with disapproval in the 1890s people who claimed a right to more relief than the guardians were willing to give.

The London poor regularly turned to welfare officials when they and their nuclear families could no longer provide sufficient food, shelter, and care. Sometimes the problems were temporary, triggered by illness or unemployment; sometimes the difficulties became permanent because of death or desertion. In both cases, the state was approached for help that normally came from kin. Historians' notion that welfare was anathema to all respectable workers ignores the many ways in which poor Londoners used the state to provide basic goods and services their families could not supply and shifted onto the welfare establishment the temporary and sometimes permanent care of those for whom they could not provide. Wives and husbands brought in requests for spouses and children; daughters demanded alms for elderly parents. Even if the state chose to limit the maintenance of families, the poor persisted in demands that would achieve that end. The availability of a variety of poor law services was well known and permitted Londoners to gain income supplements without going into the workhouse. Such aid benefited household units as well as the individuals directly aided.

The chance for free medical care led many to apply to welfare officials. The law of 1834 had authorized local guardians to appoint medical officers, and the larger London unions each employed several doctors by the late 1830s. They saw patients in the workhouse or in a local dispensary and visited the homes of those too sick to be moved. Both the demand for and the supply of medical services for the poor were high in London. The Stepney poor law medical staff of five treated about eight thousand pauper patients per year in the early 1840s. They were also responsible for midwifery and for vaccinating local people against smallpox. This latter service, which did not brand the recipient as a pauper, was intended for the entire population and drew thousands of people to poor law doctors during the 1840s. Finally, in 1853, when parents were required to vaccinate infants within a few months of their birth, poor law doctors became in effect public health officials. More by accident than design, the state very early blurred the lines between welfare, charity, and public services to which all were entitled. Although under the New Poor Law, medical aid to anyone in a family technically counted as relief and brought pauper status to all, in practice this provision was often ignored. The sick had special rights to aid, having to prove only that they could not afford a doctor.[52]

Welfare and medical services were closely linked because of the high incidence of sickness among the London poor. The cholera epidemics of 1832 and 1848–49 struck the crowded workers' areas of the East End, Southwark, and Bermondsey particularly hard, and the incidence in London of smallpox, measles, whooping cough, and scarlet fever was higher among families of laborers and poor artisans than among more affluent groups. London public health officials regularly noted the linkage between slum housing, bad sanitation, and disease that doomed workers to relatively early deaths.[53] As a result, a high proportion of applicants for poor relief were ill. Ruth Hodgkinson claims that virtually all able-bodied males who got aid were given it because they were in poor health.[54] In 1870, sick paupers constituted a third of those given outdoor relief in London, and in 1881, 40 percent of Shoreditch's and 34 percent of Camberwell's institutionalized paupers were infirmary patients.[55] The need for medical care drove many workers into the arms of the state.

The troubles of the Davis-Timcke family, Stepney residents in the 1880s, illustrate both the diseases of the destitute and their willingness to ask poor law doctors for help.[56] William Davis, a coal porter, applied for medicine for his wife, Johanna, and for outdoor relief in 1883 after the birth of a stillborn child. He needed medicine a few years later for his ulcerated leg, and the family got medical attention throughout the 1880s for a father-in-law who had a bad foot. Various family members brought poor law doctors to see an uncle who was partially paralyzed by a stroke in 1877 and a sister, whom they suspected had smallpox. Johanna Davis's sister-in-law needed infirmary care in 1887 after she bore a dead child, and her mother entered the sick asylum for bronchitis in 1884. A sister spent three weeks in the local smallpox hospital in 1881 after her mother brought the case to the attention of relief officers, and her husband was granted medicine in 1884 and 1886 for minor illnesses. Most commonly, women in the family went to the relieving officer and asked to see a doctor. After visiting the home, a poor law official ordered medicine, admission to the infirmary or workhouse, and sometimes outdoor relief. These people lived on the edge of destitution, but their most frequent demands of the state were for medical care, perhaps because it was the extra service they could not provide for themselves, perhaps because the state was willing to grant it on terms the Davis and Timcke households were willing to accept. Doctors often brought food as well as medicine, and they did not order workhouse or hospital residence except for the seriously ill. Medical care therefore was often outdoor relief in disguise, and it was popular among the poor.

Many requests for state aid came at times of crisis in family life cycles. A death in the family led workers to welfare offices because of the high cost of burial. A respectable funeral for an adult in London cost about seven weeks' wages for an unskilled laborer around 1870, and insurance plans were not universal among workers' families until the 1930s.[57] Many poor Londoners found it necessary to ask the parish to bury their children. Pauper case records from the 1890s regularly note adult males' funerals paid for by friendly societies or donations by friends, but applications were made to the union for children's and sometimes wives' interments. Burial orders were given without the demand to enter a workhouse, and infants, in particular, were less likely to be insured than adults. Poor families who spent all they had on elaborate funerals and mourning black for a father were willing, or perhaps forced, to have a simple union service for an infant or a mother.

Resentments over the form of the services sometimes surfaced but did not stop applications. Almost half of the people given outdoor relief by the Stepney guardians in 1889 whose cases were recorded in Charles Booth's interviews asked for money to bury a relative. Among these families of dock workers and low-skilled laborers, stillborn infants, children dying of fever, dependent sisters, and wives were buried with parish aid.[58]

Adult deaths, particularly those of a husband and father, catapulted many families into poverty and brought them to the relieving officer. Widows were the most frequent applicants for help, bringing requests for themselves and their children. Although widows could, and did, receive small amounts of outdoor relief throughout the nineteenth century, those grants provided no permanent security against destitution and did not provide support in the absence of other income. Entry into the workhouse was always possible, but many East End families followed another procedure in the 1890s. Since London poor law unions ran district boarding schools, the state could be used to educate and support children. Phoebe Dix, widowed in 1885, supported herself and her two youngest children on her earnings and her husband's insurance payments for three years after his death. When the insurance money ran out, she temporarily broke up the family. Her youngest daughter went to a sister's home in Yarmouth, and she petitioned poor law officers to take her ten-year-old son into a district school so that she could work as a servant. Because her eldest daughter, who was already working as a domestic, could not keep a job and seemed incapable of self-support, Dix twice got the state to admit the girl to charitable homes for adolescents and to help her find employment. When neither of these alternatives proved viable, the girl was sent into the workhouse.[59]

The temporary, selective use of state facilities for children was common among East End females attempting to survive without fathers or husbands. Ann Tanner, a widow with seven children, asked in 1886 that her two oldest sons, aged eleven and nine, be admitted to state schools. Not only was she unable to feed them, but she found them "troublesome." She and an eighteen-year-old daughter managed to support the rest of the family while another daughter took care of the younger children. When their collective earnings rose, she brought one of the sons home from the school; when they fell, he and a third son were sent away. Their mother asked that John and George Kersley be admitted to state schools when her epileptic husband lost his job and was sent to a state asylum for lunatics and incurables, where he soon died. Meanwhile, she worked as a servant, keeping a four-year-old son with her. Later she remarried and retrieved her older boys, but their reconstituted family life lasted only until her death four years later. Their stepfather, a Thames policeman, got two of the boys readmitted to the Brighton Road School on the ground that he had six other children to support and could not be held liable for the Kersley brothers.[60] Children in state schools and homes in the late nineteenth century were for the most part not orphans but children with kin in London who could not provide for them.[61] Poor families, particularly widows and stepparents, used state facilities to provide education and shelter for some of their children while they attempted to reestablish their households. During the course of the century, fewer and fewer family units entered London workhouses; they managed to find other means of survival.[62] Although case records provide limited insights into paupers' motives, families appear to have avoided joint application to the workhouse by temporarily dissolving their households. Some members of the group were sent away to increase the chances of independent survival for the rest.

The composition of a poor worker's family and household seems to have been rather flexible in the nineteenth century. Coresidence of a nuclear family was common but certainly not permanent even while children were young. The relatively high incidence of death and desertion split up nuclear families regularly, eliminating members of the original group and in the longer run bringing in a variety of stepparents, fictive kin, and extended family members. Adolescents left or were sent away to work. Those too young to fend for themselves could be enrolled in a workhouse school. Husbands and fathers sometimes traveled in search of work, leaving children with in-laws. Lodgers or elderly relatives might be taken in to help with child care and to share rent costs. Among the poor, the size and composition of coresident groups varied according to income, health, and compatibility. During times of family crisis, the weaker, less useful members were sent away, sometimes to state institutions.

In consequence, many of the poor tolerated even the hated workhouse for the services it provided. For most, it served as only a temporary refuge. A survey done for the Royal Commission on the Poor Laws showed that only 27 percent of the people on indoor relief in 1907 had remained in a workhouse for an entire year; over 50 percent remained less than thirteen weeks.[63] Some people discharged themselves in the summer, when more relatives would be employed and household income higher; others left the workhouse to gather hops in Kent in the fall, when they could earn enough to keep themselves.

This use of temporary state support was common among the elderly, who had to piece together incomes from several sources. Since the insecurity of day-to-day life prevented most workers from saving for their old age, they retreated to a combination of family and state resources when unable to work. The elderly often received partial or temporary support from several of their children, entering workhouses during periods when none of their kin were willing or able to maintain them. Although most London workhouse residents appear to have had kin in the metropolis, extended families did not take on responsibility for the elderly. The burden of caring for parents rested on nuclear families, especially daughters. Nevertheless, sickness, unemployment, and the number of their own children hampered their ability to assist; maintaining their families of procreation appears to have taken precedence over the needs of their families of origin. In any case, care did not imply coresidence. Given the small size of London workers' apartments and the English predisposition to nuclear family households, taking in an elderly parent was not obligatory, either in a legal or a moral sense. Thus children often applied for workhouse care for a parent, or the elderly presented themselves and asked for admission. Constant coresidence within a nuclear or an extended family was a luxury that the elderly poor could not afford, even if they desired it.

Demands for welfare as well as state policies were therefore closely linked to household income, health, and resources. Kin asked for help for one another with an eye to the types of public aid available because aid to one member of a group freed resources for the others. The family of an unemployed sick worker could get extra food from relief officials if medical aid was granted. By gaining a pension for an elderly parent, a son or daughter could better feed his or her own children. By sending some of her children to a poor law boarding school and then allowing the state to find work for them, widows could ensure their support and do more for the others who remained at home. Families of the poor were flexible in their composition and in their sources of income in the effort to increase the chances for survival both of individuals and of the group. Although desertion did occur, more commonly kin did not abandon responsibility for one another. Migration out of a household was usually temporary, and Londoners on welfare had frequent contact with kin. This apparent instability of families stemmed paradoxically from workers' often successful efforts to preserve families in the long run.

The London poor in their struggles for survival were not usually faced with the stark choice of entry into a workhouse or starvation. Several alternative forms of aid existed, particularly for women and children. Because administrators distinguished among applicants according to age, sex, and physical condition, different types of aid could be requested for different members of a family. Asking for relief became a negotiated process, although, to be sure, one in which the balance of power was unequal.

Low-skilled workers in London had regular dealings with poor law administrators, especially during life cycle crises. Even if they would have preferred to avoid the guardians of the poor, they needed the welfare services offered and felt that they had a right to them. As a result, the stigma of relief operated more powerfully in the minds of poor law officials than in those of their clients, who knew enough about welfare services to distinguish among them. Rather than avoid the poor law, they directed requests to the more desirable forms of aid to gain added resources for their family economies.

Notes

Research for this essay was supported by the American Council of Learned Societies. James Davis, Stefano Fenoaltea, Paul Hohenberg, Andrew Lees, and Susan Watkins made helpful comments. I thank them all.

1. Great Britain, Parliament, *Report from the Commission of Inquiry into the Poor Laws*, P.P. 1834, 27:229.
2. Edward P. Thompson, *The Making of the English Working Class* (New York: Random House, 1963), 248; Michael E. Rose, ed., *The Poor and the City: The English Poor Law in Its Urban Context, 1834–1914* (New York: St. Martin's Press, 1985), 3; Derek Fraser, ed., *The New Poor Law in the Nineteenth Century* (New York: St. Martin's Press, 1976), 21.
3. "Interviews of Inmates of Institutions," case 427, p. 653, Charles Booth Papers, B: 162, British Library of Political and Economic Science, London.
4. Ibid., case 692, p. 932.
5. The 1834 New Poor Law was administered through groups of parishes called unions.
6. "Inmates of Institutions," case 1021, p. 1222, Booth Papers.
7. This calculation uses Sidney and Beatrice Webb's estimate that the total number of aided cases in a given year was 2.2 times the number of recipients counted on the two sample days for which returns were tabulated, and it assumes only one application by the aided population during each cycle of years, which, except for the chronically ill and elderly, reflects common patterns of contact with relief officials. Poor law documents reveal the temporary and episodic character of most welfare grants. Figures of incidence of aid are contained in Table 3.1.

See Sidney Webb and Beatrice Webb, *English Poor Law History. Part II: The Last Hundred Years* (London: Longmans, 1897), 2:1051.

8. Ibid., 1:52–53, 64.

9. Great Britain, Parliament, *Report [on] the Poor Laws*, 1834, 27:127.

10. David Thomson, "'I am not my father's keeper': Families and the Elderly in Nineteenth-Century England," *Law and History Review*, 2, no. 2 (1984), 269–70.

11. London, St. Martin in the Fields, Board of Guardians, Settlement Examinations, 1847–70, cases 236, 244, 248, Greater London Council Archive.

12. R. H. Alford, "Maintenance by Relatives," *Poor Law Conferences* (London: P. S. King, 1899), 599.

13. London, Chelsea, Board of Guardians, "Inspector's Report, 1833–1834," cases 656, 578, Greater London Council Archive.

14. Ibid., case 483.

15. Ibid., pp. 2–3.

16. Great Britain, Parliament, *Abstract of Returns Relative to the Poor*, P.P. 1803–4, 13:306–7; 1818, 19:269–70.

17. Great Britain, Parliament, *Report [on] the Poor Laws*, 1834, 26, Appendix B2, Q 15: Middlesex.

18. Ibid., 27, Appendix B2, 82–185.

19. Poor Law Commission, *Annual Report* (London: HMSO, 1839), 116–18.

20. Great Britain, Parliament, *Report of the Royal Commission on the Poor Laws and Relief of Distress*, 1910, 53:636, 639.

21. M. A. Crowther, *The Workhouse System, 1834–1929* (London: Methuen, 1981), 89.

22. J. W. Innes, *Class Fertility Trends in England and Wales, 1876–1934* (Princeton: Princeton University Press, 1938); E. A. Wrigley and R. S. Schofield, *The Population History of England, 1541–1871* (Cambridge, Mass.: Harvard University Press, 1981).

23. The trend in the United States was similar. See S. H. Preston, "Children and the Elderly: Divergent Paths for America's Dependents," *Demography* 21 (1984), 435–57.

24. Karel Williams, *From Pauperism to Poverty* (London: Routledge & Kegan Paul, 1981), 205.

25. Great Britain, Parliament, *Report of the Royal Commission on the Poor Laws and Relief of Distress*, 1909, 37:38.

26. Great Britain, Manuscript Censuses of 1851 and 1881, HO 107–1484, 1516, 1553, 1577; RG 11–324, 409, 557, 679, Public Record Office.

27. Great Britain, Parliament, *Report [on] the Poor Laws*, 1834, 37, Appendix B2, 107–8, 115, 151, 168.

28. London, Chelsea, "Inspector's Report, 1833–34," case 36, Greater London Council Archive.

29. Great Britain, Parliament, *Report [on] the Poor Laws*, 1834, 36, Appendix B2, 108, 181.

30. London, Holborn Union, Board of Guardians, "Examinations, 1830–31," Greater London Council Archive.

31. Great Britain, Parliament, *Report [on] the Poor Laws*, 1834, 36, Appendix B2, 161–62.

32. J. H. Stallard, *London Pauperism amongst Christians and Jews* (London: Saunders, Otley, and Co., 1867), 203; Great Britain, Parliament, *Report [on] the Poor Laws*, 1834, 36, Appendix B2, 164, 177.

33. K. D. M. Snell, *Annals of the Labouring Poor* (Cambridge, Eng.: Cambridge University Press, 1985), 105.

34. Joanna Innes, "Social Problems: Poverty and Marginality in Eighteenth-Century England," in *The Social World of Britain and America: A Comparison from the Perspective of Social History* (Williamsburg, Va.: Institute of Early American History and Culture, 1985), 51.

35. London, St. Pancras, "Examinations, 1850–51," Greater London Council Archive.

36. Stallard, *London Pauperism*, 203.

37. London, Chelsea, Board of Guardians, "List of Outrelief Given; Settled and Irremovable Poor, 1852–1855," and "Non-Settled Poor Relief Account, 1845–1851," Greater London Council Archive.

38. London, Bermondsey, St. Olave's Union, "Signed Minutes of the Board of Guardians, 1835–1851," 1:319–24, Greater London Council Archive.

39. Ibid., 7:32.

40. Stallard, *London Pauperism*, 245.

41. London, Bermondsey, St. Olave's Union, "Weekly Returns of the Relieving Officers, 1890–1893," Greater London Council Archive.

42. Henry Longley, "Poor Relief Administration in London," *Third Annual Report of the Local Government Board, 1873–1874* (London: HMSO, 1874), 169.

43. David Thomson, "The Decline of Social Welfare: Falling State Support for the Elderly since Early Victorian Times," *Ageing and Society* 4, no. 4 (1984), 477.

44. Webb and Webb, *English Poor Law History, Part I*, 1:438–39.

45. Longley, "Poor Relief Administration," 142, 171, 204–5.

46. Edmund H. Wodenhouse, "Outdoor Relief," *Twenty-Third Annual Report of the Poor Law Board, 1870–1871* (London: HMSO, 1871), 36–37.

47. Charles Chaplin, *My Autobiography* (New York: Simon and Schuster, 1964), 26–28.

48. Norman Pearson, "The Idle Poor," *Nineteenth Century and After* 70 (1911), 917.

49. Webb and Webb, *English Poor Law History, Part I*, 2:551.

50. London, Chelsea, Board of Guardians, "Inspector's Report, 1834."

51. Paul Johnson, *Saving and Spending: The Working-Class Economy in Britain 1870–1939* (Oxford: Clarendon Press, 1985), 194.

52. Ruth G. Hodgkinson, *The Origins of the National Health Service: The Medical Services of the New Poor Law, 1834–1871* (Berkeley and Los Angeles: University of California Press, 1967), 27, 29, 275–76, 298.

53. Registrar General, *Report on the Mortality of Cholera in England, 1848–1849* (London: HMSO, 1852), clxvi–clxviii; *Report of the Royal Commission on the State of Large Towns and Populous Districts*, P.P. 1844, 17:254.

54. Hodgkinson, *Origins of the National Health Service*, 270.

55. Great Britain, Manuscript Census of 1881, RG 11, 409, 679.

56. "Interviews of Inmates," case 555, Booth Papers.

57. Johnson, *Saving and Spending*, 12, 22.

58. "Interviews of Inmates," cases 406–13, 415–16, 423–37, 773–80, Booth Papers.

59. Ibid., case 6.

60. Ibid., cases 25 and 43.

61. Lambeth Board of Guardians, "List of Persons Chargeable to the Parish on January 1, 1888," 50–75, Greater London Council Archive.

62. Crowther, *Workhouse System*, 233.

63. Great Britain, Parliament, *Report of the Royal Commission on the Poor Laws*, 1909, 37:25.

Rachel G. Fuchs

4. Preserving the Future of France: Aid to the Poor and Pregnant in Nineteenth-Century Paris

"THE POOR AND VICIOUS CLASSES always have been and always will be the most *fertile crucible* for all categories of wrongdoers," intoned a leading nineteenth-century social analyst.[1] In language evoking female reproduction, he articulated the widespread assumption that the poor women of Paris, by their capacity to become pregnant, carried in their wombs the potential for reproducing the "dangerous classes" and maintaining a cycle of poverty and immorality. As mothers, they bore essential responsibility for establishing family ties and for raising future generations. They formed an integral part of urban life. Consequently, throughout the nineteenth century the poor and pregnant were central to any discussion of the social question: what to do about the problem of poverty with its concomitant depravity, immorality, and crime. Social analysts regarded illegitimacy as a barometer of immorality and lived in a world in which illegitimacy was a visible and irritating social problem. During the first half of the century the illegitimacy rate in metropolitan Paris exceeded 30 percent of all births; throughout the century, it never fell below 24 percent.[2] Every analysis of society's ills, and the possible remedies, necessarily included discussion of the poor and pregnant, especially the unwed.

In the general shift from revolutionary France to the nation that fought in World War I, the pregnant poor played an emblematic role in focusing our understanding of the shift from charity to welfare. At the beginning of the century they were the deserving objects of charity, albeit a charity that judged them harshly. By the time of World War I they were the clearly qualified recipients of a less judgmental, yet not necessarily more generous, welfare system. A study of the poor and pregnant will elucidate that shift in society from charity to welfare. An exploration of their situation opens a window onto the general functioning of charity and welfare in Paris and furthers the study of the intrusion of social and public policy into women's lives as well as their strategies for survival.

Early in the century, the problem of the urban poor was equated with the fecundity of impoverished women who lacked morality and had children even though they could not support them or were not married. The bourgeoisie described an epidemic of illicit relationships rampant in the city, generating urban malaise, immorality, deviancy, and threats to traditional values. For the first three-fourths of the century, the morality of the poor and pregnant dominated discussions of the social question. Prevailing ideas generated religiously inspired private charity to improve the morality of the poor and to remove the threat the poor urban women posed to property, the family, and Christian morality.

Toward the end of the century, officials became less disturbed by fecundity than they were by infant mortality. French concern with depopulation cast pregnant women and their offspring in a more favorable light than earlier in the century. Poor mothers were less to be punished for their immorality; the children were more to be nurtured. This concern, as well as increasing secularization during the Third Republic (beginning in 1871), led state and municipal welfare agencies to see themselves as the protectors of the nation's children and indirectly as protectors of their indigent mothers. Specific welfare programs resulted.

Throughout the century, ideas of morality and public policy were intertwined. Each group of moralists and reformers had a vision and plan of what they should and should not do to change the behavior of pregnant women, and by extension the poor. This essay explores the shift from charity to welfare in nineteenth-century Paris as it affected urban poor mothers. It first delineates how private charity evolved and functioned in response to specific attitudes toward marriage and maternity and demonstrates how women were affected by specific charity programs. It then explains the shift from private charity to public welfare that occurred during the last third of the century and analyzes welfare programs and their female clients. This shift from charity to welfare involved new concepts of morality and a concomitant change in the recipients of aid from only married to both married and single mothers. Finally, the essay seeks to examine how private charity and public welfare affected the values and behavior of the women who were given or denied aid and how, in turn, the women may have altered the actual way charity and welfare functioned.

Private Charity

The nature of charity reflected the attitudes reformers and philanthropists held toward the poor and pregnant. The Baron Joseph de Gerando, expressing prevailing views, believed that the well-being of the laboring classes was immensely important for all of society. He argued that the population increase, the development of industry, and the inequality of conditions in the big cities imposed new tasks upon society; enlightened generosity had become an obligation if society was to prevent immorality and deviance. Following logically from such assumptions, he argued that private charity should provide for the moral rehabilitation of the poor and pregnant. It would thus prevent the contamination and corruption of their babies, who otherwise would repeat the patterns of their mothers and become a menace to society.[3]

Many philanthropists operated under the philosophy that "a Christian society is eminently charitable."[4] Religiously inspired charitable and philanthropic groups began in the early nineteenth century and grew during the 1850s and 1860s, when Social Catholicism reached its apogee.[5] The elite women who served as patrons, benefactors, and administrators of private charitable organizations for urban poor women served out of a devotion to the ideals of Catholic love and charity.[6] Because their work served the cause of motherhood and a strong hierarchical and patriarchal family, the women they aided had to be married—and married in a religious ceremony. They refused to aid unwed mothers or their illegitimate children because to do so would encourage immorality and the breakdown of traditional family ties.

Mathilde Froment Bourdon, the Comtesse A. E. de Gasparin, and the Comtesse Pauline d'Haussonville typified nineteenth-century charitable ladies ostensibly motivated by religious dictates. They believed, for example, that God ordered people to be charitable to those less fortunate, and good people, through charity, became closer to God. Charity is an arm of religion; it is a duty of all religious people.[7] Thus charity was important for the givers as well as for those who received. The bourgeois women of Paris, like those in more religious departments in France, structured their charitable work in line with their beliefs in "authority, order and the morality of domestic life," and their "exclusive concern" was the "familial problems of other women and their children."[8] Elite married women, whose primary duties were familial, became the logical group to safeguard the traditional family by alleviating some of the problems of the poor and pregnant while educating them in proper bourgeois values.

One of the oldest nineteenth-century philanthropic foundations devoted to moralizing and aiding the poor and pregnant was la Société de charité maternelle de Paris. Founded in 1784 under the patronage of Marie Antoinette, it received a subvention from the state after 1810 and continued as a private philanthropy into the twentieth century. Throughout the nineteenth century, women of title or of the upper middle classes continued as patrons, benefactors, and administrators, and the wife of the head of state usually served as chief benefactress.[9] They devoted themselves, in the name of Christian love and charity, to helping poor mothers who were married or who would marry if given financial aid.

This agency provided needy married mothers with partial payment for the cost of home delivery of the baby by a midwife, a layette, and financial aid for twelve months of nursing.[10] The society stressed the importance of nursing one's own baby. Its members believed that one cause of social misery was the weakening of maternal feelings, which they attributed to mercenary wet nursing. They subscribed to the opinion of Dr. A.-T. Brochard, a leading physician and reformer (but not a member of the society), who said, "God wanted a woman to nurse. That's why he gave her breasts with milk and placed them under her shoulders so she could press the baby to her heart."[11] Religiously inspired bourgeois *Dames de charité*, volunteering for the society, visited each aid recipient once a month to instruct her in proper religious behavior and in hygienic care of her baby and to inspect her activities and surroundings. In some respects, especially after 1874, the aid was designed to prevent depopulation by preventing the abandonment and mortality of legitimate children. It was also minimal, however, to encourage—or force—the husband to work to support his children. The society's payments to nursing mothers did not exceed what l'Assistance publique paid wet nurses to raise abandoned children or paid unwed mothers to keep their babies. Each baby received a layette, diapers, and some clothes. Financial aid ranged from four to twenty francs per month for up to twelve months, depending on perceived need and available funds.[12]

Throughout the century, the society's criteria for maternal assistance barely changed. The women had to request aid during the last two months of pregnancy, furnishing a certificate of good morals from their mayor or clergyman. They also had to be married in a religious ceremony, agree to have their babies baptized immediately after birth, and nurse their infants themselves. The society accepted women without distinction to religion as long as they fulfilled the other criteria. In 1876 a means test was added: if the husband was alive and living with the mother, they had to have at least three children under the age of thirteen, or the husband must be chronically ill, or they themselves had to be infirm with at least two children living at home. If a woman "lost" her husband during her pregnancy, however, she had to have only one other child at home to be entitled to aid. In principle, a woman living with her husband and benefiting from two incomes, or his higher wages, could support more children than could a single mother. In aiding only married women, the society sought to strengthen family bonds.[13]

Despite the investigation and inspection of the mothers' marriage, finances, and morality that the Société de charité maternelle mandated for all recipients, the number of needy Parisian mothers receiving aid increased annually from an average of 630 per year in the decade of the 1820s to approximately 1,700 per year in each decade after 1860.[14] Because of its limited resources, the society seemed more interested in moralizing many women than in alleviating the poverty of a few; as the requests for aid increased, less money was given to each mother, and the reductions were greatest during the last months of nursing. Women took the charity of the Société de charité maternelle because their need was great. Twenty or even four francs a month, plus baby clothes, provided by the society was better than nothing and enabled poor women better to manage the crisis of birth and a new infant. The relief helped get them through the extra costs and possible loss of work that the birth of an infant entailed and enabled poor mothers to avoid the deplorable conditions of the free maternity hospitals. The mothers had to tolerate visits and inspections from charitable ladies, but these visits may have been accompanied by presents and other individual acts of charity.[15]

The Société Saint-François-Régis, founded in 1826 and part of the Oeuvre des mariages des pauvres, emphasized the importance of marriage as did the Société de charité maternelle. The Société de Saint-François-Régis's leaders reflected the concerns of the social and moral economists. In 1840 the social economist H. A. Frégier complained that only one-third of the women in the needle trades were married to the men with whom they were living. The other two-thirds, living in concubinage, represented the immorality and potential danger rampant in the big city.[16] This society's leaders saw the urban areas, especially Paris, as "centers of concubinage and illicit unions among the working classes" with a resultant large number of illegitimate children. These "disordered morals," they said, "are the source of most crimes." Marriage would lead to more regulated labor and "honest sentiments in the heart." The sole aim was to "moralize" the women and legitimize the unions, thus helping to end the "plague of concubinage that threatened" the city.[17]

The Société Saint-François-Régis facilitated and funded civil and religious marriages among poor Catholic couples living together. It required couples seeking aid to appear at the headquarters of the society on a Sunday afternoon, carrying a recommendation from their mayor or clergyman attesting to their established residency, age, and good morality. If the man was under twenty-five years old, or the woman under twenty-one, they had to have parental consent to marry. Counselors later interviewed the couple in their living quarters with the instruction to "penetrate the couple's hearts and inspire religious sentiments."[18]

By enabling couples to marry, the society had some success, especially toward the end of the century. From 1826 to 1875 the society conducted 53,936 marriages and legitimized 29,551 children. Between 1826 and 1841, the 7,165 couples receiving aid to legitimize their cohabitation represented one-eighteenth of all marriages in Paris.[19] But between 1856 and 1887, it funded one-ninth of all marriages in the Department of the Seine.[20] The society's work had been made easier and less expensive by the law of December 18, 1850, on the marriage of indigents. The law was designed to preserve the family, especially in big cities, by facilitating the marriage of indigents and the legitimation of children. After a mayor or priest certified the couple's indigence, the cost of marriage, birth, and legitimization certificates was eliminated and the required notarial fees were reduced. During the second half of the century, the Société Saint-François-Régis implemented the law and assisted more couples to marry. In keeping with its philosophy, the society also provided each couple with a religious ceremony.

Poor and indigent cohabiting couples lived together without a legal marriage by necessity rather than choice. Marriage was costly, and securing the papers necessary for registering a marriage was both a large expense and an onerous burden. For example, in 1876 the necessary birth certificates for a couple cost 2.55 francs each and the marriage certificate cost 3.30 francs. This did not include the notarial fees, the papers signifying the necessary parental approval for either person who was under age, and the expense in getting parental approval if the couple lived far from their parents—as was frequently the case for cohabitants in Paris. The overall cost of completing the necessary paperwork for getting married ranged from 40 to 100 francs, not including fees to recognize legally (9.38 francs) or legitimize (3.75 francs) a child born before the marriage.[21] If they had to go back to the countryside to get parental approval, the couple had the additional financial burden of losing wages. Getting married cost more than one month's wages for a poor working couple in Paris who barely had enough for the necessities of survival. Saving for marriage was beyond their financial ability. For many women in Paris, cohabitation was the nonrealization of the goal of marriage—a marriage strategy that failed.[22]

Of the impoverished couples receiving aid to legalize their cohabitation and legitimize their children, most were employed and in long-term, stable unions. Over one-third of all the couples had been living together for more than six years. Only 22 percent had been living together less than one year; 24 percent had been together one to three years; and 20 percent had been together for three to six years. They were able-bodied, "deserving" poor. Only 6 percent of the men were marginally indigent; 27 percent were *menu peuple*—domestic servants, day laborers, cooks, street vendors, and shop clerks, and 64 percent were manual laborers. Most of the women in these stable unions worked in the needle trades (78 percent), 8 percent were "without profession," and 13 percent worked at heavy labor.[23] These couples could not afford the fees necessary to get married because their combined income approximated between three and five francs a day.

The Société Saint-François-Régis did not intend to alleviate poverty; it gave no financial aid before or after the marriage and did not financially aid those who most needed it. It fulfilled the consciences and sense of duty of the donors more than it alleviated the economic need and suffering of the poor. Since women essentially were in common-law marriages, legalization did not *ipso facto* provide the needed second income and may not have made a difference in the family economy. The Société Saint-François-Régis legitimized many children and secured women in marriage, thereby helping them achieve their goal of marriage. Under Napoleonic law, marriage gave women legal recourse to paternal child support not available to unmarried mothers.

Whether the mothers were married, cohabiting, or living alone, the problem remained of providing for the care of their babies if they had to work outside the home. Crèches, or infant day care centers, though apparently a form of charity for infants, in reality served the mothers—the married ones. The religiously inspired Société des crèches, by accepting only legitimate children, hoped to encourage single mothers to marry. Crèche founders and organizers believed that the acceptance of illegitimate children, just as assistance to unwed mothers, would encourage single mothers—a sure sign of debauchery—and tend to destroy the traditional family of two parents under God. The society put great emphasis on the piety of mothers and children and on family ties; it aimed to make the children good workers, good citizens, and even good soldiers—under the influence of God.[24] The first crèches, designed to prevent abandonment and mercenary wet nursing of legitimate babies, appeared in Paris in 1844. According to Firman Marbeau, the organization's founding father, the crèches moralized the family (especially the mother), protected family ties against abandonment and wet nursing, and favored work. "Work is, after faith, the most powerful moralizing factor in the world. . . . Work makes a mother virtuous."[25] By putting her baby in a crèche, the mother could work, periodically nurse her baby, and avoid abandoning her infant and causing its probable death. Mothers' alternatives to a crèche were leaving their babies alone all day, with neighbors, sending them to wet nurses, or abandoning them. Marbeau argued that babies had a greater chance of survival in a crèche than they did under these other conditions.

Each crèche accommodated, at any one time, only about twenty infants ranging in age from fifteen days to three years, at a cost to the parents of twenty centimes per day.[26] Authorities considered twenty centimes affordable because it was the price of a loaf of bread, and the average wage for a working woman in Paris was about one and a half francs a day. Private donations and bequests, as well as state, departmental, and municipal subventions, supported the crèches. Few crèches existed. In 1853 there were twenty-five crèches in Paris, in 1868 there were twenty-one sheltering 880 babies, and in 1870 there were twenty-three accommodating 810 babies. Until late in the nineteenth century, few mothers took advantage of the crèches because the few that existed were overcrowded, far from the mothers' homes, and did not accept children of single mothers. Generally, private charity did not aid unwed mothers. It devolved upon l'Assistance publique to offer them relief.

During the first three-fourths of the century, private charity, almost all under religious auspices, dominated aid to the poor and pregnant. Although the directors of the charities determined their recipients and controlled their resources, they were not independent of public funds. For example, the Sociétés de charité maternelle, des crèches, and Saint-François-Régis received annual appropriations from departmental, municipal, and national governments. Furthermore, the Société Saint-François-Régis occasionally received money from the Bureau de bienfaisance of an arrondissement because it "regularized" the relationships of so many indigents living in that arrondissement.[27] Private charity was driven by the perception of the unwed poor and pregnant as immoral and the desire to encourage marriage and traditional moral and religious values. In short, charity and welfare up to 1870 served to defend the conservative trinity: family, property, and religion.

Depopulation and Poverty, 1870–1914

With the beginning of the Third Republic, private efforts were overshadowed by new secular welfare programs. The assumptions about who was responsible for charity and welfare changed, as did the motivations behind the programs. The idea that France was a Christian nation gave way to the secular concept of France as the totality of its citizens. As Henri Monod, a leading Republican welfare official, said, "If charity is an individual virtue, then public assistance is a state virtue."[28] If the state embodied all its citizens, then it was the state's responsibility to provide welfare for all. As a result of the laic transposition of the former Christian virtue of charity, the Third Republic developed social welfare policies and programs designed for the single "debauched" as well as the married "moral" poor. The paternalism of the bureaucracy replaced the maternalism of bourgeois, charitable women.

During the Third Republic, public welfare developed in Paris, and by extension in France, primarily because the population crisis contributed to a change in attitudes and led to a redefinition of the "social question" in such a way that state and local governments could take legislative and programmatic action. The crushing defeat of France by the Prussian army in 1870 shocked the French. Officials of the new Third Republic sought to explain the loss and examined the nation. Demographers showed that the population of France was not growing as fast as that of Germany or even England. They feared a depopulation of France based on voluntary limitation of family size and on one of the highest infant mortality rates in Europe. Faced with a strong, united, and growing Germany, officials sought to increase the French population. Reformers and officials stopped criticizing the poor for having so many babies, mostly illegitimate, and began to concern themselves with high infant mortality. Philanthropists, as well, recognized the depopulation problem and supported programs for single mothers and their children. The new social question became "the causes of infant mortality and how to prevent it."[29] Officials now wanted to make sure the babies lived to be hardworking, moral citizens who supported the Republic. Social reformers no longer castigated the unwed mother for her immorality but instead viewed her as a victim. If she was not a sinner but a victim, with proper guidance and welfare she could raise and nurse a child, thus contributing to the child's (and France's) chances for survival.[30]

The confluence of three other major concerns, along with fear of depopulation, contributed to the growth of social welfare for single mothers. First, the government feared that the poor, socialism, and antirepublican clericalism might overthrow the fragile Republic. The Paris revolutions of 1830, 1848, and especially the Commune of 1871 struck fear in the hearts of the controlling groups. These fears spurred legislation for social programs. Second, the Third Republic was avowedly and ardently anticlerical. Private charitable organizations had been associated with the church and religious individuals. In raising the next generation of secular republican French citizens, public officials sought to limit the role of the church. For example, in 1877 and 1883 the government curtailed subventions to the Sociétés Saint-François-Régis and Charité maternelle ostensibly because of the heavy church influence in the societies and over the minds of those they aided. Finally, active groups committed to reform (such as doctors, social hygienists, and welfare organizations) achieved an element of power. New attitudes engendered by these groups led to increased government involvement in the lives of the poor.

Public Welfare: Bureaux de bienfaisance

Modern public welfare in the Third Republic had its antecedents early in the nineteenth century and evolved in response to new ideology and conditions. The Bureaux de bienfaisance provided the earliest form of public welfare, although it was specifically designed to help the poor and pregnant. An ordinance of July 1, 1816, created one Bureau de bienfaisance for each arrondissement of Paris to distribute secours à domicile (assistance to the needy at home). Laic charitable women and nuns distributed the aid. The bureaus paid doctors, surgeons, midwives, teachers, and legal experts, who staffed the bureaus as needed.

Local revenues from each arrondissement provided the bulk of the resources. The richer the arrondissement, and the proportionally fewer poor, the more resources accrued to the local bureau. The bureaus that needed funds the most had the fewest resources. To overcome such inequalities, the Municipal Council and l'Assistance publique of Paris gave subventions to the local Bureaux de bienfaisance in proportion to the indigent population in each arrondissement.[31] The structure, function, and format of the Bureaux de bienfaisance changed little during the century except for the proliferation of substations throughout each arrondissement.

The bureaus provided deserving indigents with temporary help or regular, long-term aid. Nursing mothers with other children to care for and no means of support, heads of families with at least three children under the age of fourteen, widows and widowers with at least two children under fourteen, orphans under sixteen, and pregnant women, along with the sick and wounded of both sexes, received short-term assistance; the paralyzed, blind, infirm, and aged required long-term aid. Until 1895, assistance took the form of work (finding jobs for the able-bodied), goods (such as food, clothing, and heating fuel), or services (such as midwife or other medical care). In 1895 monetary aid replaced goods.

The bureaus did not aid all who sought help. The needy had to fulfill conditions of residency in Paris, sobriety, cleanliness, vaccination, and morality. Those cohabiting or unwed mothers except in childbirth normally did not receive aid. Hardworking, repentant unwed mothers who promised to keep and nurse their babies could be delivered for free by one of the bureau's midwives. The local bureau assigned a midwife to each qualified poor woman in her ninth month of pregnancy, and the women were to go to the midwives to whom they were assigned. The women, however, through their networks, sometimes had greater confidence in one midwife over another and went to the one they preferred.[32] Or they chose one with whom they were more likely to have a "stillbirth" if that was their strategy.

The number of poor and pregnant women delivered at home by a bureau midwife increased from 7,400 in 1865 to approximately 12,000 by the end of the century.[33] This increase of 62 percent does not reflect an increase in the birth rate. It far exceeds the 2 percent increase of total births in Paris or the 20 percent increase in the total births in the Department of the Seine for the same time period.[34] The increase partially results from the policies of l'Assistance publique and the Department of the Seine that sought to keep women out of hospitals by allocating funds to the Bureaux de bienfaisance to provide free midwifery care. Bureaux de bienfaisance policy indicates the increasing concern with preserving the lives of infants and preventing mortality and child abandonment. In philosophy (aside from the absence of a deep religious element) and even in revenue, the bureaus differed little from private charity until the Third Republic.

Public Welfare: Aid to Unwed Mothers

Private charity and the Bureaux de bienfaisance did little to alleviate social concern over the large number of illegitimate and abandoned children, except to encourage the women to marry and to discourage them from abandoning their babies. Philanthropic reformers believed that aiding the unwed mother would only encourage her sin and debauchery. Before the 1870s, public welfare for these women came primarily from free childbirth facilities offered by the general hospital system, created at the end of the eighteenth century to house indigents.

Major hospitals, such as the Hôtel-Dieu, la Charité, and la Maternité, provided free childbirth. La Maternité was the largest free, state-run maternity hospital in the Department of the Seine. Until late in the century it was the only hospital strictly for obstetrics, and it was always the largest, admitting between two thousand and six thousand women each year. Pregnant women giving birth in la Maternité were the very poorest women in Paris. Only those who could not afford a midwife or did not qualify for midwifery services from their local Bureau de bienfaisance sought hospital admission as a last resort. Women feared giving birth at la Maternité, especially from the 1850s through the 1870s, because of the high incidence of puerperal fever and maternal mortality.[35]

The profile of the women giving birth at la Maternité changed little over the century. Fewer than one-fifth were born in Paris. The age of women admitted remained fairly constant, ranging from sixteen to forty-four; most, however, were in their mid-twenties and the average age was twenty-five. That is close to the average age at first marriage and first child for women in Paris. The marital status of the women entering la Maternité changed slightly during the century and indicates the influence of public policy. From 1837 to 1860 roughly 85 percent of the women admitted were single. Some were in stable consensual unions, and on rare occasions the father took the baby if the mother died at the hospital.[36] Beginning in 1869 there was a gradual diminution in the percentage of single women and a corresponding increase in that of married women to almost 30 percent of total admissions. This change did not reflect the marriage rate, which remained fairly constant.[37] The institution was becoming a major women's hospital and treated women for gynecological problems as well as childbirth. In addition, alternative childbirth options such as more state-paid midwives (previously available for home births only to married women) were becoming accessible to single women.[38]

Throughout the century domestic servants constituted the largest occupational group of women entering the hospital, followed by seamstresses
and day laborers. If seamstresses and those listing their occupations in one
of the needle trades are taken collectively, they outnumber domestic servants. None were registered prostitutes, although unwed mothers and
prostitutes came from the same working-class female population.[39]

The women who entered la Maternité typified working-class women of
nineteenth-century Paris. They exhibited no identifiable differences from
the female urban population; they just happened to be pregnant. They gave
birth in a free maternity hospital more by necessity than choice. If they were
single, could not afford a midwife, and did not (or could not) take advantage of marriage supported by a charity, they had little alternative. Often,
they gave birth in la Maternité because of the secrecy it afforded and the
reputed ease of abandoning a child from there. For example, Anastasie S.,
twenty-four years old, a laundry worker born in the Department of the
Yonne and a Paris resident for two years, was engaged to marry a soldier
who was away and with whom she had a son whom she kept. While her
soldier was away, she had a brief affair with an Italian painter and got
pregnant. She planned to go to la Maternité and abandon her child—all in
secrecy.[40]

Until the 1870s single mothers had few sources of charity or welfare to
enable them to keep their babies.[41] Beginning in 1837, the private philanthropic Fondation Montyon, working with officials of la Maternité, offered
aid for four months, plus an infant's layette, to mothers who delivered their
babies at that hospital and who promised not to abandon them. A select
few single mothers who gave birth in la Maternité received aid from the
Fondation Montyon; that private charity, like the others, preferred to assist
married women. In 1838, 1,272 women received relief before they left la
Maternité. The possibility of financial aid to keep their babies may have
affected women's decisions to enter la Maternité; the number of women
giving birth there rose from 2,935 in 1837 to 3,388 in 1838.[42] This represents
an increase from 10 to 11 percent of the total births in Paris and from 30 to 36
percent of the illegitimate births in that city. The amount of aid, however,
was too small and of too short duration to affect most women greatly. The
aid was only about forty centimes a day; between 1837 and 1869 women
received approximately five francs a month for up to four months. To put
these figures in perspective, in midcentury, the average monthly salary of a
domestic servant was twenty-five francs a month and that of a day worker
was a franc a day, taking into account seasonal unemployment.[43] A one-

pound loaf of bread cost about twenty centimes, and first-quality white bread was thirty-one centimes a kilogram.[44] The aid to prevent abandonment was thus insufficient to allow a woman to stay home and nurse her baby.

Aside from this modest effort, welfare for single mothers was rare before the 1870s. Public welfare, like private charity, operated under the principle that giving assistance to unwed mothers would encourage single motherhood. Public officials did, however, want to limit abandonment; an abandoned child was an economic burden on the state, municipal, and department treasuries. Initially, most welfare programs restricted women's options rather than enhanced them. For example, starting in 1852, women who delivered their babies in la Maternité were required to stay there eight days, nurse their babies, and take their babies with them when they left. The motive was more to strengthen maternal ties and inhibit abandonment than to assist the mothers. The mothers received little financial support. Furthermore, if they stayed the required eight days, they might lose their jobs and their apartments because they could not pay the rent. As a minor form of aid, hospital authorities gave some mothers a baby's layette when they left.

Starting in 1856 l'Assistance publique provided one month's payment to a wet nurse—usually thirty francs—for both legitimate and illegitimate babies who were in danger of being abandoned. Very few women received this assistance, and most of them were married. A one month payment for a wet nurse was meaningless because the mothers could not maintain the payments after the first month and could not take their babies back and continue to work. Most often the babies were abandoned with their wet nurses, and such aid merely delayed abandonment. The percentage of mothers who left the maternity hospital with their babies but later abandoned them increased more than fifteen times from 1830 to 1869—from 2 percent in the 1830s to 31 percent in 1869.[45] Furthermore, there was nothing to prevent a mother from keeping the money and either keeping her baby or abandoning it. Maxim DuCamp, a critical observer of the Parisian scene, asserted that when women left la Maternité or the foundling home with the thirty francs for the first month's payment to the wet nurse, they encountered their lovers, who were waiting to take the money.[46]

Policy toward unmarried mothers changed with the beginning of the Third Republic primarily because reformers and public officials became more concerned with the related issues of depopulation and child welfare. They advocated programs to offer help and advice to impoverished single mothers in attempts to ensure the health and lives of their babies, alleviate their poverty, and make the lifestyle of the poor more in keeping with bourgeois morality. They believed that although unwed mothers might have been victims of moral, physical, and financial distress, their children suffered much more victimization. Doctors recognized that the weakness and mortality of newborns resulted from the terrible conditions mothers faced as well as the system of mercenary wet nursing.[47] Public officials decided to aid the children while "moralizing" the mothers by increasing the number, scope, and financial resources of programs called "aid to unwed mothers to prevent abandonment" that their predecessors had begun decades earlier. They favored maternal nursing to decrease infant mortality. Programs reflected the increasing influence of social scientists, the Academy of Medicine, and individual doctors, who saw the alleviation of social problems as one of their major functions.

In 1875 l'Assistance publique of the Department of the Seine began a comprehensive program to provide for "children born outside of marriage." The children aided were "the infants whom their mothers, despite their meager resources, agreed to keep and to raise."[48] The administration of l'Assistance publique decided to aid these single mothers in an effort to prevent child abandonment and reduce infant mortality. Its programs during the Third Republic dispensed aid in a variety of forms that attempted to deal with the issue of depopulation and also addressed some specific problems of single mothers in Paris.

L'Assistance publique continued and expanded the program of providing a lump sum of money, equivalent to the first month's wages of a wet nurse, to mothers (predominantly single), who upon leaving a maternity hospital or a midwife could not, or would not, keep and nurse their babies themselves. As earlier in the century, this form of aid merely postponed abandonment, although, in a few cases, l'Assistance publique continued making payments to a wet nurse until the baby was ten months old. In addition, women who threatened to abandon their babies at a maternity hospital or at the foundling home could receive money immediately (usually thirty-five francs) if they agreed to keep their infants. Furthermore, women who were temporarily unemployed or ill were entitled to assistance of ten to fifteen francs a month for up to four months if they requested it at the main offices of l'Assistance publique and threatened to abandon their babies.[49] Although direct evidence is lacking, it seems clear that women knew of these forms of relief and could feign illness or manipulate the system by threatening a behavior that was discouraged such as child abandonment to maximize the assistance they received. Public welfare, with the goal of discouraging abandonment, forced women to threaten abandonment to get the aid they needed.

The most important and influential maternal welfare program during the Third Republic was that of regular monthly monetary payments to mothers to enable them to keep and nurse their infants themselves and thereby prevent abandonment. Initially, only single mothers were eligible for this program because they were most likely to abandon their babies. But toward the end of the century, especially after 1892, authorities made little distinction between married and single mothers in determining who was qualified for aid. Only the distribution of aid differed: married women went to their local Bureau de bienfaisance (which received a special allocation from l'Assistance publique to aid these women); single mothers went directly to l'Assistance publique.[50]

To receive monthly "aid for maternal nursing to prevent abandonment" women had to make the same formal request and informal threats that women made to receive other forms of assistance. They requested aid at the offices of l'Assistance publique, or gave birth in a public hospital and threatened to abandon their babies, or went to the foundling home with the avowed intention of abandoning their babies. Officials then questioned each mother about her family, morality, and need and inspected her living quarters to find evidence that despite her single motherhood she was essentially moral. Authorities admitted a problem in determining who to aid. They argued that some women did not want to admit that they needed to abandon an infant because of their poverty. Others, authorities complained, pled poverty and threatened to abandon their babies just to get aid.[51]

The program was large in scope but small in aid. In the early years women were offered from ten to twenty-five francs a month for up to three months with continuation each month based on need and morality. In 1881 three months of aid seemed to be the maximum; in 1894 it was six months. By the end of the century, in principle, women could receive up to thirty francs a month for up to two years, but most still received assistance for less than one year. Demand for aid was always almost triple the number of women receiving it, and in any given year aid was requested for between one-fourth and two-thirds of all births in the Department of the Seine.[52]

To improve the efficacy of the public assistance program to assist newborn babies and "moralize" their mothers, the administration created a system of inspection. Public assistance officials, rarely physicians, were in principle to visit annually each child and mother who had received public assistance in the past year and determine whether the mother was indeed indigent and deserving of aid and whether the aid should be continued. In actual fact, the only regular inspections were made by salaried women (*dames visiteuses*) who visited aid recipients once a month and submitted reports to the male inspectors.[53]

The morality of single mothers remained a major concern to the administrators and inspectors of l'Assistance publique's programs, but it was secondary to the welfare of the children. Officials did not refuse a woman aid if a man was found in her apartment, or even if they viewed her morality as questionable. Even women living in a *ménage irrégulier* were given aid because "it is really the infant who is the victim."[54] Inspectors saw their role, and that of the *dames visiteuses*, to "try to lead the women to a more regular conduct by advice or even sometimes by threats. But one must not forget that it is the child, and not the mother, whom we aid and that the morality of the mother must only be a small part in the motives for giving aid."[55] Some inspectors sought to eliminate aid if the mother was obviously cohabiting or entertaining several men with purchases of liquor from her monthly payments. Most inspectors did not, however, eliminate the aid, even when they found men engaged in drinking and eating with the mothers in their rooms.[56] They wanted to control such behavior, not in the interest of the mother's morality but in that of the child.

The mothers were not entirely passive in behaving as officials would have liked even though the *dames visiteuses* affirmed that the "mothers are generally docile and observe the instructions they are given."[57] *Dames visiteuses* came once a month at a prearranged time to ensure that the mothers would be home. Since the mothers knew in advance of the visits, it was a simple matter for them to hide traces of their lover or cohabitant and appear to be doing what the *dames visiteuses* had asked them to do. Abuse of the system was possible, but if mothers did so, it generally went unreported except for one extant case. A mother of twins went to the offices of l'Assistance publique and received monthly assistance for maternal nursing to prevent abandonment. She later went to the foundling home and threatened to abandon her twins so she could receive payments for a wet nurse.[58]

Inspectors' statistics show that between 70 and 90 percent of the aid recipients were single mothers living alone; fewer than 3 percent were in a *ménage irrégulier*, and under 5 percent were married. Almost one-fifth of the mothers lived with their families, usually their mothers.[59] These data are of limited accuracy because mothers knew of impending visits from the inspectors. Inspectors contacted the concierges for information about the aid recipients, and it is likely that news of the inspectors' visits spread through the districts and buildings in which the mothers lived. The women may have tried to hide their liaisons from the inspectors for fear of losing aid.

Inspectors used persuasion, and mothers were passive resisters. More women than the figures show had to have been living with families or with a cohabitant out of financial necessity. The annual estimated minimum cost of living for a worker ranged from 850 to 1,200 francs a year.[60] Single mothers received 20 francs a month from l'Assistance publique and earned an average of 1 franc per day (taking into account seasonal unemployment), giving them an annual income of 565 francs. For them to make ends meet financially, without family support or a cohabitant, would seem impossible. Couples may not have regularized their *ménage irrégulier* because of the fear of losing aid from l'Assistance publique.[61] They were correct; l'Assistance publique continued to show preference in giving aid to single mothers because they were the ones most likely to abandon their babies. Public welfare, by giving too little aid and only to single mothers, may have encouraged clandestine cohabitation, inhibited marriage, and perpetuated a cycle of poverty.

The policies of l'Assistance publique in giving aid to unwed mothers to prevent abandonment recognized and accommodated the very lifestyle earlier reformers had sought to eliminate. From 1875 to 1892 women had to remain single, rather than marrying the fathers of their children, as a condition for aid. L'Assistance publique encouraged single motherhood, even though since 1889 inspectors and *dames visiteuses* reiterated that "never is marriage a cause for suppression of aid."[62] One inspector stated, "It is necessary . . . that all those in *ménages irréguliers* know that the Administration does not consider the marriage of unwed mothers as necessarily and incontestably leading to the cessation of aid," and he encouraged mothers to legitimize their children through marriage.[63] They made it clear that the women did not lose aid just because they married; if they did lose aid upon marriage it was supposedly because their husbands worked and earned an income that the inspectorate judged sufficient to provide for the child without help from l'Assistance publique.

Despite administrative exhortations to marry, mothers may have remained single for a variety of reasons. Marriage remained expensive and time-consuming, even with the reduction in cost made possible by the 1850 law on the marriage of indigents and with the efforts of the Société Saint-François-Régis. It was also time-consuming, and perhaps humiliating, to be investigated for indigence and morality. Inspectors may have turned a blind eye to cohabitation, but despite their protests to the contrary, they frequently terminated a married woman's regular monthly aid. A mother may have been able to conceal a lover and his income and thus retain aid on the grounds of need, but she could not conceal a legal husband and his wages. After 1892 l'Assistance publique made no distinction in marital status of recipients of aid for maternal feeding to prevent abandonment except that married women received their aid directly from their local Bureau de bienfaisance. An interesting response to that change occurred from 1892 through 1895. In those years almost one-fourth of the terminations of aid from l'Assistance publique were because the "father returned."[64] One assumes that those whose aid from l'Assistance publique was terminated were not without any aid but received it from their Bureau de bienfaisance. The data may indicate that until 1892 fathers stayed away so that the women could receive aid, or that the women denied the existence of the fathers. Most aid recipients, however, remained single. It appears that the women knew how the system worked, and that knowledge gave them power to exert passive resistance to maximize their aid and assure some sustenance.

In effect, l'Assistance publique during the Third Republic completely reversed the criteria for aid stipulated by private charity during the first three-fourths of the century. Administrators recognized that in the nineteenth-century Parisian culture of poverty many mothers did not marry but lived in long-term consensual unions. Some unions became a legal marriage when a mother died and left one or more children; marriage in extremis was not unknown.[65] If administrators and public officials wanted to save infants' lives, they had to work within the mothers' culture. Morality in caring for children rather than marital morality became the key in welfare for mothers.

L'Assistance publique's programs for maternal infant feeding were the most extensive programs for the poor and pregnant, but other public institutions developed toward the end of the century. In addition to la Maternité, the maternity clinics Baudelocque and Tarnier opened to receive poor women who had lived in Paris for at least one year. Women were admitted in their ninth month of pregnancy. In 1900, these three hospitals admitted almost sixteen thousand pregnant women. The hospitals did not have enough beds to meet the demand, so l'Assistance publique employed ninety-five midwives to deliver needy women and care for them for nine days after delivery. The demand for hospital beds exceeded the supply because by the 1890s the use of antiseptics and asepsis made hospitals safer places to have babies than they had been before. With the use of anesthesia in childbirth limited to hospitals, they became a place of choice, not of last resort, for married women as well as for the single women whom the institutions had previously predominantly served.[66]

Several smaller institutions, created and supported by the city and l'Assistance publique of Paris, housed poor and pregnant women during their last weeks of pregnancy. The 200-bed Asile Michelet, particularly for unwed mothers, admitted women up to six weeks before the expected birth of their babies. In 1904 approximately 1,800 women spent an average of twenty-two days there.[67] The Asile Fessart (established in 1890), with 257 beds, housed both single and married indigent abandoned women. These and the Asile Georges Sand (with 97 beds) fed, housed, and clothed pregnant women for several weeks up to delivery. These women were without work and a place to live during their last month of pregnancy. While there, they did general kitchen or cleaning jobs, laundry, or seamstress work until their date of delivery. In 1898 approximately 1,200 women requested admission, but there was only money enough to support 857.[68] One, perhaps typical, resident, had come to Paris in 1906 from Brittany to work as a domestic. She was fired because she broke a vase. Embarrassed to return home, she then lived in a furnished room, where, "defenseless," she became pregnant. As a result of the pregnancy, she could not go home. Reduced to sleeping on the streets, she sought the Asile Fessart.[69] Asile Ledru-Rollin, created in 1892 by the Municipal Council of Paris after a donation from the widow of the Republican politician Alexandre Ledru-Rollin, had 50 beds to accommodate convalescent women and their newborn babies for fifteen days after childbirth. Admission to all these institutions was without cost to the women, and all beds were always filled. L'Assistance publique of Paris designed these homes for indigent, predominantly unwed mothers, in response to the fear of depopulation. They sought to reduce infant mortality by sheltering homeless indigent women in their last month of pregnancy, assuring safe childbirth, reducing abandonment and mercenary wet nursing, and educating poor mothers about nursing and proper infant hygiene.

In the last decades of the nineteenth century, the concern with saving infants' lives through welfare for their mothers as a means of combating depopulation was so great and the public revenue allocated for such welfare so insufficient that municipal and departmental agencies worked together

with private charity—provided the charity was secular and did not discriminate against single mothers. As a result, during the early decades of the
Third Republic, charitable organizations increased in number and scope
and extended their interests to include single women. Even philanthropists
worried about depopulation. If the charities were not church-dominated,
they often had financial and organizational support from l'Assistance publique. The secular Société philanthropique, which had since its inception in
1780 offered shelter to single as well as married mothers, grew in the last
decades of the nineteenth century and received allocations from the department and city. Of the seven philanthropic organizations it funded and
directed, two were devoted to the poor and pregnant—the Asile maternelle
and the Asiles de nuit.[70] The *asiles de nuit* increased in number and capacity
in the 1880s. They were designed for young women who left their homes in
the countryside in search of work in Paris and then encountered "decep-
tions" or fell ill or suffered unemployment and found themselves alone and
without resources on the sidewalks of the big city. By 1900 the Société
philanthropique had established three *asiles de nuit* in Paris, each with about
20 beds and a special dormitory for pregnant women. The women temporarily housed in these shelters for the homeless were single mothers as well
as married women who had been abandoned by their husbands. Pregnant
women sheltered in an *asile de nuit* often gave birth in la Maternité.
Between 2 and 5 percent of women giving birth in la Maternité gave an *asile*
as their home address.[71] These unfortunate women had no other home.

The Asile maternelle, founded in 1886 under the auspices of the Société
philanthropique, augmented the Asile Ledru-Rollin. It sheltered some
women without husbands who delivered babies at la Maternité. Women
could stay in the Asile maternelle up to fifteen days. During that time a
doctor and a counselor would instruct them in nursing and proper infant
care, and other counselors would help them find jobs so they could support
themselves and nurse their babies. From 1886 to 1900 about 50 percent of
women in the Asile maternelle found work by the time they left. From 1903
to 1906 the efforts of the Société philanthropique increased and five-sixths
of the women found work.[72]

Single mothers who kept their babies and received welfare had to work
to survive. Many could do piecework in their rooms, but most had to work
outside the home as garment workers, day laborers, and *femmes de ménages*.
They had a problem finding care for their babies. A small percentage could
leave their children with their families, but many left their infants alone all

day or with a neighbor. Crèches became increasingly available but were too few, not open long enough hours, or not in working-class neighborhoods for women to take advantage of them. Mothers also had an antipathy for institutional care for their babies. Crèches cost only twenty centimes a day, but despite the increase in their number, low cost, and increasing acceptance of illegitimate children they were basically unavailable to single mothers.

Starting in the 1870s private crèches became willing to care for illegitimate children, and secular municipal ones were started. A regulation encouraging municipal crèches, approved in December 1874, was to protect the infant from death with a wet nurse or from artificial feeding. The regulation allowed a woman to nurse her infant at a crèche and gave women who worked outside the home the possibility of nursing their infants themselves without giving up work. At the same time, those in charge of the crèches gave the mothers advice and education and provided regular medical examinations for the infants. In response to changing state philosophy and the priority accorded to saving babies' lives, even private crèches began to admit children of unmarried women, who by their good conduct deserved pardon. As Marbeau admonished: "You will take the hand of the repentant as the divine Master has done."[73] In 1892, sixty-seven public and private crèches provided for 6,312 legitimate and illegitimate infants.[74] Crèches closely fit the aims of the Third Republic. In allowing for maternal nursing and hygienic and medical care of the babies, crèches were designed to reduce infant mortality. They also encouraged mothers to work. Finally, crèches became all the more necessary with the application of the law on obligatory primary instruction for boys and girls; the crèches relieved older sisters of child care duty and enabled them to go to public schools.[75]

The proliferation and expansion of philanthropies and private charities for single and married women at the end of the century indicated a new morality that gave preference to saving infants' lives over insistence on marriage and religion. Major philanthropies, such as the Société philanthropique and the Société des crèches, were accompanied by the proliferation of many smaller charities providing infant care, assistance in childbirth, free milk and medical consultation, and free lunches to unwed mothers as well as to the married. Since 1874 members of the Academy of Medicine, the Société protectrice de l'enfance, the Société de charité maternelle, and the Société des crèches became members of the national Comité supérieur de protection des enfants du premier age.[76] All had the greater goal of saving infants' lives. And all were willing to sacrifice the liberty of the women to the surveillance and inspection that accompanied the welfare and to shift ideological and programmatic emphases from individual liberty to life.[77]

Conclusion

Throughout the century private charity and public welfare were mutually supportive. Once charitable programs were started by bourgeois or aristocratic religious men or women, the state, department, and city of Paris often gave subventions. And throughout the century, private charitable donations went to public assistance. By 1900 traditional private charity and the modern public welfare state overlapped. Public welfare dominated assistance programs to mothers and infants, but private charity helped implement public policy programs. Both sought to save infants' lives and preserve the future of France, but they wanted to mold that future according to modern views of health and hygiene and were less motivated by traditional views of morality that had so preoccupied them in the past. The emphasis of both charity and welfare during the Third Republic was still on maternal love and maternal feeding, but less in the name of God and the religious sanctity of the family and more in the name of increasing population and promoting Republican ideals. The depopulation issue engendered new attitudes toward women, poverty, crime, and morality and led to philanthropic and public efforts to aid illegitimate children and indirectly their mothers during the Third Republic.

The motivations of philanthropists and welfare bureaucrats in establishing programs for the poor and pregnant differed from the needs of the women themselves. Middle- and upper-class philanthropists and Republicans had a vision of appropriate moral, maternal behavior—married, religious, and nurturing. This vision dictated the nature of the relief they gave: assistance in getting married, in having a baby, and in keeping and nursing babies. Private charity and public welfare officials were more concerned with improving morality and ending depopulation than with alleviating the poverty of the mothers in Paris. The women, however, were mired in poverty. Their behavior reflected the economic realities of their lives and not always the intentions of the donors of charity and welfare. To the impoverished women, single motherhood was not the stigma it was to the middle-class officials; it was a fact of life engendered by poverty, by their vulnerability, and by their inability to enforce a marriage with a man of their choice. Only at the end of the century did philanthropists and public assistance leaders realize this and accept the nonmarital status of the women. Although they still provided insufficient money or training to enable the mothers to rise from poverty, they no longer predicated maternity benefits upon marital status. Single motherhood remained a poverty trap.

The poor adapted to the requirements for relief, but in maintaining their way of life they also helped shape programs. To a limited extent, the women could make choices and alter the actual way charity and welfare functioned. At the most basic level, they were not forced to accept any of the programs and could choose among them. Making a choice implies that the women had a strategy, and having a strategy implies knowledge of various alternatives. Poverty made their lives so precarious that they had to know what was available to help them survive and how to work within the system. If they wanted to marry, they could have gone to the Société Saint-François-Régis. If they were pregnant and married, they received benefits from the Société de charité maternelle for help in crisis management during pregnancy and for a few months after birth. If marriage was not a possibility, women had few recourses to charity or welfare until late in the century. They gave birth in la Maternité if they could not afford a midwife, and some received a short-term payment for a wet nurse for their babies. After 1875, however, remaining single entitled them to the same, or more, relief than married women. L'Assistance publique established a broad program of aid to unwed mothers to prevent abandonment, and single mothers sought support from that government agency. But there were insufficient resources allocated to single mothers. Either because of economics, l'Assistance publique's programs, or their culture of poverty, women remained in consensual unions despite the urgings of philanthropists and welfare officials for them to marry. By 1900 the preoccupation with saving infants' lives was so great that both charity and welfare officials accepted women's nonmarital behavior patterns and accommodated their programs to those patterns.

To some extent, the women had systems imposed upon them by the complicated requirements to qualify for any particular welfare program. Mothers had to demonstrate desired behavior patterns, but they were not forced to receive aid except in the sense that their economic situation was so desperate that their survival depended on it. The closest women came to having a system imposed upon them was if they really wanted to abandon their babies. Then they were discouraged and in some cases prohibited from abandonment and forced to accept a form of aid to prevent it. After the period of aid expired, however, there was little to stop them from abandoning their babies—except the maternal ties that may have developed. If such ties prevented abandonment, then the charity and welfare donors realized one of their major goals.

Charity and welfare affected the behavior more than the values of the mothers and met some of the needs of a few of the poor. Even though their avowed goal was population growth and moralization of the poor, charity and welfare spoke to real needs: marriage, help in childbirth, and financial aid in the months after the birth of a child. Women took advantage of whatever program was available to them. They may not have liked the welfare machinery, but they used it when it was compatible with their lives. Neither charities nor welfare ever had enough money or facilities to meet the demand. Programs may have been designed to control the urban poor, either directly or through religious and moral training, but some urban poor women benefited in a small way. However onerous and demeaning the task of applying for assistance and submitting to interrogation and inspection may have been, many women realized a goal of marriage and of keeping their babies and not having them die in infancy. But until late in the century, assistance was too minimal to enable women to break out of poverty and available to too few women to do much good.

Nineteenth-century charity and welfare were designed to imbue the working classes with bourgeois values, and this required that public officials, the bourgeoisie, and the state intrude into private lives. Intrusion of the state into women's private lives implies that the women were compelled to accept the aid or had to change their behavior to receive it, but this was not always the case. Jacques Donzelot's explanation of middle-class intervention in the family as a form of social control has limited validity.[78] It is a simplified picture of the nineteenth-century Parisian world. It is necessary to go beyond the social control explanation of charity and welfare. Intervention by middle-class reformers and the state may initially have been designed to "moralize," and thereby control, a subgroup of the population, but such intervention improved living conditions and saved people's lives. State welfare, with its emphasis on the collectivity and on the lives of the citizens rather than on their individual liberties, may have emerged because the recipients maximized to their own advantage the welfare they so desperately needed.

Notes

I wish to thank Elinor Accampo, Gay Gullickson, Leslie Moch, and Philip Nord for their helpful criticism and suggestions.

ABBREVIATIONS
AAP   Archives de l'Assistance Publique
ADS   Archives de la Ville de Paris et Département de la Seine
AN   Archives Nationales
APP   Archives de la Préfecture de Police

1. H. A. Frégier, *Des classes dangereuses de la population dans les grandes villes, et des moyens de les rendre meilleurs*, 2 vols. (Paris: J.-B. Baillière, 1840), 1:9, 2:201; emphasis added. Frank Jellinek in his translation of Louis Chevalier, *Laboring Classes and Dangerous Classes in Paris during the First Half of the Nineteenth Century* (New York: Howard Fertig, 1973), translates the phrase as "productive breeding ground" (p. 141). The female reproductive imagery remains.

2. The data are for the Department of the Seine. See Rachel G. Fuchs, *Abandoned Children: Foundlings and Child Welfare in Nineteenth-Century France* (Albany, N.Y.: State University of New York Press, 1984), 72–76.

3. Joseph de Gerando, *De la bienfaisance publique*, 4 vols. (Paris: Jules Renouard, 1839), 1:lxv, lxxvii–lxxxii, 317–18, 417–18. De Gerando's prize-winning treatise reflected predominant opinions both of the time in which it was written and of the subsequent decade; it became the most frequently cited writing on poverty and charity.

4. For example, Société des crèches, Septième Séance publique annuelle (Paris: Guiraudet et Jouast, 1853), 8; F. Gille, *La Société de charité maternelle de Paris* (Paris: V. Goupy et Jourdan, 1887). For a recent brief discussion of the Catholic and moral economist views on poverty, charity, and the social question see Katherine A. Lynch, *Family, Class and Ideology in Early Industrial France: Social Policy and the Working-Class Family, 1825–1848*, (Madison, Wisc.: University of Wisconsin Press, 1988), ch. 2.

5. Ferdinand Dreyfus, *L'assistance sous la Séconde Republique, 1848–1851* (Paris: Edouard Cornély, 1907), 102, 170–71. Charitable efforts focused on the twelfth arrondissement, the poorest section, and the one most feared by the bourgeoisie after the insurrection of June 1848. See also Henri Rollet, *L'action sociale des catholiques en France, 1871–1914*, 2 vols. (Paris: Desclée de Brouwer, 1958).

6. For an excellent discussion of charity among the bourgeoises, see Bonnie G. Smith, *Ladies of the Leisure Class: The Bourgeoises of Northern France in the Nineteenth Century* (Princeton: Princeton University Press, 1981), ch. 6. Important primary sources indicating the attitudes of both Catholic and Protestant women toward charity include Mathilde Froment Bourdon, *La charité en action* (Lille: L. Lefort, 1859); and Bourdon, *Charité, légendes* (Paris: Amboise Bray, 1864). The latter work was reprinted ten times from 1864 through 1902. Com-

tesse A. E. de Gasparin, *Il y a des pauvres à Paris . . . et ailleurs* (Paris: L.-R. Delay, 1846), provides a leading Protestant view of charity.

7. Pauline d'Harcourt d'Haussonville, *La charité à travers la vie* (Paris: Gabalda, 1912); Bourdon, *La charité en action*, x, 112; Bourdon, *Charité, légendes*, vi, 71; Gasparin, *Il y a des pauvres*, 8, 107.

8. Smith, *Ladies of the Leisure Class*, 138.

9. See Gille, *La Société de charité maternelle*, Liste Alphabétique des Dames protectrices, des Dames administrantes et des Trésoriers de 1784 à 1885, pp. 283–98. This society existed in many major cities. La Société de charité maternelle de Paris lost its state subvention in 1883 because of its distinct religious component but received state subvention again in 1887 and kept it for most of the remainder of the century.

10. The society insisted on home delivery to avoid contagion and possible death from puerperal fever at the maternity hospitals. See AN F15 3894, Société de charité maternelle, Compte moral et financier, 1871.

11. A.-T. Brochard, *Education du premier age. Utilité des crèches et des sociétés de charité maternelle*. Conférence faite par M. le Dr. Brochard, Chevalier de la Legion d'Honneur . . . en faveur de la Société de charité maternelle de Saint-Etienne (Saint-Etienne: Théolier Frères, 1876).

12. AN F15 2564–65, 3561, 3806–13, 3894, Société de charité maternelle de Paris, Comptes rendus, 1810–76; and Léonce de LaMothe, *Nouvelles études sur la législation charitable* (Paris: Guillaumin et c^ie^, 1850), 70. Here, and in later usage, I have kept the French spelling of l'Assistance publique to refer to a particular government agency and not to public assistance in general.

13. AN F15 3799–3811, Société de charité maternelle de Paris, Compte Rendu, 1866, 1876; Gille, *La Société de charité maternelle*, 12–56, 76.

14. Gille, *La Société de charité maternelle*, 71, 85, 100, 120, 161, 220, 274.

15. The writings and novels of Mathilde Froment Bourdon, as well as those of others, always indicated that religiously motivated charitable women gave worthy recipients extra gifts of clothing and food when they visited them. For example, see Mathilde Froment Bourdon, *Quelques nouvelles* (Lille: L. Lefort, 1864), and her novel, *Antoinette Lemire, ou l'ouvrière de Paris* (Paris: Putois-Cretté, 1861); see also Jules Gossin, *Que la religion est aimable! ou Récreations de la jeunesse catholique* (Paris: Gaume frères, 1851).

16. Frégier, *Des classes dangereuses*, 2:101.

17. Oeuvre des mariages des pauvres, *Rapports et compte rendu* (Paris: Au secrétariat de la Société de Saint-Vincent de Paul, 1876), 3–5. This society aided only Catholics. The Oeuvre evangélique des mariages funded Protestant and mixed marriages (ADS, VD6 1909, no. 3). For greater detail see Jules Gossin, *Manuel de la Société charitable de Saint-Régis de Paris* (Paris: Au secrétariat de la Société de Saint-Vincent de Paul, 1851).

18. Oeuvre des mariages des pauvres, *Rapports*, 5. Counselors also found out the couple's occupation; date and place of birth; number, ages, and sex of their children; the existence or death of their parents; and their degree of religiosity.

19. Computed from the number of marriages in the Department of the Seine for

each year. See *Annuaire statistique de la ville de Paris* (Paris: G. Masson, 1881–1900). The volume for 1900 contained retrospective data.

20. Angus McLaren, *Sexuality and Social Order: The Debate over the Fertility of Women and Workers in France, 1790–1920* (New York: Holmes and Meier, 1983), 174.

21. Oeuvre des mariages des pauvres, *Rapports*, 13; APP DB/90, proposals to amend the law of 1850 on the marriage of indigents, 1876, 1890.

22. Michael Frey, "Du mariage et du concubinage dans les classes populaires à Paris (1846–1847)," *Annales: E.S.C.* 33 (1978), 803–29.

23. Ibid., 804.

24. AN F15 3812–13, Société des crèches, Séance publique, February 28, 1875.

25. Ibid., seventeenth annual public meeting, May 1869, and *Rapport et compte rendu*, 1854 in AN F15 3812–13.

26. Ibid.

27. Administration générale de l'Assistance publique à Paris, *Rapports des Bureaux de bienfaisance des vingt arrondissements de Paris* (Paris: Henon, 1900). In 1855 and 1858 the Bureau de bienfaisance of the sixth arrondissement gave one hundred francs.

28. Henri Monod, *L'Assistance publique en France en 1889* (Paris: Imprimerie nationale, 1900), 13.

29. *La Revue Philanthropique* 1 (1897), 901.

30. For a discussion of the role depopulation played in Third Republic politics, especially as it affected poor women, see the following works: Rachel G. Fuchs, "Rich Man, Poor Women: Paul Strauss and the Politics of Motherhood in Third Republic France," paper presented at the Pacific Coast Branch of the American Historical Association, August 1988; Joseph Spengler, *France Faces Depopulation* (1938; rpt. Durham, N.C.: Duke University Press, 1979), ch. 10; and Karen Offen, "Depopulation, Nationalism, and Feminism in Fin-de-Siècle France," *American Historical Review* 89 (June 1984), 648–76, esp. 649–53, 658–59. For a more detailed discussion of welfare in Third Republic France see Mary Lynn [Stewart] McDougall, "Protecting Infants: The French Campaign for Maternity Leaves, 1890–1913," *French Historical Studies* 13 (Spring 1983), 79–105; John H. Weiss, "Origins of the French Welfare State: Poor Relief in the Third Republic, 1871–1914," *French Historical Studies* 13 (Spring 1983), 47–78. For contemporary literature emphasizing the link between infant mortality and depopulation see Jacques Bertillon, *La dépopulation de la France* (Paris: Felix Alcan, 1911); *Gazette Hebdomadaire de Médecine et de Chirurgie* 4 (1870), 53–57; Emile Levasseur, *La population française*, 3 vols. (Paris: Arthur Rousseau, 1911); René Marjolin, *Mémoire sur la necessité du rétablissement des tours* (Paris: A. Picard, 1878); and especially Paul Strauss, *Dépopulation et puériculture* (Paris: Charpentier, 1901). Strauss's views are similar to those expressed in the Procès Verbaux of the Commission des enfants assistés of the Conseil général de la Seine, Séance October 12, 1892, ADS. Strauss, as senator from the Department of the Seine, was also the reporter for the national Commission de la dépopulation, sous-commission de la mortalité and submitted the *Rapport général sur les causes de la mortalité* (Melun: Imprimerie Administrative, 1911), in which he linked infant mortality with depopulation.

31. Seine (Département), Administration générale de l'Assistance publique, *Rapport général sur le fonctionnement des vingt bureaux de bienfaisance* (Paris: Henon, 1899).

32. Procès Verbaux, Bureau de bienfaisance, sixth arrondissement, January 23, 1852, AAP.

33. Seine (Département), *Rapport général sur le fonctionnement des Bureaux de bienfaisance*, Appendix.

34. Data collected from the *Annuaire statistique de la France* and the *Annuaire statistique de la ville de Paris* for 1865 to 1900.

35. For a literary example see Edmond and Jules de Goncourt, *Germinie Lacerteux*, trans. Leonard Tancock (London: Penguin, 1984). See also Paul Delaunay, *La Maternité de Paris* (Paris: Jules Roussel, 1909).

36. All information on the demographic profile is calculated from a random sample of two thousand women from the Registres d'admission of la Maternité for selected years from 1830 to 1900.

37. The marriage rate was computed by dividing the number of marriages in Paris by the total population. It is a crude measure because it does not take into account age specificity. Accurate age-specific data for women in Paris or the Department of the Seine do not exist.

38. For a complete analysis and presentation of the data see Rachel G. Fuchs and Paul E. Knepper, "Women in the Paris Maternity Hospital: Public Policy during the Nineteenth Century," *Social Science History* 13 (Summer 1989), 187–209.

39. Alain Corbin, *Les filles de noce: Misère sexuelle et prostitution aux XIXe et XXe siècles* (Paris: Aubier Montaigne, 1978), 75–76, 80, 203; and Jill Harsin, *Policing Prostitution in Nineteenth-Century Paris* (Princeton: Princeton University Press, 1985).

40. ADS, Cours d'Assises, 1880. She had been accused and acquitted of infanticide.

41. They could always abandon their babies and have the children raised by wet nurses or foster parents at state expense, as a form of maternal or child welfare, but that is a different issue. See Fuchs, *Abandoned Children*.

42. AAP, l'Hôpital Port Royal, Registres d'admission; and Fuchs, *Abandoned Children*, 82.

43. Theresa McBride, *The Domestic Revolution and the Modernization of Household Service in England and France, 1820–1920* (London: Croom Helm, 1976), 61; Paul Leroy Beaulieu, *Le travail des femmes au XIXe siècle* (Paris: Charpentier, 1873), 73.

44. Jeanne Singer-Kerel, *Le coût de la vie à Paris de 1840 à 1954* (Paris: A. Colin, 1961), 299; Othenin d'Haussonville, *Salaires et misères de femmes* (Paris: Calman Lévy, 1900), 9.

45. Rachel G. Fuchs, "Legislation, Illegitimacy and Poverty: Child-Abandoning Mothers in Nineteenth-Century Paris," *Journal of Interdisciplinary History* 18 (Summer 1987), 54–80.

46. Maxime DuCamp, *Paris, ses organes, sa fonctions et sa vie dans la seconde moitié du XIXe siècle*, 6 vols. (Paris: Hachette, 1869–75), 4:124.

47. M. Chauffard, "Academie de Médecine. Addition à la séance du 28 décembre, 1869," *Gazette Hebdomadaire de Médecine et de Chirurgie* (January 28, 1870), 53–57.

48. AAP, Conseil général de la Seine (Session de 1875), *Rapport* présenté par M. Clemenceau au nom de la 3[é] Commission sur le service des enfants assistés. Extrait du procès-verbal de la Séance du 24 November 1875 (Montevrain: Impr. Ecole d'Alembert, 1876).

49. ADS, D.1X4(21–25), Service des Enfants assistés de la Seine, Rapports d'Inspection, présenté par l'inspecteur principal à M. le Préfet de la Seine, 1875–1898 (hereafter cited as Rapport de l'inspecteur principal, with the date).

50. For greater detail on this welfare program see Rachel G. Fuchs, "Morality and Poverty: Public Welfare for Mothers in Paris, 1870–1900," *French History* 2, no.3 (1988), 288–311.

51. AAP, Administration générale de l'Assistance publique à Paris, Service des enfants assistés de la Seine, *Rapport* presenté par le directeur de l'Administration générale de l'Assistance publique à M. le Préfet de la Seine, 1888 (Montevrain: Impr. Ecole d'Alembert, 1889) (hereafter cited as *Rapp. Ann.* with the year).

52. ADS, D.1X4(21–25), Rapport de l'inspecteur principal, 1881, 1894, 1897.

53. These reports provide sufficient details of the women's lives to enable us to go beyond the perceptions of those in power to understand something of the conditions of poverty and the lives of the recipients of welfare.

54. ADS, D.1X4(26–27), Rapports d'Inspection sur le Service des enfants assistés de Paris, Manuscrits, Bernard, 1890 (hereafter cited as ADS, Rapports, Mss., author and date).

55. ADS, Rapports, Mss., Forgeot, 1890.

56. Ibid., 1891.

57. ADS, Procès Verbaux, Commission d'inspection des enfants assistés, Conseil générale de la Seine, Séance February 14, 1906.

58. Ibid., Séance October 31, 1879.

59. ADS, Rapports, Mss., Roualt, 1890, 1891, 1895, and Rapports de l'inspecteur principal, 1881. The variation in the percentages depends on the year and the inspector making the report.

60. Othenin d'Haussonville, *Misère et remèdes* (Paris: Calman Lévy, 1892), 214; Lenard R. Berlanstein, *The Working People of Paris, 1871–1914* (Baltimore: Johns Hopkins University Press, 1984), 39–52, 201.

61. ADS, Rapports, Mss., M. Montravel, 1890.

62. *Rapp. Ann.* (1889), 29.

63. ADS, Rapports, Mss., Roualt, 1890. The name of the program had been changed from "aid to unwed mothers" to "aid for maternal feeding" in part to remove the fear that if an unwed mother married she would lose aid and in part to stress the effort to combat depopulation.

64. Rapports de l'inspecteur principal, 1886–1899.

65. AAP, l'Hôpital Port Royal, Registres d'admission, 1830–1900. In a sample of approximately two thousand women admitted, four were married *in extremis* at that hospital.

66. Fuchs and Knepper, "Women in the Paris Maternity Hospital."

67. J. Fauconnet, *L'Assistance aux filles-mères et aux enfants illégitimes du premier age en France*, Thèse pour le doctorat (Paris: V. Giard et Brière, 1907), 74.

68. *Rapports des Bureaux de bienfaisance*, 270.

69. APP, DB/90, extract from *Le Journal*, June 27, 1906.

70. The other philanthropic activities were *asiles de nuit* (shelters for the homeless) for men; medical and surgical outpatient centers for women, children, and the sick of both sexes; aid for economical housing for men and women; furnished housing for women and young girls; and soup kitchens (*cantines*) for both sexes.

71. AAP, l'Hôpital Port Royal, Registres d'admission, 1880–1900.

72. Société philanthropique de Paris, *Rapports et Comptes Rendus, Annuaire de 1906–7* (Paris: Bureau de la Société, 1906), 146.

73. AN F15 3812–13, Speech of Marbeau before the Séance Publique, Société des crèches, 1875.

74. Paul Strauss, *Paris Ignoré* (Paris: Maison Quentin, 1892).

75. AN F15 12529, Letter to Ministre de l'instruction publique from Mairie du Temple asking for support for a "spectacle" to raise funds for a crèche in his arrondissement, 1882.

76. Gille, *Société de charité maternelle*, 178–79; AAP, Fosseyeux 686.

77. For an important analysis of the paradigmatic shifts from an emphasis on liberty to an emphasis on life and from private charity to obligatory public welfare see François Ewalt, *L'Etat providence* (Paris: Bernard Grasset, 1986), 16–25.

78. Jacques Donzelot, *The Policing of Families*, trans. Robert Hurley (New York: Pantheon, 1979), *passim*.

Bruce Bellingham

5. Waifs and Strays: Child Abandonment, Foster Care, and Families in Mid-Nineteenth-Century New York

CHILDHOOD, AS FAMILY HISTORIANS THINK OF IT, was gradually "invented" as a new category of bourgeois experience during the eighteenth century; it provided the rationale for the nineteenth-century ideology of middle-class "domesticity"; and it finally established a universal norm of loving or psychological parenthood in the West in the twentieth century.[1] But public policy, no less than private sentiment, was involved in this cultural invention, and the resulting norms to which caretakers are now held refer more to the universal civil status of children as bearers of rights, including "nurturance rights," than to the quality of their particular family ties. Some seem to shrug off change in the quality of parental sentiments, arguing that "what is most remarkable" about the Western ideology of childhood "is that it entails a passionate concern with the welfare of *other people's children*."[2] When the invention of childhood is treated in welfare or educational history rather than in family history, the emphasis is on broad public responsibility for children irrespective of kinship. Interpretation may celebrate or disapprove child-saving interventions, but there is agreement that reforms re-formed, seizing upon and changing vernacular patterns of child life according to new policy designs.

Interest in child welfare during the rise of industrial civilization is not fully met by separate discussion of either private feeling or public responsibility. The "useless but priceless" sentimental view of childhood expressed a developing pattern of private relationships inside the middle-class home and simultaneously served as its rationale.[3] The problem is that this model of private feeling was simultaneously promulgated as a public ideology—a standard of morality to which others were held accountable—and it was deployed in aggressive public crusades, both symbolic and practical. Private meanings shaped in the bosom of family life were also shaped in the crucible of civic controversy, as cultural ideals of psychological parenthood were used to foment social rivalries. The very authenticity and rightness of these new meanings owed as much to the force of invidious comparison with others as to the functional fit between domesticity and the bourgeois condition. The virtuousness of middle-class parenthood was, in part, defined in contradistinction to the neglect or abuse ascribed to working-class families.

Descriptions of the public invention of childhood in child-saving reforms are as abstract as accounts of the evolution of private sentiments. However critical their tone, they are essentially administrative and intellectual, not social, histories. Top-down, coercive policies of family reorganization seem to proceed in a pristine social field cleared of agonistic and combative groups, or truculent or wily individuals, or the passions of communal solidarity. Accepting the organizational fiction that helping agencies encounter individual clients whom they process according to their specialized mandates, welfare history cast in the idiom of social control hardly attempts to explain the most significant political question: how did charity accommodate working-class families to the economic or demographic miseries of early industrial society? Instead we are presented with a world apart of professional help or control—power—abstracted from the normal experience of class in private lives. However militant their stance, histories of which official or elite said what to whom and why substitute accounts of nominal policy for the reconstruction of struggle and accommodation.

In this essay I present information on the charitable practice of the New York Children's Aid Society in the middle of the nineteenth century and the behavior of the society's clients, in order to discuss two aspects of the history of childhood: the politics of private relations and the politics of public responsibility. The first concerns the definition of working-class family life as a Victorian social problem. I will argue that the problem of child abandonment arose at midcentury because family coping strategies were suddenly seen and reacted against as instances of impaired or even defunct filiation. Parents who did not maintain continued custody of their children were deemed neglectful by the urban middle classes, who were coming to avoid discontinuities in the care of their own children and who imputed reprehensible motives to parents for whom discontinuities in parenting were a matter of course. Childhood as constructed by the private culture thus entitled children to newly regulated jural rights as well as newly prescribed feelings. From the jural perspective, modern childhood imposed on parents, as a settled matter of public morality, obligations that—I will try to show—the lower-class population could not have met and did not accept.

The second issue is the implementation and effectiveness of an early attempt to solve the supposed problem of bad parenting, especially child abandonment. The program of modern fostering and adoption pioneered by the Children's Aid Society was distinguished from old-style indentures as a radical social policy that would permanently transfer custody of "homeless" children to substitute parents for proper resocialization, education, and sponsorship to upward mobility. In examining the early fostering and adoption records, I found, however, much mutual accommodation of helper to helped and few dramatic changes in the trajectory of the children's careers. Child savers talked about "breaking up" families but—I will show—did not do so in this period. And what they did was so surprisingly evocative of unreconstructed charity assisting the normal coping efforts of working-class families that I argue their hidden agenda was the subvention of social reproduction. Others have noted the Children's Aid Society's hostile description of the children's parents,[4] but I found that the problem of neglectful, abandoning parenting was substantially made up. The panacea of transporting city children wholesale to "good Christian homes" in the country has been criticized from its inception as an intrusion. Judged against the standard of what the families would have done anyway, I argue it was not much of an intervention.

The Problem: Child Abandonment

Routine abandoning behavior, more perhaps than the confused frenzy of violence, seems to epitomize the idea of a radical discontinuity in the lives of children between past and present and between the core urban-industrial societies and others on the periphery of the world economy today. Summarizing the arguments for the "invention of childhood" thesis, which she disputes, Linda Pollock states, "the indifference and cruelty of parents are derived from the practice of such behaviors as infanticide, abandonment, wet-nursing, swaddling and the sending of children away on apprenticeships."[5] Abandonment, wet nursing, and apprenticing involve the transfer of parenting functions from natal parents to proxies. A more global argument is that surrogate care is associated with low parental "investment" in "middle-range" agrarian and artisanal societies, whereas in simple hunting and advanced industrial societies parents invest more and take care of their own. The Western invention of childhood is cited to show that the difference is evolutionary, not a regional cultural preference:

> The parent caretaking system that is now normative in many parts of the industrialized world has developed from a far different set of domestic relationships than those characteristic of our recent historical past. . . . Such practices as primogeniture, wet nursing, child fosterage, and the widespread use of lower status surrogate caretakers led to pronounced inequalities in the treatment of offspring and to greater risks in the lives of children.[6]

Here three of the four indexes of traditional child care are delegations.

Although parents unable to devote themselves to intensive nurturance doubtless adopted other expedients to rear their children, the description of routine middle-range fosterage patterns is made lurid by transparent moral condemnation of a pattern of behavior and values without considering either the circumstances or the spirit of the actions. Modern family ideals— and implicitly the means to achieve them—are taken as transcendent standards of parenthood. Pollock, for example, defends the good character of parents in the past by arguing away all evidence that the offending behavior ever occurred, accepting the cultural absolutist ideals of psychological parenthood as readily as any historian of sentiments. The hostile formulation that parents who delegated care of their children exposed them to "greater risks" begs the question: greater than what? The only sensible yardstick is whether the hazards were greater than those that would have followed from not delegating. For American and British parents in the popular classes there is no evidence that delegations securing substitute homes for noninfant children, occupational training, or even institutional care were not preferable to the looming alternative: homeless indigency.[7]

Of course, these "hazards" are a red herring: the objection to fosterage is cultural, not epidemiological, and historians of physical welfare explain juvenile health problems on the basis of nutrition, sanitation, and working conditions, not kinship patterns. The determination to interpret this one aspect of group life out of its contemporary context—when far more outlandish practices are treated "from the native's point of view"—testifies to the enduring cultural force of Victorian-era ideals of domesticity. In this perspective undelegated nurturance and socialization are the measures of love, and love is the criterion of true, psychological parenthood.[8] Victorian child-saving reforms invoked the ideology of psychological parenthood and helped shape an enduring critique of fosterage by assigning the older, rather instrumental pattern of delegated child care new meaning as child "abandonment." Reformers then cited working-class practice—the failure to love, or *really* to love—as a negative foil against which the propriety of bourgeois standards was further refined.

Seen through the lens of "domesticity," historical fosterers did no better than abandoners. In a representative statement about the origins of American adoption in the place-out schemes of the mid-nineteenth century, Margaret Mead and Rhoda Metraux wrote that "some children were lucky. The families to which they were sent accepted them not just as small laborers, but also as members of a family community, with rights to physical care, education and affection. A great many others, about whose fate we know relatively little even today, were simply exploited."[9] The worst is assumed unless they "adopted" their charges in the modern sense, assuming *all* parental functions, for the absolutist cultural understanding of "family" insists that the status of household members be clarified according to an in or out dichotomy. Because modern adoption statutes did not exist in any American state until 1851 or in the United Kingdom until 1926,[10] it follows that fosterers who failed to meet this anachronistic criterion (or almost all of them) were wicked exploiters of child labor. In a more general discussion of the way cultural ideals of parenthood determine possible adaptations to constraints, such as delegations to proxy parents, Esther Goody explains:

> The meanings attached to a birth-status identity and the rearing roles determine what parental strategies are seen as beneficial and indeed as possible. (This rather abstract formulation may be clearer if one substitutes the current Western definitions of parent roles. We see nurturance and socialization as necessary elements of "true parenthood" and thus are able to argue . . . that parents who do not fill these rearing roles "cannot really deserve their children"—for us they cease to *be* parents. But given West African definitions of the parent role, this is no longer true.)[11]

Contemporary descriptions of "abandonments" in the nineteenth century were colored by an ideological bias, which is replicated in historians' accounts of the invention of childhood that ignore the essentially political, hectoring dimension of the new definition. In this essay, I look at the course and consequences of the abandonment of child custody to fosterage in the 1850s. The evidence shows delegated parenting strategies and discontinuity in the roles of children and conceptions of parenthood. Widespread abandonment of child custody was no myth, and if we count informal custody delegations to friends, its incidence was probably greater than family history recognizes. But the practices do not have the lurid emotional character or biographical fatefulness often attributed to them. Some of the almost four hundred children in my sample had unkind parents, and this was probably affected by the stresses of poverty. The question is whether abandoning children to the agency's foster care was part of a normative and reasonable family strategy for coping with the economic and demographic viscissitudes of proletarianization.

The Solution: Child-Saving Deployments and Parental Interests

Child savers denounced working-class family life for its widespread, en-cultured parental neglect. This problem called for an organized solution: radical intervention in families to promote alternative, rehabilitative social-ization of children. Convention in the history of philanthropy holds that institutionalized charities and reform efforts of the middle and late nine-teenth century were hitched to a program of humanitarian help or repressive social control.[12] The historiographic use of the omnibus term *reform* suggests the imposition of a new, ambitious design, in implicit contrast to a traditional charitable practice bound up with social reproduction. David Thomson disputes this emphasis on discontinuity, arguing the continuity of "welfare relations,"[13] by which he indicates a history of selective but respectable subventions from charity and local government to mitigate the rigors of life, particularly those associated with life crises. By social reproduction I simultaneously refer to economic strategies for mitigating health problems, catastrophic reverses, and routine misery and mechanisms of social replacement, including sponsorship to adult roles and kinship identities. The notion of a transformative design in welfare supplanting the old process of mobilizing resources to succor misery also underlies occupational narratives of progress from charity to social work.

Victorian child saving figures in the history of welfare as a milestone of institutional dissociation of philanthropy from vernacular interests, herald-ing the triumph of "policy" design over routine adjustments. Child saving purported to drive a wedge between the client and his or her flawed background. Jacksonian asylums were to remove children from depraved influences for resocialization; Victorian fostering and "adoption" schemes were to replace those influences altogether. Citing welfare history as authority, Michael Grossberg writes that the bench sanctioned fostering schemes because they were allegedly part of a modernizing policy trend of social control:

> Judicial authorization for state intervention in dependent poor families, so counter to the bench's general antebellum tendencies, may well have been encouraged by the asylum movement. . . . Old institutions that had perpetuated misery and crime would be replaced by new public institutions of reform and rehabilitation. It was an easy corollary that dependent poor families should be superseded by state-provided benign environments.[14]

Thus the rhetorical ideal of child-saving policy is understood as being set dead against the logic of family reproduction, corresponding instead to the ideology of psychological parenthood. It is as the sine qua non of radical, transformative intervention that child saving marks a disjunction between a traditional, client-influenced adjustment process and a characteristically modern design of social engineering. Echoing the self-serving critique of such Progressive reformers as Homer Folks, Judge Benjamin Lindsey, or their predecessors, some welfare historians hold that the excesses of Victorian-era radical interventionism were subsequently tempered, and a more highly professionalized generation of Progressive career helpers assumed an avuncular demeanor toward immigrant families and adjusted treatment to the individual.[15] But this was from a vantage of institutional ascendancy initiated by earlier reformers, and it occurred under the aegis of a secularized and therapeutic doctrine that owed its authority to the Victorian-era ideal of transformative policy.

I argue that policy ambitions to police families, transform character, socialize reproduction, colonize private life, inculcate labor discipline, and so forth had little to do with the actual practice of child saving by this leading agency. The Children's Aid Society accommodated unreconstructed family purposes, piggybacking an effort to promote sentimental adoptions as a child-saving intervention onto the normal, temporary fosterage transactions that poor families pursued independently. Some aspects of the family relations of the poor or the life trajectory of their children might have been changed in the process, but the overwhelming impression conveyed in the midcentury case records is of continuity. Like the problem of child abandonment, the solution of child-saving reform was substantially an illusion of nominal policy and public ideology.

The New York Children's Aid Society and the Victorian Child-Saving Movement

The Victorian child-saving movement was epitomized by Charles Loring Brace. Thomas Bender argues that Brace's influence as a writer helped shape the modern "urban vision."[16] Paul Boyer, too, judged that "on anyone's list of dominant figures in the history of moral control a place near the top" would go to Brace.[17] In 1853 Brace turned from missionary work with New York's "street Arabs" to establish the Children's Aid Society, which was oriented primarily to practical amelioration rather than to the evangelism of city missions. Like so many other commentators of the last century, Brace placed working-class children in the category "orphan." His originality lay in his advocacy of their wholesale "emigration" to "good Christian homes" in the rural West. In claiming that placement in foster families improved character, he established novel, child-centered "developmental" goals for policy. The plan started as a tentative variation of the old practice of placing dependents in the households of local tradesmen and farmers. But Brace's originality was marked by the emergent familistic claim that, through transfer of parenting functions, the foster home provided substitute parents, not just governance in a domestic work site; by the scale of his work and the great distances he sent children; and by his refusal to bind charges of the agency in legal indentures to their guardians.[18]

Brace retained his position as a preeminent urban reformer and humanitarian until late in the century. During his tenure of almost forty years as secretary of the Children's Aid Society, Brace claimed to have personally overseen the emigration of more than one hundred thousand city children. Many other agencies followed the same practice, though by the 1880s foster placement was less important in the agency's work than programs that sought to reform city youths and their families rather than transplanting and disrupting them. There is some consensus that Brace's familism achieved ideological dominance even though the policy of foster care was less important than institutional confinement until the twentieth century.[19] But even his rivals tried to routinize Brace's charismatic familism through "cottage plan" measures, replete with housemothers and fathers mimicking conjugal family structure.[20] In the following two sections I examine case record data from the founding year of the New York Children's Aid Society, the preeminent child-saving institution in the United States in the nineteenth century. The sample consists of the 383 usable case histories in the 399 numbered cases in the society's Record Book number one, covering the period from April 1853 to September 1854. The sixteen discarded cases were scratched-out partial entries or blank but numbered records.

These case histories do not represent all child abandonments by impoverished working-class families in New York City. The only representative sources would be census enumerations, which do not contain information on parental transactions or the contacts of working-class families with benevolent institutions. Like all information on the popular classes, the agency records are colored by the viewpoints of the recorders. This problem may be less bothersome than usual because, unlike official reports, the source was not intended for publication; because facts at this time were compiled by immediate entry in a running ledger, without the delay or reflection of a composed case analysis; and because the collective biography that emerges is so unlike the rhetorical story the child savers were promoting. I am sure they censored but doubt they fabricated, for they would surely have made up something more consistent with their public iconography of cruel, dissipated parents and "homeless orphan children." Through his journalistic reports on the "dangerous classes of New York,"[21] Brace has influenced American social historians' view of the underclass of Victorian New York City,[22] so there can be scant grounds for not examining the raw material on which he drew for his social portraits.

Circumstance and Motive in Child Abandonments

In his public speeches and in published vignettes and illustrations, Brace conveyed a stereotypic image of the homeless orphan children served by the agency. The idealized passage from abandonment through placement to adoption is depicted in Figure 5.1, from the frontispiece of the society's 1873 Annual Report. This image of relatively young, homeless, and friendless waifs entering care through the active intervention of agents is inconsistent with the characteristics of abandoned children described in the operational records.

Most of the real children were older than their official image in Figure 5.1, as Table 5.1 shows. The median age at which custody of the children was surrendered to the agency was 13 years. For boys the median was 13.2 and for girls 12.1. The age distribution of the children entering care shows that only 14.5 percent were 10 years old or under. Sixteen percent were 17 years old or over. The remaining 70 percent of the cases may be divided into age groups 11 to 13 years (34 percent) and 14 to 16 years (36 percent). Carl F. Kaestle

FIGURE 5.1. The Work of the Children's Aid Society, frontispiece of the society's 1873 Annual Report.

TABLE 5.1   Age of Children at Time of Custody Surrender, 1853–1854

	Panel A	Panel B	
	All Children	Boys	Girls
Median Age	13.0	13.2	12.1
Age Distribution			
0–10	53 (14.5%)		
11–13	131 (35.8%)		
14–16	138 (37.7%)		
17+	44 (12.0%)		

reports that the New York school system regarded 14 as the normative age for most pupils to leave school.[23] Thus, with respect to American age grade structure in the Victorian era, 52 percent of the youthful clients were not of an age to be considered as children. They were in a stage of youthful "semiautonomy," having entered some adult roles but not having nearly completed the entire set of transitions to adulthood.[24]

Neither had most of the real children been homeless in the lurid sense suggested by the illustration. It is true, as Table 5.2 shows, that only 12 percent of the children were surrendered from intact, two-parent families, but 64 percent were living "at home" at the time they were surrendered: 53 percent with one or both parents and 12 percent under the household governance of an adult "friend" in the nineteenth-century usage.[25] Of the remaining 36 percent, only 16 percent were homeless; the remainder were youths residing in paid lodgings or in an institution of some sort. Most frequently those who were in institutions were older youths who had been sleeping in a police station house but were not incarcerated there. The age and residential circumstances of these abandoned children suggest an ordinariness or normality that does not jibe with the received image. This impression of normality is reinforced by evidence on the specific reasons why parents surrendered child custody. A summary of the motives cited in the records appears in Table 5.3.[26]

In about a quarter of all cases (23 percent) parents are reported surrendering children because of the trauma of recent widowhood or marital separation, poor health, or poverty. Following Goody, I call this crisis fostering.[27] Children were also surrendered by parents (and even surrendered themselves) in hopes of developmental benefit: 9 percent of cases report moral control goals. Almost 34 percent were hoping for advantages

TABLE 5.2   Residential Situation of Children at Time of Custody Surrender, 1853–1854

	Panel A	Panel B	
	All Children	Boys	Girls
Living in a Home	234 (64.1%)	151 (61.6%)	83 (69.2)
Median Age	12.3	12.5	11.7
With Both Parents	43 (11.8%)	22 (9.0%)	21 (17.5%)
Median Age	12.6	13.1	12.2
Father Only	47 (12.9%)	36 (14.7%)	11 (9.2%)
Median Age	12.9	13.1	11.5
Mother Only	79 (21.6%)	57 (23.3%)	22 (18.3%)
Median Age	12.0	12.0	12.0
Parent + Stepparent	23 (6.3%)	11 (4.5%)	12 (10.0%)
Median Age	11.5	10.8	11.8
With "Friends"	42 (11.5%)	25 (10.2%)	17 (14.2%)
Median Age	12.0	12.8	10.5
Not in a Home	131 (35.9%)	94 (38.4%)	37 (30.8%)
Median Age	14.1	14.5	13.1
In Institution	47 (12.9%)	20 (8.2%)	27 (22.5%)
Median Age	13.8	15.0	12.8
In Lodgings	25 (6.8%)	23 (9.4%)	2 (1.7%)
Median Age	15.0	14.9	18.0
Homeless	59 (16.2%)	51 (20.8%)	8 (6.7%)
Median Age	13.9	14.1	13.3
Total N	365 (100%)	245 (100%)	120 (100%)
Missing Cases	18	18	

in job training or entry into the labor force. These motives reveal a pattern similar to what Goody calls purposive fostering. In only 16.2 percent of all cases did Children's Aid Society record-keepers even allege the unloving parental behavior (violence, drunkenness, and indifference) that their own public imagery presented as the characteristic motive for child abandonment. This lurid public and literary image of abandonment has been accurately relayed by sentimental historians, but the picture disclosed by the routinely generated records is so inconsistent with the image of aban-

TABLE 5.3   Motives for Custody Surrender, 1853–1854

| | | | Panel A | | Panel B | |
			All Children	Median Age	Boys	Girls
Var A.	Dis-	Yes:	62 (16.2%)	11.3	32 (12.5%)	30 (23.6%)
	organization	No:	321	13.1	224	97
	Total N		383 (100%)		256 (100%)	127 (100%)
If	Violence		15 (3.9%)		9 (3.5%)	6 (4.7%)
Yes	Drinking, No					
	Violence		17 (4.4%)		10 (3.9%)	7 (5.5%)
	Other Neglect		30 (7.8%)		13 (5.1%)	17 (13.4%)
Var B.	Family	Yes:	88 (23%)	11.8	59 (23%)	29 (22.8%)
	Trauma	No:	295	13.3	197	98
	Total N		383 (100%)		256 (100%)	127 (100%)
If	Widowhood					
	Desertion		21 (5.5%)		13 (5.1%)	8 (6.3%)
Yes	Health Problems		19 (5%)		12 (4.7%)	7 (5.5%)
	Poverty, Not					
	Healthy		48 (12.5%)		34 (12.3%)	14 (11.0%)
Var C.	Moral	Yes:	35 (9.1%)	12.6	18 (7.0%)	17 (13.4%)
	Control	No:	348	13	238	110
	Total N		383 (100%)		256 (100%)	127 (100%)
Var D.	Seeking	Yes:	129 (33.7%)	14.1	102 (39.8%)	27 (21.3%)
	Job/Training	No:	254	11.9	154	100
	Total N		383 (100%)		256 (100%)	127 (100%)
Var E.	Recent	Yes:	43 (11.2%)	15.5	39 (15.2%)	4 (3.1%)
	Immigration	No:	340	12.7	217	123
	Without					
	Parents					
	Total N		383 (100%)		256 (100%)	127 (100%)
Missing Cases		0		0	0	

donment that I will use the less familiar term *surrender* to avoid these connotations. Here I draw on standard usage, not the bureaucratic distinction in child welfare between "surrendered" children, whose parents signed custody surrender forms, and "abandoned" children for whom no form was signed. The bureaucratic distinction lumps together the few dramatically abandoned children left in lobbies or ejected from home with those whom incapacitated parents had placed out with friends, or even with those officially removed from natal homes for various reasons over parental protests.

Parents often surrendered their children to secure for children the parental function of nurturance in times of family trauma: food, shelter, and other physical care and socialization to the cultural idiom. Such circulation of children between households figures in Louise A. Tilly and Joan W. Scott's description of a family economy and in Richard Wall's recent qualification of that model.[28] Within the trauma category, desertion and widowhood, health problems, and extreme destitution were three common reasons for surrendering custody of a child. Table 5.3 shows that desertion or widowhood was the cause in 5.5 percent of cases, health problems preceded surrender in 5 percent of cases, and grinding poverty was mentioned in 12.5 percent of cases. Most families in contact with the Children's Aid Society were, of course, poor in some sense, but for this 13 percent poverty was an immediate, pressing motive mentioned to explain surrender.

Narratives of Need: Crisis and Purposive Fostering

Notations in the records citing poverty tended to be laconic. A thirteen-year-old American Protestant boy (case number 1.64) was surrendered because his widowed mother was "too poor to support him." August Schurz (1.70), a thirteen-year-old German boy, was the "son of a poor man—can't take care of him." When widows had to relinquish custody for reasons of privation, the record often contained an exonerating note. Mrs. Nind, a widow, worked as a nurse and was deemed "a worthy Protestant woman too poor to keep her large family together." She gave up two of her sons (1.71 and 1.72), aged ten and eight. Washwomen, nurses, and needle workers were described in the records as poor but deserving, and their decision to surrender children was recorded with no hint of censure.

In the 5 percent of cases in which children were surrendered because of health-related family trauma, there were several emergencies—a recent death from cholera, an industrial accident—but the usual reason was a chronic disability. Before the welfare state, disability meant that parents who could not draw on kin resources, or who had exhausted their resources, had to give up their children to substitute families or institutions. Typical health-related cases of trauma were those of a father who surrendered his child because he was a "broken down laborer" (1.50); another boy came because he was the son of an "old, poor Scots laborer" (1.54). Another boy's entry to care was explained by his father having had rheumatism for two years (1.102).

My characterization of surrender as a coping strategy designed to secure nurturance for the child is illustrated in the case of Albert Wallace, a fourteen-year-old American Protestant. The Wallace family used the agency for the temporary safekeeping—moral as well as material—of the child. Albert's mother, a widow, had to take work as a lady's nurse. Because she could not then keep house for her son, he went to the Children's Aid Society office, declaring that he wanted to "live with a farmer." In April 1854 he was placed with a farmer in Connecticut. He wrote that he liked farming and continued in school and that the farmer and the farmer's parents, who lived nearby, were very nice to him. He was called home by his mother, now living in New Jersey, after twenty months in foster care. Albert continued to correspond with Brace. In September 1856 he was still with his mother, and he thanked the society for his "preservation from ruin."

Girls were surrendered and then allowed to return home under similar circumstances. Eliza Chaplain's widowed mother (1.276), an American Protestant living at 4 Horatio Street, room 6, sewed and washed for a living. She "has six small children to support by her own hard earnings—often sits up three nights in a week sewing for the slop shops. Eliza has been religiously trained by her mother, who is a member of the Methodist church." Eliza went to a place on Long Island and returned to her mother sixteen months later.

Purposive fostering to secure for children the benefits of education, moral training, and entry into the labor force were other motives attributed to parents. One-third of placements cited entry to the labor force and 9 percent cited moral control as reasons for surrender. Some boys or their parents tried to manipulate an advantageous entry to the labor force. A thirteen-year-old American (1.106) was removed from a sweated sash and blind shop by his widowed mother and then surrendered. He stayed at a farm in New Jersey for three years, then his mother retrieved him to put him to a trade after an extended dispute in which she unsuccessfully tried to have the farmer arrange for the boy to enter a trade locally. Many parents wanted their older children to "learn a trade" or to "earn something beyond their keep" and stipulated terms of compensation under which their children could be placed out.

There is a danger of anachronism in assuming that the lives of older children and youths in the nineteenth century were routinely ordered by plans for a career. Many just wanted work. The parental function of arranging training shaded off into a search for work in agriculture or rural industry on the part of youths, especially those in their mid-to-late teens, who would in the normal course of events expect to reside semiautonomously under the household governance of an employer or other adult.[29] Thirty-four percent of the children wished to use the Children's Aid Society as an employment agency of sorts, as shown in Table 5.3, and as may be deduced from their fairly advanced ages. These children were of an age to work but found nothing in the city, or the positions they already had would never lead them to stable adult occupations.

In my coding scheme, moral control motives indicate an explicit wish to conserve or alter the child's demeanor in line with prevailing notions of rectitude. Mrs. Leary was a very poor Irish seamstress from 600 Grand Street whose oldest son had just "fallen into prison." She feared for her thirteen-year-old son, Will (1.79), and surrendered him for preemptive reformation. Because he was totally illiterate and would not benefit from school, she asked that he be placed where he would get something besides board and school. Brace placed him at a tan yard in rural New Jersey. Ward Stanley (1.251) was surrendered because his father was out of work, which reduced his family to poverty. A moral stipulation was included in the request, as Ward's mother gave up her twelve-year-old son saying that she wanted a "God fearing home as he has been religiously brought up." In another case of parental moral control, eleven-year-old Jesse Toliver, an American Protestant, was surrendered by his father, a carpenter (1.277), who stipulated that he be placed "where God and the sabbath are feared." Brace evidently found such a place, for in giving notice of Jesse's arrival at his farm, William Little of Orange County, New York, expressed the dour hope that the boy would "prove useful to himself and others." Apparently pleased, the elder Toliver returned some days later to surrender Jesse's older brother Will (1.298). Girls for whom parents felt concern about moral control were more often surrendered reactively than proactively. Their cases show parental frustration and despair over incorrigibility or "stubbornness" and fears for their sexual honor. One Irish Catholic father wanted his daughter (1.338) placed out to get "education [etc.] until of age," averring she was "not a bad girl, just wild."

Neglect and abuse by parents were cited as motives for surrender, but only occasionally. Parents who had married for a second time, gaining a stepparent to the children, were in a particularly unhappy condition. Their children represented 6.3 percent of the agency's intake, and they were the youngest group. These stepfamilies do seem to have used surrender to unburden themselves in an abandoning manner. The agents suggested that twelve of the twenty-three surrenders from stepfamilies were motivated by disorganization. Families headed by stepfathers seem to have been particularly troubled. Although one must be cautious in drawing conclusions from such a small number of cases, it is impressive that for ten of the twelve children surrendered by households headed by a stepfather disorganization was cited as a motive for surrender. Writing of an earlier period in European history, Tilly and Scott say that "sometimes the price of remarriage was the abandonment of [the woman's] children, since a prospective husband might be unwilling to contribute to their support. But even this alternative might seem preferable to the precarious existence of a widow on her own who might have to abandon her children anyway."[30] This appears to be equally true of the Victorian period in America.

There would be little to gain in rehearsing the litany of parental misdeeds cited in the 16.2 percent of the case histories in which disorganization was alleged. In these instances, the "push" of unloving parenting might reinforce the "pull" of a simultaneous crisis or purposive motive. Thirteen-year-old Michael Mullin (1.80) was brought to the agency by his mother, who feared that the boy's father, an Irish Protestant bookbinder employed at 20 Nassau Street, "would kill the boy sometime." Michael, whom Charles Loring Brace rated "the smartest boy we have ever had in the office," had a good job with a publisher and earned $3 per week, but according to the boy and his mother the father always spent it on drink. Michael said he tried to "lay some up," but his father always got it. The boy and his mother wanted him apprenticed to a newspaper, which Brace was able to arrange.

The evidence of the midcentury Children's Aid Society records suggests that surrenders were, for the most part, rational family responses to normal if unpredictable economic and demographic constraints or mechanisms to negotiate a transition from the status of dependent child to semiautonomous youth. The character of the parent-child relation was not notably ambivalent or rejecting at surrender, and it was sometimes even solicitous and purposive. But though parents had compelling or expedient reasons for surrendering their children, they did so with an alacrity that distinguishes their attitudes from those of normal middle-class parents today and probably from middle-class parents at the time. The parents were seriously concerned about the welfare of their children, but the children did not seem to be dear to them in the "sacralized" sense that Vivian Zelizer argues was established as a norm in the early twentieth century.[31] Before that time a very different "utilitarian" or "instrumental" value was placed upon children, she says, and reading the archival evidence I was indeed struck by the matter-of-factness with which abandonments were transacted. I do not doubt Zelizer's cultural analysis of changing values, but I wish to make a different argument about the concrete, material transaction that was child surrender rather than the normative ideals framing conduct. The portrayal of casual, brisk, but responsible surrender may seem more plausible once we have examined the character of the relationship between natal and foster family that followed.

The Child-Saving Relationship:
Negotiation, Conflict, and Cooperation

At its origins the modern system of child fosterage typically entailed a temporary surrender, followed by the child's return to the natal parents' household or to independence, depending on the child's age. This pattern probably followed the course of informal fosterage at the time. Of the 127 children who resided with a parent at the time of their surrender and who were sent out of New York City, 70 percent (89) are known to have returned, as Table 5.4 shows, and some of the remainder surely did so unbeknownst to the society, which at the time only followed up placements by post. By contrast, 42 percent (57 of 130) of children without parents who were transported subsequently returned to the city. A total of 48.5 percent of all children were positively identified as returning. The return of large numbers of surrendered children is unremarked in the historiography of child welfare for the very good reason that child savers did not admit it, though any demographer familiar with "circular" or "return" migration patterns would likely have predicted it. This pattern, together with the motivational evidence presented above, is the basis for my argument that child "abandonment" was really "surrender": an expedient and morally respectable strategy of the natal family trying to balance its economy.

TABLE 5.4   Whether Children Are Reported Returning Home to New York, 1853–1854

	Panel A	Panel B		Panel C	
	All Children	Boys	Girls	Resided with One or Both Parents	Resided with Friends or Out of a Home
Return	150	101	49	89	57
Noted	(48.5%)	(49.5%)	(46.7%)	(57.0%)	(40.2%)
No Return	118	77	41	38	73
Noted	(38.2%)	(37.7%)	(39.0%)	(24.4%)	(51.8%)
Placed in	41	26	15	29	11
New York	(13.3%)	(12.7%)	(14.3%)	(18.6%)	(7.8%)
Total N	309	204	105	156	141
Missing Cases	74	52	22	86	

Children left placements under a variety of circumstances, but the case histories of the 34 who were reported retrieved from placements by the direct initiative of their kin (11 percent of the 318 cases in which an outcome was discernible) give particularly clear insight into the fosterage transaction. In a situation of shared parenthood, ultimate possession of child custody was ambiguous. So too was ultimate responsibility for caretaking and the child's welfare. The common pattern is revealed in the case of John Quig (1.1), aged thirteen, the first child to be placed out by the society. He had lived with his widowed mother. Brace sent him to East Woodstock, Connecticut, in April 1853, where he stayed for an unusually long time. He attended school, and his foster father reported him "improved as much as could be expected." But in December 1855, after two years and eight months, he was retrieved by his brother at the behest of his mother and brought back to New York City. The foster father felt ill-used in this transaction, complaining to Brace that he had been kind to the boy. He would have liked a more effective familial relation, one that supplanted the relation with the family of origin, but in the nineteenth century fostering and "adoption" (as such placements were referred to) rarely had this enduring character. In only a handful of cases did the society, the foster family, or any other "agent of social control" attempt to prevent a birth parent from retrieving his or her child from a placement, and in only one case was it successful. In four other cases the society was actively uncooperative with natal parents.

Two basic stories emerge from the histories of retrieved children. One is that children were retrieved explicitly to assume family duties or because of a change in the circumstances of the family. The second is that the family of origin simply asserted a prerogative to reclaim custody, sometimes in face of opposition from foster parents. The first situation is illustrated in the case of a twelve-year-old German girl, Mary Ring (1.306), who was surrendered by her parents and then retrieved two months later because her parents' "circumstances have improved." The same phrase was repeated often. Leni Pfeiffer (1.306), a twelve-year-old German girl, was sent upstate to a household in July 1854. But in two months the foster family reported that she had "returned to her parents whose circumstances have improved."

In some cases the issue was less that the parents became more able to provide nurturance than that demands were placed on the child to return and help the family. A fourteen-year-old Irish Catholic girl had lived with her parents, who surrendered her for placement in Connecticut. About ten months later her mother died, and she "returned to take charge of the family." A similar picture of filial obligation emerges from the case of Susan Rowlands (1.332). Her mother had been a shirtmaker in England but could not find much work in the city and relied on her oldest son's earnings. Because he was out of work, she had to surrender Susan, then fifteen, to a domestic position in New Jersey. Only a month later her brother died and Susan was retrieved "as her mother needed her to help with the family." After Mary Murrell (1.140) spent nine months in Connecticut, her mother died, and Mary promptly returned to her father's home "to take charge of the family."

For boys the retrievals were most often automatic or routine assertions of residual rights in the child by the birth parent. These retrievals, terminating placements of short duration, are the logical outcome of strategic crisis fostering: they helped the family weather some reverse. Mrs. Peters worked as a domestic after her husband deserted her and went to New Orleans. The entry reads that she had seen nine of her twelve children die and now "gives up all she has." But she did not give them up for good. After ten months she was once more in a position to keep house and reclaimed her son James (1.292), now aged twelve. This scenario was repeated in the case of twelve-year-old Ward Stanley (1.251), whose father lost his job. His mother's paltry income was all they had, so they surrendered Ward, demanding a "God fearing home." After four months the boy was "taken away by his father."

Even if the child was accepted into intimacy with the foster family, the ambiguity about who had custody was resolved in favor of the natural parents without dispute or demand for explanation. Charles Tremblay (1.4), a ten-year-old French stepson, whose natural father was blind, was sent to a farmer in New Jersey, who gave him board, clothing, and schooling. This placement worked well for two and one-half years. The relationship was affectionate. The farmer reported that Charles was "addicted to lying but is likely to get rid of this bad habit as his disposition seems naturally good." That the boy was included in the family circle and was not just an employee is clear from the fosterer's comment that Charles "is fonder of attending Church than his books. He would consider it a great punishment to be sent back to New York." But in October 1855 he was retrieved home with a good recommendation from his foster father.

There is no indication that the reformers were opposed to such reunions for the priority of the family of origin fit into established norms of child work. In the case of Charles Gallagher (1.40), the society agreed to acknowledge this priority. His father was at sea, and the stepmother, who was poor, agreed to surrender the eleven-year-old on the condition that the father could reclaim him on his return. The society accepted these terms without hesitation.

Birth parents and foster parents sometimes negotiated the conditions of a boy's labor and remuneration between themselves, informing the society after the fact. In October 1853 Christopher Mathiessen (1.106), aged thirteen, was removed from the sweated shop where he worked and surrendered to the society by his single mother. In 1856 Mrs. Mathiessen told the farmer her son was living with that she wanted him removed and put to a trade. This did not suit the farmer, who thought Christopher "a stout, healthy boy and is able to do a good deal of work for his age"—a considerable compliment. He defended his fair treatment of the boy, saying that he would have saved money from his wages except that "he is fond of gratifying his palate. Spends his money on cigars, ice cream and candy." In January 1857 Mrs. Mathiessen went to New Jersey and retrieved her son so she could put him to a trade but could find him no job in the city and returned to the society later that month requesting that he be sent to the West, which he was. In cases like this, both the natural and the foster parents saw the child's labor as an economic contribution that should be exchanged for a benefit.

The farmer wanted to pay directly, but the mother wanted training for her son. They accepted the principle of reciprocity but disagreed on the terms.

The original and the foster parent might negotiate over the distribution of the benefits of child labor accruing to the two family economies. Shared parenting need not involve the child's welfare alone, for at this time material reciprocity between parent and child was not a one-way transaction. Robert Wilson (1.127), a thirteen-year-old Irish Protestant, was with his aunt when his father was in the hospital. The mother was alive in Ireland. The aunt could not keep him and turned him out. By the time he came to the society with his ten-year-old sister, Robert was "willing to go anywhere and do anything to get a living." He was sent to a farmer in Seneca County, who said he wished to keep him until he was twenty-one. The farmer's brother took Robert's sister. The instrumental view of childhood is evident on the part of both the birth and the substitute parents in this case. When Robert arrived, the farmer wrote Brace that the boy "may answer to my purposes." After a year he was reported having run away "from his work on the farm" (not from his "home"), returning subsequently "as morose as ever." The boy's father returned to Ireland when discharged from the hospital, but he reemigrated to the United States two and a half years later and successfully exacted payment from the farmers for the services of his children, then disappeared again. This sad instance of shared parenting illustrates the strength of the father's residual rights in custom even though he provided no nurturance.

Not all of the natural parents wished to interfere with or curtail the foster placements. A common interest between the birth parent and the foster parent could lead to cooperation. When Mrs. Prentice, an American seamstress, was deserted, she surrendered her two boys, William, aged eleven, and Troy, nine (1.334). William went to Westport, Connecticut, to a farmer in August 1854 and ran away to return to his mother in June 1856. His mother took him straight back to the farmer, but the man would not have him, and the boy ended up staying with a neighboring farmer. In another case of apparent serendipity James Hogg (1.304), an Irish boy aged twelve, had a widowed mother with five children. He was sent to a farmer in Chicopee, Massachusetts, in June 1854. In November 1855 he came to New York to visit his mother, and she later told the society that James went back "much pleased with the prospect of returning to his good boss again." Such cooperation did not undercut the natal parent's claim, for in April 1856 he returned to the city on his mother's instructions.

Even when placements were of long duration, the tenacity of the mother-child tie could be extraordinary if fosterers cooperated. When Benjamin Moore (1.212), aged twelve, was brought to the office in April 1854, Mr. Macy, a society agent, described him as "an intelligent, smart boy." He was sent upstate. The foster family liked his appearance when he arrived and sent the society several good reports on him. In 1857, almost three years after his placement, Benjamin's aunt in New York City told the society the boy was still at his placement and that his mother had visited him there. Benjamin's filial constancy was outdone by that of Arthur Turner (1.33). This American Protestant boy was sent to Vermont at age twelve in June 1853. Two years later he was in New York to visit his mother, and he dropped by the society office to report that he was "still doing capitally." He thanked the society for helping him and returned to Vermont. The success of the placement did not undermine the tie to his mother, for in 1856, at age fifteen, he took his mother back with him to Vermont. The last time he dropped by the office was in April 1859, when he was twenty and preparing to return to Vermont again. It is not clear that his mother relocated permanently to Vermont. She may have visited there and returned to the city (perhaps explaining Arthur's presence in the city in 1859). In either case, it is clear that the relation with his mother was retained in cooperation with the foster family.

Fosterage as a Family Strategy and Child Welfare as a Resource

Evidence that parents used the child-saving agencies as a resource in forming survival strategies suggests that their "abandoning" behavior was normative, reasonable, and possibly the least detrimental option open to them. It argues against both the culture shock idea that such abandonments indicated novel anomie and disorder caused by modernization and the evolutionary idea that they were attitudinal holdovers from a traditional regime of parental indifference and cruelty before the invention of childhood. Two points remain to be argued. The first is that these custody surrenders fit into a family pattern of fosterage independent of child saving and philanthropy. It could be that fosterage was a radical intervention that was not as fateful as it claimed to be but still transformed the experience of its clients. Second, if it is accepted that abandoning parents were really "surrendering" their children in the sense that I have described, the widespread agrarian and working-class cultural toleration of delegation of parenthood may have been uniquely well suited to American conditions. The questions, in sum, are, Why ought we to think that widespread fosterage was a normal part of American kinship outside the middle classes, and why might this have been so?

To address the prevalence of parental delegation one would need information on fostering arrangements made by parents on their own, showing that their transactions were similar to those mediated by child-saving institutions. No one has studied fosterage transactions that were not mediated by charities,[32] and the data needed to do so are unlikely to be found, so the only way to approach this issue is to infer the plausibility of my interpretation by examining related topics.

Anthropological findings show that fosterage is common in societies at a particular stage of development.[33] Conditions that seem to produce fosterage are a social hierarchy but weak caste barriers between the lower and the middle ranks, relatively weak reliance on clans and other social groups based on lineage, little concentration of capital, and few social distinctions based on formal credentials. Under these circumstances, fostering parents do not risk losing their children because birth-status identity and reciprocities of early nurturance are not culturally threatened by subsequent surrogate care. Fosterage under these conditions is unlikely to be condemned and may be a positive norm because educational advantages may accrue to the child, and his or her resource network for sponsorship to adult roles may be augmented. Rose Laub Coser proposes that fosterage is a special case of the "weak ties" that sociologists have found important for entry to the labor force.[34] Anthropologists also note the creation or reinforcement of an interfamily "claims system" linking the adults of the natal and foster families through the circulation of children,[35] though this was largely precluded in the cases I examined by the mediation of the society between parents and proxy parents. Since the social structure widely associated with fostering coincides with some abstract features of "settler societies"[36] like the United States, might the anthropological view of abandonment and fosterage be applicable to the American case? A caveat here is that labor recruitment based on fictive kinship is liable to gross exploitation with the transition to capitalist agriculture, but this effect seems to turn on the immobility of labor and isolation from alternative job markets. Neither of these conditions would apply in the case of the Children's Aid Society's emigration schemes.

There are two reasons for believing that abandonment and fosterage were very important features of the nineteenth-century family economy of laborers and yeomen in America. The first may be considered the supply-side evidence. From evidence on demographic constraints we can infer that fosterage was common in America throughout the nineteenth century, as it was in the colonies and the United Kingdom before and as it seems to be in many agrarian societies. Mary Ryan states that "in a number of historical situations demographic conditions were such that only a minority of the population could be housed in nuclear families," and sometimes "most children spent some time living as orphans."[37] Peter Laslett gives as a conservative estimate that a third of all English children in the last century lost one or both parents while minors.[38] Peter Uhlenberg has shown that high mortality rates in the last century, combined with late childbearing through the mother's thirties and even into her forties, produced large numbers of half or fully orphaned children surviving the deaths of parents.[39] Many surviving widowers had no older daughter available or willing to step into the deceased mother's shoes,[40] and a widowed mother employed as a seamstress, domestic, nurse, or washwoman would very likely find it impossible to keep her family intact without some disruptions unless she could move the lot in with a relative. There was, of course, no adequate welfare "net" to fall back on before widows' pension plans in some states beginning in the 1920s.[41]

If family structure problems gave some parents incentive to surrender child custody, at least temporarily, others were willing to take the children in for the value of their labor contributions to the productive household. Census-based demographic studies of household composition from the middle to the late nineteenth century report that, at any given time, between 20 and 35 percent of farm homes contained children other than those of adult household members.[42] Several circumstances could lead to this outcome, but it is surely plausible to infer that widespread fosterage among kin and friends was prominent among them.

Legal adoptions might seem to argue against my "adaptive" interpretation of the delegation of the parental role since the ideology of adoption reform placed an accent of the transformative, anti-natal-family ideal that children would totally change their birth-status identities. This was the reform theory, but in his examination of legal adoptions Jamil S. Zainaldin found that only 52 percent of legal adoptions in Boston between 1851 and 1875 were "modern" or sentimental stranger adoptions.[43] Forty-eight percent of children whose parents could not cope or had died were adopted by friends and kin. Of the almost half of all adoptees whom Zainaldin classified as adopted through a traditional "family process," 90 percent were legitimate and 65 percent had one or both parents alive at the time of adoption.

By a heroic feat of record-linkage, Zainaldin found that family-process adopters were more often workers or immigrants, the children were older, and the children were less likely than those adopted by strangers to be coresiding with their "adoptive" parents at a later date. They presumably returned to their natal families or experienced semiautonomy in an employer's household. These family-process adoptions were thus similar to the fosterage transactions I describe. The term *adoption* was freely used as a synonym for *foster* in the Children's Aid Society records, but the terms *service*, *indenture*, and *apprenticeship* were never used in this context.

In line with indications of demand, the agricultural historian David Schob reports that residential "plow boys" or "chore boys" were ubiquitous in the nineteenth century.[44] Economic historian Stanley Lebergott reports that there was very little wage labor in the agrarian economy and that more children "meant more income per family."[45] Further reason for hypothesizing a demand for foster children comes from demography, as bearing and begetting children is not the only way to augment household size. Demand for the labor of young people, especially boys, is important for theories of rural fertility. In the nineteenth century the American birth rate was very high. On the farm, fertility shot up strikingly, but the general decline in fertility over the course of the century was, paradoxically, accounted for very substantially by declining fertility among farm families. This anomaly was resolved by stressing the factor of land availability used to sponsor children to ownership.[46] This would make fosterage a particularly appealing method of augmenting the domestic labor force as sponsorship obligations would not necessarily be incumbent on the fosterer, though stable reciprocity exchanges can be identified and some children were indeed sponsored.

Conclusion

The evidence I examined is hard to square with either the view that the invention of childhood installed a regime of love in place of the negligent indifference epitomized by child abandonment or the view that such a dramatic installation was the early child savers' project, even though they rhetorically held that it was. Many parents abandoned their children, temporarily at least; and many household heads incorporated stray children into their families. A fraction of this child circulation was mediated by charitable institutions that kept records on the transactions, but the circulation of children between households orchestrated by the Children's Aid Society appears to have been of a piece with a common family strategy and not a transformative effect of philanthropy.[47]

Distorted views of both abandonment and subsequent placement in a "good home" rest on a normative opposition between work and love and place such a premium on uninterrupted continuity of care that it becomes the core symbol of performance of the parental role. Interpretations that embrace the developmental norms of "psychological parenthood" presume that global desiderata of parenthood informed both the evolution of personal relationships and the imposition of public policy in Victorian America. These values are not "presentist" retrojections; they were part of an emergent family ideology of domesticity that the Victorian-era middle classes were adopting in their own lives and advocating for others. But the family relations of the poor were not adequately described in those terms, and institutional child-saving practice had to accommodate itself to the reality of these family relations in order to recruit and roughly satisfy clients. The cooperation of early child savers with families adapting to constraints is startling only if one assumes that charitable institutions constituted a world apart and that their agents were blinded by doctrine to the conditions that brought clients to them. In short, the society's clients were normal in this period; and they were not "normalized" in Jacques Donzelot's sense.[48]

The first point is straightforward and, once said, probably not surprising as it fits with the literature on family economies. But the second may seem odd in that child saving helped crystallize a middle-class ideology that stigmatized these sorts of adaptive family strategies. Is it not confounding that, in practice, the Children's Aid Society facilitated the coping strategies it decried? It may seem that I am criticizing the twin conventions that child saving helped children escape their miserable backgrounds or coerced their families, only to replace them with an obverse notion that families and youths manipulated reformers. It might well be asked, What of the "agency" of these charity workers? Did they passively acquiesce in the rout of their programs while continuing to devote lives of service to the effort? Two answers can be given to this challenge, one predictable and the other perhaps less so.

The predictable answer beats a retreat along the well-worn path to the unforeseen consequence. Child welfare always had a project of moral regulation and did indeed change social relations "from the top down," but with results that turned out very differently from what the reformers envisaged. Programs might have been used as strategic resources by families while also furthering transformative ideals of policy. Brace and the society agents, and their midcentury contemporaries, arguably established the grounds on which parents really were deprived of child custody decades later and on a selective basis. In five cases out of almost four hundred discussed here, some permanent severing of natal ties occurred as a result of the society's efforts. Mothers or guardians suspected of prostitution were deprived of custody rights, as were male relatives when young girls were orphaned.

In the more typical cases, the placements found by the agency were farther-flung and perhaps a notch or two above what the parents might have arranged for themselves, and foster families were almost invariably Protestants. Zainaldin's evidence on noninstitutional family-process legal adoptions shows, in contrast, that natal and proxy parents had very similar social standing and ethno-religious affiliations.[49] The Children's Aid Society was uncompromising in its insistence that compensation for children's work was owed the child (in schooling and keep or in wages), not to her or his parents. This may have violated custom and have had an emancipatory influence, but we should not automatically assume that nonresident children normally shared their wages with parents. Conceivably, even the temporary placements that seem to speak most clearly against the transformative ideal may have had some effect on children who returned home. For example, some children who had absconded from placements grew dissatisfied at home and returned to the agency to be placed out again (though they would have left home anyway in due course). And some children were fully orphaned and available for sentimental adoption (and a few of them got it).

My other, less predictable suggestion is that the most dramatic contributing influence of child saving to the triumph of domesticity lay in the promotion of fictive kinship in fosterage arrangements, which occurred in tandem with the invention of adoption in legislation enacted by the American states beginning in 1851 and with changes in the law of custody dispositions that first disempowered fathers and then natal parents by the introduction of judicial discretion and a "best interest" standard. Children had always circulated through households. Brace's innovation—the idea that kinship identities ought to change in consequence of child circulation—was no less revolutionary for not being widely implemented. As a publicist and ideologue Brace represented the novel standard that continuity of care was in the "best interests" of the child, a standard that came to serve as a universal symbolic criterion of the family bond as such. In this top-down change in the cultural meaning of kinship, the blood tie was formally and openly rivaled by another, equally valid or even more valid symbolism of loving conduct that might supplant the claims of blood kin who cease to be symbolically "real" for failure to satisfy a code for conduct. The institutionalization of this new symbolic standard of filiation eventually became the nexus of class and ethnic conflict over the family—as it remains today—though it had little practical effect in the 1850s, when domesticity was still a proselytizing lifestyle, not a transcendent standard of virtue.

If all history is history of the present it is reasonable that the history of child saving is read for evidence that programs changed families. The limits of private rights and the legitimacy of official interventions are critical issues at present. The central issue that welfare history poses to social theory is the "Foucault paradox" that the expansion of citizenship rights to material security and improvement was associated with expanded regulation through surveillance and administration.[50] This paradox sharpens our interest in the idea that the culture of kinship was altered by middle-class reformers and moral entrepreneurs like Brace. The symbolism of "blood" sanctifies natal claims to rights in children whereas the defining symbolism of a code for conduct like continuity of care legitimizes official intervention in the child's best interests. But the overwhelming implication of the midcentury evidence—that surrendering families were normal and were not "normalized"—is at odds with emphasis on the rise of therapeutic social control.

When we take leave of that evidence to engage the current interest, the history of the present is threatened by anachronism in adhering to a notion of authoritative "public welfare" that "rose" in the last half of the nineteenth century and was fixed in the unprecedented "welfare state" at some point toward the middle of the present century. Against this, Thomson argues for the continuity of "welfare relations" in the English case, noting that writers at diverse points of the current political compass believe in the rise of the welfare state and counterpose it to a prior condition of self-sufficient "family-based" social reproduction that is, on several scores, implausible; and they sustain this belief by studying the discourse of welfare, not its practice: who got what from whom under what circumstances? On partial evidence, he argues that, as a percentage of the average worker's wage, subventions to the aged decreased under the welfare state.[51] I can offer nothing so dramatic in suggesting that child saving was by and large consistent with a long and demographically inescapable pattern of subventions to families experiencing crises; that persons such as the socially conscious clergymen and professionals' wives who did the work of the Children's Aid Society were precisely the sort of people who had long occupied themselves with charitable tasks; that the much discussed change from purely spiritual missionary efforts to "practical evangelism" that inspired the society rests on a bogus dichotomy; and that the novel ideological vocabulary Brace indubitably promoted is simply not as interesting or as sociologically important as the continuity of his society's practical articulation with family strategies.

Notes

1. Philippe Ariès, *Centuries of Childhood* (New York: Vintage, 1962); Elisabeth Badinter, *Motherlove: Myth and Reality* (New York: Macmillan, 1981); John Demos, *Family Life in Plymouth Colony* (New York: Oxford University Press, 1970); Carl F. Kaestle and Maris Vinovskis, "From Fireside to Factory: School Entry and School Leaving in Nineteenth-Century Massachusetts," in Tamara K. Hareven, ed., *Transitions: The Family and Life Course in Historical Perspective* (New York: Academic Press, 1978); Lloyd de Mause, "The Evolution of Childhood," in de Mause, ed., *The History of Childhood* (New York: Psychohistory Press, 1974); Christopher Lasch, *Haven in a Heartless World: The Family Besieged* (New York: Basic Books, 1977); Ivy Pinchbeck and Margaret Hewitt, *Children in English Society*, 2 vols. (London: Routledge & Kegan Paul, 1969–73); Edward Shorter, *The Making of the Modern Family* (New York: Basic Books, 1976); Lawrence Stone, *The Family, Sex and Marriage in England, 1550–1800* (New York: Harper & Row, 1977).

2. Robert A. LeVine and Merry White, "Parenthood in Social Transformation," in Jane B. Lancaster, Jeanne Altmann, Alice S. Rossi, and Lonnie R. Sherrod, eds., *Parenting across the Life Span: Biosocial Dimensions* (New York: Aldine de Gruyter, 1987), 274.

3. Vivian Zelizer, *Pricing the Priceless Child: The Changing Social Value of Children* (New York: Basic Books, 1985).

4. Steven Schlossman, "The Culture of Poverty in Ante-bellum Social Thought," *Science and Society* 38 (1974), 150–66; Christine Stansell, *City of Women: Sex and Class in New York, 1789–1860* (New York: Knopf, 1986), 193–216. In the same vein, see Bruce Bellingham, "The 'Unspeakable Blessing': Street Children, Reform Rhetoric and Misery in Early Industrial Capitalism," *Politics and Society* 12 (1983), 303–30.

5. Linda Pollock, *Forgotten Children: Parent-Child Relations from 1500 to 1900* (Cambridge, Eng.: Cambridge University Press, 1983), 10. Stone, *Family, Sex, and Marriage*, 193, illustrates his argument that parents failed to emphasize the individuality of their children between 1450 and 1630, saying that most upper-class parents as well as many lower down fostered out their infants and were in

general unmoved by the death of infants. For the transition period, when the middling sorts were engaged with their offspring, Stone describes the top aristocracy as "negligent" because they still gave out their children to nurses and teachers. For more on this subject, see Michael Mitterauer and Reinhard Sieder, *The European Family: Patriarchy to Partnership from the Middle Ages to the Present* (Chicago: University of Chicago Press, 1982), 110. Roger Thompson, *Women in Stuart England and America* (London: Routledge & Kegan Paul, 1974), 155, says boarding out children in others' households was "hardly calculated to encourage intimacy between parents and adolescent children." De Mause, ed., *History of Childhood*, 33, concurs, saying, "Abandonment motives were behind the custom of fosterage. . . . The parents gave every kind of rationalization for giving their children away. . . . Sometimes they admitted it was simply because they were not wanted." The more orthodox psycho-historians see "ambivalence," not outright disinterest, in traditional parenting: the wish to retain and at the same time reject offspring. John Walzer, "A Period of Ambivalence: Eighteenth-Century American Childhood," in de Mause, ed., *History of Childhood*, feels that this concept is illustrated by the alleged paradox that American mothers and fathers were genuinely interested in their children but still sent them away to school or to live with relatives.

6. Patricia Draper and Henry Harpending, "Parent Investment and the Child's Environment," in Lancaster, Altmann, Rossi, and Sherrod, eds., *Parenting across the Life Span*, 226.

7. Michael Anderson, *Approaches to the History of the Western Family, 1500–1914* (London: Macmillan, 1980), 59, complains that the "sentiments" school of social historians often fails to distinguish behavior toward infants from that toward older children. This is so for abandoning behaviors, the meaning of which may be highly variable depending on the child's age. In a discussion mostly devoted to infant foundlings, Shorter, *Making of the Modern Family*, 173–74, mentions divorcing mothers, who did not want child custody (showing the "clearly visible . . . tip of this iceberg of traditional indifference") and cites reports on women "kicking out their children, who would 'run about in bands of three and four, at the mercy of public charity'." In this essay I am discussing only abandoning behavior toward children. There is little information on American infant abandonments. Paul A. Gilje, "Infant Abandonment in Early Nineteenth-Century New York City: Three Cases," *Signs: A Journal of Women in Culture and Society* 8 (1983), 580–90, cites mostly European studies or infanticide cases as background for the three instances he reports. Shorter, *Making of the Modern Family*, plate VI, gives a picture of a New York abandonment but no discussion, and the picture is not self-explanatory. Peter L. Tyor and Jamil S. Zainaldin, "Asylum and Society: An Approach to Institutional Change," *Journal of Social History* 13 (1979), 23–48, permit the inference that infant abandonment was actively solicited by pioneer adoption agents, who recruited through a network of upper-class adopters and employers of servants, but they do not directly address the issue of abandonment as a social phenomenon independent of adoption brokering. No one suggests that infant abandonments were a mass phenomenon in the United States as they were in France.

On this see George D. Sussman, "The End of the Wetnursing Business in France, 1874–1914," in Robert Wheaton and Tamara K. Hareven, eds., *Family and Sexuality in French History* (Philadelphia: University of Pennsylvania Press, 1980), 224–52; and Rachel Fuchs, *Abandoned Children: Foundlings and Child Welfare in Nineteenth-Century France* (Albany: State University of New York Press, 1985).

8. Despite its contemporary sound, American legal historians trace this doctrine of "psychological parenthood" to a spate of decisions that began in the early nineteenth century and were consolidated as precedent by the 1850s. In concrete disputes this value hurt men in comparison to morally unblemished women, for patriarchal ownership of children was subordinated to relational issues; but more especially continuity of care indexed relational quality such that recent caretakers—usually mothers and maternal in-laws—might defeat the claims of fathers wanting their children back as a right following a separation. And the new doctrine hurt working-class parents, who, like noncustodial middle-class fathers, were liable to condemnation as abandoners if they could not keep their households together. In the odd case in which proxy parents wanted their children, the parents might be denied all claims to them. On custody history see Michael Grossberg, *Governing the Hearth: Law and Family in Nineteenth-Century America* (Chapel Hill: University of North Carolina Press, 1985), 234–85; and Jamil S. Zainaldin, "The Emergence of a Modern American Family Law: Child Custody, Adoption and the Courts, 1796–1851," *Northwestern University Law Review* 79 (1979), 1038–89. The facts of the cases reviewed by Zainaldin, if not the principles on which the dispositions rested, suggest that the "child-centered" innovations often mitigated the consequences for grandchildren of bourgeois daughters' marital misalliances or the downward mobility of their husbands, who were liable to be seen as unfit fathers in consequence of their status impairments. The early "best interests" doctrine in custody disputes then regulated property transmission to children or their status inheritance. Grossberg, *Governing the Hearth*, 263–68, stresses that courts did not employ the "best interests" standard in dealing with lower-class children's interests in custody disputes arising from involuntary apprenticeships.

9. Margaret Mead and Rhoda Metraux, "Adoption: Adopting Parents, Adopted Children: A Real Family?" in *Aspects of the Present* (New York: William Morrow, 1980), 304.

10. The incomparability of ancient and modern adoption is stressed by Jack Goody, *Production and Reproduction: Comparative Studies of the Domestic Domain* (Cambridge, Eng.: Cambridge University Press, 1976), 66–85, who says that ancient Eurasian adoption was an heirship strategy to assure lineal continuity, property succession, and care in old age. In *The Development of the Family and Marriage in Europe* (Cambridge, Eng.: Cambridge University Press, 1983), Goody argues that the range of compensatory Eurasian heirship strategies, including adoption, was interdicted by medieval canon law and that there was no legal adoption in the West until American state legislatures started passing adoption statutes in 1851. Jamil S. Zainaldin, "The Origins of Modern Legal Adoption: Child Exchange in Boston, 1851–93" (Ph.D. dissertation, University of Chi-

cago, 1976), argues that legal adoption was new only in that it guaranteed proxy-parental rights against natal claims. In the absence of natal claims, name changes and testamentary bequests to adoptive children were not interfered with in nineteenth-century England. Going back farther, Barbara Hanawalt, *The Ties That Bound: Peasant Families in Medieval England* (Oxford: Oxford University Press, 1986), 252, says that there was no incentive to adopt children because they circulated between households anyway and peasant surnames were unstable and symbolically unimportant, but legal "adoptions" of adults by old people were common, enabling the adoptees to inherit tenancies on condition that they provide for the "parent" in old age. Early state statutes, and the individual adoption acts that preceded them, are the topic of Stephen Presser, "The Historical Background on American Law of Adoption," *Journal of Family Law* 11 (1972), 443–516. Presser thinks legal adoption was a standardization of acts the legislatures were routinely granting to individual petitioners and something of a response to placing-out schemes like that of the Children's Aid Society: with so many children getting substitute homes, something had to be done to legitimate the phenomenon. Although the placing-out schemes and adoption legislation were expressions of domesticity values, I doubt that they were as directly related as Presser suggests, for few of these foster placements were long term and fewer of these were legally legitimated. My argument is that the placements were twisted to predomestic, instrumental purposes by both the working-class natal families and the agrarian foster families. Zainaldin, "Emergence of a Modern American Family Law," sees an extension of the "psychological parenthood" principle spurred by changes in custody law: customary rights invested in the biological facts of bearing and begetting gave over to new judicially allocated privileges reflecting parental conduct and relationships that judges valued above kinship. Once biology ceased to be the criterion of legal kinship, the law was ready to "receive" modern adoption.

11. Esther Goody, *Parenthood and Social Reproduction: Fostering and Occupational Roles in West Africa* (Cambridge, Eng.: Cambridge University Press, 1982), 279.

12. David Rothman, "Social Control: The Uses and Abuses of the Concept in the History of Incarceration," *Rice University Studies* 76 (1981), 21–42; Walter I. Trattner, "Introduction," in Trattner, ed., *Social Welfare or Social Control? Some Historical Reflections on Regulating the Poor* (Knoxville: University of Tennessee Press, 1983), 3.

13. David Thomson, "Welfare and the Historians," in Lloyd Bonfield, Richard M. Smith, and Keith Wrightson, eds., *The World We Have Gained: Histories of Population and Social Structure* (Oxford: Basil Blackwell, 1986), 355–78.

14. Grossberg, *Governing the Hearth*, 266.

15. Ann Vanderpol, "Dependent Children, Child Custody and the Mother's Pensions: The Transformation of State-Family Relations in the Early Twentieth Century," *Social Problems* 29 (1982), 221–35.

16. Thomas Bender, *Toward an Urban Vision: Ideas and Institutions in Nineteenth-Century America* (Lexington: University Press of Kentucky, 1975), 131–57.

17. Paul Boyer, *Urban Masses and Moral Order in America* (Cambridge, Mass.: Harvard University Press, 1978), 94.

18. Kristine E. Nelson, "The Best Asylum: Charles Loring Brace and Foster Family Care" (Ph.D. dissertation, University of California, Berkeley, 1980), 174–210. Even if it did not affect many of the children's birth-status identities, the effectiveness of Brace's familistic ideology on his society's work is evident in contrast to the large-scale British placing-out schemes that developed later in the century and lacked this transformative, democratic ethos. See Joy Parr, *Labouring Children: British Immigrant Apprentices to Canada, 1869 to 1924* (Montreal: McGill-Queen's University Press, 1980), reporting findings from late nineteenth- and early twentieth-century case records of the Barnardo Homes and several smaller efforts to place English children with Canadian farm families.

19. Martin Wolins and Irving Piliavin, *Institution or Foster Family: A Century of Debate* (New York: Child Welfare League of America, 1964).

20. Steven Schlossman, *Love and the American Delinquent: The Theory and Practice of "Progressive" Juvenile Justice* (Chicago: University of Chicago Press, 1977).

21. Charles Loring Brace, *The Dangerous Classes of New York and Twenty Years' Work among Them* (New York: Wynkoop and Hallenback, 1872).

22. James Bennett, *Oral History and Delinquency* (Chicago: University of Chicago Press, 1981), 93–99; Stansell, *City of Women*, 210–14.

23. Carl F. Kaestle, *The Evolution of an Urban School System: New York City, 1750–1850* (Cambridge, Mass.: Harvard University Press, 1973), 96.

24. Michael B. Katz, *The People of Hamilton, Canada West: Family and Class in a Mid-Nineteenth-Century City* (Cambridge, Mass.: Harvard University Press, 1975), 212, 307; Michael B. Katz and Ian E. Davey, "Youth and Early Industrialization in a Canadian City," *American Journal of Sociology* 84 (1978 Suppl.), s81–s119.

25. Alison Prentice, "Education and the Metaphor of the Family: The Upper Canadian Experience," *History of Education Quarterly* 12 (1972), 281–303.

26. A case history might cite several motives. For example, a mother might say she gave up her son because the father beat him, while simultaneously stating that she wanted him to learn a trade or avoid criminal associates. I have not tried to select the best or most important motive when more than one was cited. Each of the five regularly cited motives is a separate dichotomous variable. I have altered clients' names in the narratives that follow for reasons of confidentiality.

27. Goody, *Parenthood and Social Reproduction*, 23.

28. Louise A. Tilly and Joan W. Scott, *Women, Work and Family* (New York: Holt, Rinehart and Winston, 1978); Richard Wall, "Work, Welfare and the Family: An Illustration of the Adaptive Family Economy," in Lloyd Bonfield, Richard M. Smith, and Keith Wrightson, eds., *The World We Have Gained: Histories of Population and Social Structure* (Oxford: Basil Blackwell, 1986), 261–94.

29. Katz and Davey, "Youth and Early Industrialization," s88.

30. Tilly and Scott, *Women, Work and Family*, 52.

31. Zelizer, *Pricing the Priceless Child*, 21.

32. Mead and Metraux, "Adoption," admit they make their condemnation of the care of placed-out children "about whose fate we know relatively little even today." Apparently anticipating this problem, Goody, *Production and Reproduc-*

tion, 115, pleads that in "examining . . . domestic relationships we need to look at a wider category of roles (e.g., . . . orphans, foster parents and foster children), for people have been too long imprisoned by the idea of the terms for kin as a bounded genealogical set." Lutz Berkner, "Recent Research on the History of the Family in Western Europe," *Journal of Marriage and the Family* 35 (1973), 395–406, seems to agree, asking of augmented households: "Who were these people and what were they doing in the household?" Barbara Laslett, "Family Membership, Past and Present," *Social Problems* 25 (1978), 476–90, similarly laments that the "qualitative character" of "the extent to which non-relatives were integrated into the family's life and affairs" cannot be known from the census data used to identify augmented households. Demographic information that is uninformative on relationships and transactions remains the canonical data source of family history.

33. Goody, *Production and Reproduction*, 66–85; Goody, *Development of the Family and Marriage in Europe*, 40–44, 191; Goody, *Parenthood and Social Reproduction*, 250–81.

34. Rose Laub Coser, "Review of Goody," *Contemporary Sociology* 13 (1984), 189–90.

35. I have found no instances of this function in the records of the Children's Aid Society, either in the midcentury population on which this report is based or in two other samples extending to 1894 and 1923.

36. Donald Denoon, "Understanding Settler Societies," *Historical Studies* 18 (1979), 511–27.

37. Mary Ryan, "The Explosion of Family History," in *Reviews in American History* 10 (1982), 187.

38. Peter Laslett, "Parental Deprivation in the Past: A Note on Orphans and Step-Parenthood in English History," in *Family Life and Illicit Love in Earlier Generations: Essays in Historical Sociology* (Cambridge, Eng.: Cambridge University Press, 1977), 160–73.

39. Peter Uhlenberg, "Death in the Family," in Michael Gordon, ed., *The American Family in Social-Historical Perspective*, 3d ed. (New York: St. Martin's Press, 1983), 169–77. Tilly and Scott, *Women, Work and Family*, 23, observe that in eighteenth-century Europe most orphanage inmates actually had parents alive. In one Aix-en-Provence orphanage only one-third of the inmates were full orphans. Sometimes parents retrieved one child, depositing another in his or her place, rather like juggling savings and checking accounts. They say, "Families used the orphanage as a temporary measure, enrolling a child and then withdrawing him or her as economic circumstances allowed." It would help if we knew whether a substantial proportion of orphanage inmates in America were surrendered after infancy because of such "push side" family problems. There are no statistics on orphanage residency or other receptacles of such children in the 1850s. Rachel B. Marks, "Institutions for Dependent and Delinquent Children: Histories, Nineteenth-Century Statistics and Recurrent Goals," in Donnell M. Paffenfort, Dee Morgan Kilpatrick, and Robert W. Roberts, eds., *Child Caring: Social Policy and the Institution* (Chicago: Aldine, 1973), citing the first statistics of the U.S. Bureau of Education (1884), say that

of the 25,170 children in American orphanages in 1884 for whom parentage was given (there were another 11,000 whose institutions did not report parentage), only a third were full orphans. Over half had one parent and 10 percent had two parents.

40. Linda Gordon, "Incest and Resistance: Patterns of Father-Daughter Incest, 1880–1930," *Social Problems* 33 (1986), 253–67, discusses the sexual consequences that could follow from this routine assumption by older daughters of the wifely role.

41. Vanderpol, "Dependent Children"; Muriel W. Pumphrey and Ralph E. Pumphrey, "The Widow's Pension Movement, 1900–1930: Preventive Child Saving or Social Control?" in Trattner, ed., *Social Welfare or Social Control?*, 51–66. But see Frances Fox Piven and Richard I. Cloward, "Humanitarianism in History: A Response to Critics," ibid., 114–48, who deny that an effective net was strung until the 1960s. All parties to the debate could be mistaken; none can answer what would seem to be the first question: did the incidence and duration of filial deprivations actually decline relative to the population at risk of disruption? A policy consensus to support natal family integrity when possible may not be taken as evidence that disruptions were therefore proportionately reduced.

42. Barbara Laslett, "Social Change and the Family: Los Angeles, California, 1850–1870," *American Sociological Review* 42 (1977), 268–91, reports that 27 percent of the households headed by whites in rural Los Angeles County were augmented; Crandall A. Shifflet, "The Household Composition of Rural Black Families: Louisa County, Virginia, 1880," *Journal of Interdisciplinary History* 6 (1975), 235–60, puts the figure at 25 percent of whites in Louisa County, Virginia, in 1880. Using the 1855 state census, which gives all persons' relation to their household head, Michael B. Katz, Michael J. Doucet, and Michael J. Stern, *The Social Organization of Early Industrial Capitalism: Themes in the North American Experience* (Cambridge, Mass.: Harvard University Press, 1982), 305, reports that about 25 percent of farm households in Erie County, New York, were augmented by kin (including but not restricted to children) and an additional 6 percent and 11 percent were augmented by nonrelatives in what they define as the middle and late family cycle stages respectively. If about 35 percent of households were augmented at any particular time (an unstated proportion by fostered children), then over time a very large proportion would have been so augmented. James Q. Graham, "Family and Fertility in Rural Ohio: Wood County, Ohio, in 1860," *Journal of Family History* 8 (1983), 269, uses the 1860 federal census to estimate that 17 percent of families in this Old Northwest area were augmented by nonrelatives, an unstated proportion of whom were youngsters. An additional 13 percent were augmented by relatives, but many of these could also be augmented by nonrelatives as Graham gave relatives analytic priority in constructing his types. For estimating fosterage the best data come from David Gagan, *Hopeful Travellers: Families, Land, and Social Change in Mid-Victorian Peel County, Canada West* (Toronto: University of Toronto Press, 1981), 64, who reports that in Peel County, Ontario, in 1851 28 percent of households were augmented by "servants, employees, other chil-

dren," a group he distinguishes from relatives, boarders, and visitors and from a second conjugal family. Clearly, the figures presented are imperfect measures of the prevalence of child fosterage. Because the concern of family historians studying household composition has been with variation in household composition, we do not know the proportions of households that were augmented at a given enumeration by fostered children, related or unrelated.

43. Zainaldin, "Emergence of a Modern American Family Law," 224–48.

44. David E. Schob, *Hired Hands and Plow Boys: Farm Labor in the Mid-West, 1815–60* (Urbana: University of Illinois Press, 1975), 190.

45. Stanley Lebergott, *Manpower in Economic Growth: The American Record since 1800* (New York: McGraw-Hill, 1964), 49. Richard A. Easterlin, "Population Change and Farm Settlement in the Northern United States," *Journal of Economic History* 36 (1976), 60, reports that "over ninety percent of farm laborers were males under age 30," while Schob, *Hired Hands and Plow Boys*, 268, found most to be aged sixteen to twenty.

46. Easterlin, "Population Change and Farm Settlement in the Northern United States," 45–47; Easterlin, "Population Issues in American Economic History: A Survey and Critique," in Robert E. Galman, ed., *Research in Economic History, Suppl. 1: Recent Developments in Business and Economic History* (Greenwich, Conn.: JAI Press, 1977); Yasukichi Yasuba, *Birth Rates of the White Population of the United States, 1800–1860: An Economic Study* (Baltimore: Johns Hopkins University Press, 1961); Colin Forster and G. S. L. Tucker, *Economic Opportunity and White American Fertility Ratios, 1800–1860* (New Haven: Yale University Press, 1972); D. R. Leet, "Human Fertility and Agricultural Opportunity in Ohio Counties from Frontier to Maturity, 1810–1860," in David C. Klingaman and Richard K. Vedder, eds., *Essays in Nineteenth Century History: The Old Northwest* (Athens: Ohio University Press, 1975), 138–58; R. M. McInnis, "Child Bearing and Initials in Original Land Availability: Some Evidence from Individual Household Data," in Ronald D. Lee, ed., *Population Patterns in the Past* (New York: Academic Press, 1979), 201–27.

47. There is some evidence that early asylums played a similar family support role, possibly to the chagrin of their managers. Barbara Brenzel, *Daughters of the State: A Social Portrait of the First Reform School for Girls in North America, 1856–1905* (Cambridge, Mass.: MIT Press, 1983), 80, writes that "the girls at Lancaster do not appear to have been brought in at the initiative of the impersonal and bureaucratic state. In fact, a conservative estimate indicates that at least half of the 1856 girls were brought to Lancaster as a result of action taken by relatives." Michael Katz, *In the Shadow of the Poorhouse: A Social History of Welfare in America* (New York: Basic Books, 1986), 105, makes a similar point about the uses of orphanages.

48. Jacques Donzelot, *The Policing of Families* (New York: Pantheon, 1979), 70–82. This aspect of the uses of charity is elaborated further in Bruce Bellingham, "Institution and Family: An Alternative View of Nineteenth-Century Child Saving," *Social Problems* 33 (1986), s33–s57; see also Julie V. Brown, "Peasant Survival Strategies in Late Imperial Russia: The Social Uses of the Mental Hospital," *Social Problems* 34 (1987), 311–29.

49. Zainaldin, "Origins of Modern Legal Adoption," 220.
50. Nicholas Abercrombie, Stephen Hill, and Bryan Turner, *Sovereign Individuals of Capitalism* (London: Allen & Unwin, 1986), 148–52, 180.
51. Thomson, "Welfare and the Historians," 373, does concede that from the late 1860s there was a "lurch towards the family pole of the continuum of welfare responsibilities" and diminution of public support for social reproduction.

Ellen Ross

6. Hungry Children: Housewives and London Charity, 1870–1918

WHEN CHARITABLE VISITORS called at the homes of the London poor in the generations before 1918, it was almost always a woman who came to the door. Despite the determination of many private and state agencies to make husbands act like the men of the house, it was the wife (or widow or eldest daughter) who spoke to the visitor, attended the hearing, or visited the caseworker's office.[1]

The overwhelming evidence of housewives' inventiveness and determination in pursuit of their central project of sustaining their households cannot be reconciled with an image of charity recipients as passive objects of reformers' zeal and demands an exploration of the material uses to which wives put eleemosynary goods and services as a complement to political and administrative readings of late nineteenth- and early twentieth-century charity.[2] Looking at housewives' use of charity obliges us to register an image blurrier and more contradictory than the idea of the "popularity" of welfare measures can convey[3] and challenges as well the more theoretically sophisticated vocabulary of the social control model.[4] Charity and welfare,[5] as they were experienced by the London poor in the two generations before World War I, were not quite so bad as they look to some of the contributors to *Social Control in Nineteenth Century Britain*, or to their own contemporary critics from the ranks of socialism or the labor movement. But they were by no means as good as they looked in their own annual reports. They did supply, in London at least, a surprisingly large proportion of the resources on which poor people drew, and this despite all the waste occasioned by their seasonal balls and palatial headquarters. To create "deserving" objects of charity out of their rough and varied clientele, philanthropists readily used persuasion, even coercion, of which working-class wives were the main targets. The wives, in turn, however, often reshaped the philanthropists' gift into something they could really use.[6] The first section of this essay assesses London charity's contribution to household survival for the poor. Next, to illuminate the material and social meanings of charitable gifts, I look closely at children's school dinners, a large-scale charitable enterprise that carried out a quintessentially maternal responsibility.

London wages were not large or regular enough, in general, to insulate households from the occasional, if not chronic, need for charity. Real wages in the metropolis, as elsewhere in Britain, had risen since the middle of the nineteenth century. Wages went up in the 1880s and 1890s, and London workers were generally paid more than those elsewhere in the country. Even many well-paid trades had slack seasons, however, as in most kinds of work on the docks, in gasworks, and in the clothing and building trades. There were also general slumps (1884–87, 1892–95, 1901–5, 1908–9), which threw thousands out of work for longer periods. The higher wages were eaten up in many London districts by the area's terribly high housing costs, which, in 1891, drove nearly a fifth of London households to occupy homes of only one room compared with a figure of less than 5 percent nationally.[7]

The sexual division of labor in London working-class households was, in this period, powerful and relatively inflexible, delegating to wives almost sole responsibility for daily household maintenance. In London's (and, in general, Britain's) characteristic "internal wage" system, most husbands handed their wives the largest part of their weekly earnings, retaining pocket money for their own use. They generally expected the woman to handle virtually all household expenses out of this "wage." This money "belonged" to the wife, and the husband took no further interest in it. The transfer of cash was simultaneously a delegation of work and authority, leaving to wives such major decisions as when and where to move the household or when to remove teenagers from school and put them to work and such minor ones as whether to call in a district nurse or to seek school dinners for the children. This domestic arrangement, which sometimes burdened wives beyond endurance, also endowed them with domestic power and, if we judge from the autobiographies written by their children, special psychic significance.[8]

Although domestic relationships between women and men probably changed only a little in the generations I am describing here (fairly similar patterns were found by researchers in London and other towns in the middle of the twentieth century), there was a shuffling of resources between government bodies and poor households in the period between 1870 and the conclusion of World War I which certainly had a bearing on the meaning of charity.

The structure of public (poor law) relief was changing in the period under discussion. From its establishment in 1871, the Local Government Board (LGB) campaigned to eliminate outdoor relief (that is, relief in cash or kind in clients' own homes rather than in the workhouse), and to replace it with private charity, a goal with which local poor law guardians were urged to cooperate. Thousands of women, who as widows or the elderly had been the primary recipients of outdoor relief, lost access to public funds; by 1891 the number getting outrelief had been cut by two-thirds. Workhouses in London were subsidized from 1867 through the Metropolitan Common Poor Fund, but outrelief, financed through local rates (taxes), was much more at the discretion of the unions, whose policies on providing it varied. West Ham, Poplar, and, in the 1900s, Lambeth were among the most generous. Poor law medical care was upgraded from the 1870s if not earlier, and after 1885 both in- and outpatient medical services could be used without disfranchisement. Poor law homes for children improved, and after the mid-1890s outdoor relief for the poor began to increase, with elderly workhouse residents getting such "privileges" as visitors and ordinary street clothing. Yet the provision of outrelief for London women supporting children was still limited and compared very unfavorably with that of the rest of the country.[9]

The welfare measures of the Lloyd George–Churchill era supplied millions of households with new sources of cash or services: the old age pension for which nearly half a million were qualified at its introduction in 1909; national health insurance (which went into effect in 1913); the maternity benefit, which was attached to it; and unemployment insurance, covering 2 million mostly skilled male workers in 1914, about a quarter of the work force, a few years after its implementation. But except for the old age pension, the aid these programs offered was most effective for regularly employed or skilled workers. Casual workers and most women workers, widows, and older people under seventy—all those living daily under the economy of expediency—experienced little change.[10]

Large families, which students of poverty such as B. S. Rowntree and A. L. Bowley were vividly aware caused poverty, were decreasing in the years considered here. In London as a whole the legitimate fertility rate (based on the married female population aged between fifteen and forty-five) declined by about a quarter between 1870–72 and 1910, and the illegitimate birth rate declined 45 percent. But in poor boroughs like Poplar and Southwark, declines in fertility were very slow in the nineteenth-century decades; in Poplar, for example, the decline between 1880–81 and 1900–1901 was only 6 percent. The decline accelerated in the 1900s, but families remained large. In Bethnal Green, for example, in 1881 there had been 313 births per thousand married women aged fifteen to forty-five, which meant that nearly a third of the women in this group were giving birth every year. By 1934 the rate in Bethnal Green had declined to less than a third of that, but it was still as high as 226 per thousand in 1909–11.[11] Families of one, two, or three children that predominated by the 1930s were rare in the population who used London charities before World War I. For them the declines meant families of five or six children rather than eight or ten. Feeding these children remained a major undertaking, and charity was one of the resources mothers used to do it.

London Charity and Household Survival

Charity was big business in late Victorian and Edwardian Britain. In the 1870s eleemosynary contributions were greater by far than the whole national expenditure on poor relief. In 1885 donations to charities in London alone (some of this money was spent in other towns) were worth more than the entire national budgets of a number of nation-states, Portugal, Sweden, and Denmark among them. Though there were changes over time in the ways philanthropists spent their money, neither David Lloyd George's extension of the income tax nor the general expansion of state services had diminished the British enthusiasm for philanthropy by 1914. London was the hub of English charity (raising the question of the applicability of this study of charity in the metropolis to other towns at the same period). By the turn of the century there were nearly a thousand private charitable agencies based there, and in private or public services of various kinds—medical care for mothers and babies, clinics, and school meals among them—several London boroughs were among the leaders in Britain.[12]

London charities in the late nineteenth and early twentieth centuries made available to various categories of poor people a wide assortment of goods and services, which changed over the period studied here. Breakfasts and noontime dinners for children were offered in larger and larger numbers and eventually accommodated a large minority of the board (state-run) school population of the metropolis. As the great London teaching hospitals expanded, they provided ever more free hospital visits and absorbed an increasing proportion of the money spent on charity; medical charities received about half of the nation's charitable donations in the years before 1914.[13] In 1887, about a fifth of the Greater London population used a hospital in- or outpatient service at one of the region's ninety-one hospitals; in 1901, a quarter used the services of ninety-two hospitals, and more than three hundred thousand more people took advantage of charitable dispensaries.[14] Organizations new and old made charitable contributions: police court "poor boxes" supplied the needy at the magistrate's discretion; vestry or borough sanitary officers offered free disinfectants and whitewash; church- or settlement-sponsored "mothers' meetings" ran clothing, boot, blanket, or coal "clubs," through which members saved for these necessities a penny at a time for goods purchased wholesale. Several district nursing services operated in inner-London neighborhoods, not counting the midwives and nurses employed by the large maternity charities attached to major hospitals. For children there were Sunday school teas and "treats," similar Band-of-Hope events, evening and after-school clubs, and, by the later decades of the nineteenth century, summer holidays, only partly covered by fees paid by parents and which by 1899 supplied nearly thirty-four thousand London schoolchildren with two weeks at farm or seaside, a number that had increased to forty thousand in 1908.[15]

The variety and profusion of charitable activity in London at the turn of the twentieth century is well exemplified in Jeffrey Cox's catalog of those sponsored by churches or chapels in the borough of Lambeth alone. The list included

> *at least* 57 mothers' meetings, 36 temperance societies for children, 36 literary or debating societies for young men, 27 Bible classes, 27 girls' or young women's clubs, 25 cricket, tennis, or other sports clubs, 25 savings banks or penny banks, 24 Christian Endeavour societies, 21 boot, coal, blanket, or clothing clubs, 19 adult temperance societies, 17 branches of the Boys' Brigade or Church Lads' Brigade, 13 vocational or adult classes, 13 men's clubs, 10 gymnasiums (usually devoted to recreational classes of some sort), and 10 maternity societies. There were 16 nurses and two part-time doctors as well as a part-time dentist in addition to those sponsored by the provident dispensaries which were closely linked to the churches. Furthermore there were two "servants' registries," two lodgings registries, two "industrial societies" which employed women at needlework, one burial guild, one convalescent home, one hostel for the dying, one invalid kitchen, cripples' classes, a children's playtime, a day nursery, a "prostitutes' institute," several libraries, and dozens of Sunday Schools in addition to the extensive work of extra-parochial and transdenominational organizations.

About half of the Nonconformist chapels and all of the Anglican parishes in the borough also provided relief to the poor in cash or kind.[16]

Access to this and other charity was related not only to religion and church affiliation but to such chance factors as borough of residence (three-quarters of London hospital beds were within a mile and a half of Charing Cross, for example)[17] or the school the children attended (some of which had teachers or school managers particularly active in charity for the pupils).

Despite its source outside working-class communities and the alien principles governing its distribution, charity has to be viewed as a neighborhood resource. Given the huge variety and small scale of most charities, probably the single most important element determining access to them was information. For London wives, it was primarily neighbors who supplied this information; both knowledge of charities and beliefs about their moral acceptability were embedded in women's street culture. Margaret Nevinson and Beatrice Potter, both rent collectors in the 1880s in different apartment blocks run by the East London Dwellings Improvement Company, found that their tenants were very prone to exchanging information (that is, gossiping) about the rent collectors' "favoritism"—their willingness to let some tenants' rent fall into arrears.[18] Poor law guardians complained in the late 1880s that outdoor relief granted to one woman generated a chorus of neighbors demanding equal treatment, and school officials had the same problems with half-time certificates, which allowed children to hold jobs while attending school part-time. Recruitment to Ranyard mothers' meetings was by word-of-mouth as members brought in their neighbors, and the Ranyard nurses noted that landladies or neighbors often referred them to patients.[19] Westminster women pleased with the services of a preschool medical center there in the 1910s brought neighbors and friends with them when they returned for their second visits.[20]

From the housewife's vantage point, it was not the distinction between state welfare and private charity that was important but the contrast between official philanthropy and help supplied by kin and neighbors. "The charity of the poor to the poor," much of which took the form of daily exchanges between female neighbors, was immensely fascinating to middle-class spectators. The secrecy that surrounded bourgeois monetary affairs may have added piquancy to their discovery of the open channels along which the poor freely passed information, goods, cash, and services.[21] Neighborhood help was efficient. It appeared in response to specific needs reported in daily gossip, assessed at a glance, or requested directly: no dinner on the table; husband out of work; a black hat needed for a funeral. A Tower Bridge magistrate of long experience estimated just

before World War I that a deserted wife could "drag along" with neighborhood aid for perhaps a fortnight, quite an achievement considering the
neighbors' own lack of any surplus.[22] Many observers indeed came to view
working-class neighborhood exchange as a significant element in household survival. South London vicar Arthur Jephson, describing the response
of his parishioners after a major flood of the Thames in the early 1900s,
wrote of the "unstinted and abounding charity of the poor to the poor. . . .
So long as one person has anything to share, they are willing to share it."
Helen Bosanquet said less sentimentally that this "self-charity" was tanta-
mount to a "tax" levied by the poorest on those of their neighbors who
were slightly better off. Indeed, working-class charity stood "between . . .
civilisation and revolution," according to more than one outside observer.[23]

Yet the precise extent of this form of charity eluded even the most eager
and sympathetic students of working-class household budgets. Margaret
Loane, a district nurse with years of experience in London as well as in
several other parts of England, was contemptuous of the charities' claim to
be "'thoroughly investigating' cases at the rate of about twenty an hour."
Nurses, she said, often worked with families for weeks or months before
they were able to piece together the invisible sources of a household's
comfort, sources ranging from extra wages to garden produce to neighbors' contributions. London investigators of the budgetary effects of wartime inflation in 1915 and 1916 were sure that neighborhood sharing provided the key to the survival of households whose cash incomes were utterly
inadequate, especially those of old people. But working-class "donors"
were unwilling to disclose the nature of their giving: "Them's the things
one don't speak about," the economists heard repeatedly.[24]

Middle-class visitors to the slums often observed, too, that working-class
neighborhood charity did not "demoralize" its receivers. By this they
meant, no doubt, both that it implied no moral inferiority on the part of the
receiver and that it was built on the relative transparency of poor neighbors
to each other. The latter was, of course, not entirely true; women did think
it important to keep up appearances before neighbors. One has only to
think of the Walworth wife, who, early in this century, rattled her dishes in
her kitchen for the neighbors' benefit on the Sundays when she had no hot
dinner for her family.[25]

Like other face-to-face encounters between rich and poor, those involving charity called for special, carefully orchestrated performances on the
part of the working-class recipients. Maud Pember Reeves was painfully

aware of the effect her ladylike (though socialist) presence had on the Lambeth women who participated in a study carried out in the 1910s by the Fabian Women's Group:

> At the beginning of each case the woman seemed to steel herself to sit patiently and bear it while the expected questions or teaching of something should follow. She generally appeared to be conscious that the strange lady would probably like to sit in a draught, and, if complimented on her knowledge of the value of fresh air and open windows, she might repeat in a weary manner commonplaces on the subject which had obviously been picked up from nurse, doctor, or sanitary inspector.[26]

Working people knew that middle-class probing demanded circumspection. A new mother who lamented the birth of a ninth baby too loudly in the doctor's presence might find, if it should die, that the coroner would send someone to investigate. Children who complained that they were hungry might unwittingly set off a visit from the "Cruelty man" from the National Society for the Prevention of Cruelty to Children, so many poor parents instructed their children to watch their words.[27]

Accents and vocabulary were, of course, barriers when middle-class agents tried to help the poor. H. H. Snell, assigned to the Woolwich branch of the Charity Organization Society (COS) in the 1890s, was aware of the linguistic barriers. "What an inexperienced social worker might possibly have regarded as wilful falsehood was due in part, but not always, to a restricted vocabulary, and to ignorance of the exact value [to a middle-class ear, he should have said] of the words and phrases used." Even very sympathetic observers found working-class women's ubiquitous medical malapropisms highly amusing; they were actually emblems of the strangeness of the middle-class linguistic code to their ears: "nervous ability," "accepted knee," "cosmic asthma," and "pisis" were what Devons Road, Poplar, women heard when doctors spoke to them. At the school clinic she ran, Bow Common settlement worker Clara Grant pointed out, doctors had to learn to "talk simply" to the mothers. "It was interesting . . . to hear a school dentist talking to a mother ascend from 'deciduous' to 'temporary' and thence to 'milk' teeth."[28]

Relationships involving reciprocity and some degree of friendship and trust, however, could certainly grow across the barrier of class. The charity workers had needs, too, which the poor could sometimes satisfy. Settlement workers needed children and young people in their clubs; rent collectors wanted information; clergymen needed bodies in any form, for their offerings were not very attractive to the London poor. In one case, in South London, a mutually satisfying relationship grew up between a young parson and a struggling housewife. Mrs. Robinson, a nonchurchgoer who moved to cramped quarters in the parish of St. Marks, Walworth, as her husband's trade as a hansom cab driver declined, was "visited" one day a little after the turn of the century by the young Reverend Austin Lennox Watt. On his first visit the Reverend Watt chatted with the woman for half an hour and left her a half sovereign saying he believed he could trust her to buy food with it. In subsequent weeks Mrs. Robinson got more coins from the clergyman. He also offered her places for two of her sons in the church choir, for which the boys were paid 5s. quarterly; the son's account suggests that the boys' attending Sunday school regularly was a part of the deal. Mrs. Robinson gradually became a pillar of the parish, joining the mothers' meeting and delivering the parish magazine.[29] Beatrice Potter, as a rent collector for the Katherine Buildings in the mid-1880s, tried to establish similar relationships with some of her tenants. In one case she offered a man a post at Toynbee Hall on condition that he stop drinking. For a time, too, Potter seemed to have some sort of partnership with the wife of a police constable, who, as a policeman's wife, could provide her with information about her fellow tenants, which, Potter wrote, "has proven valuable in some cases." The woman, in turn, borrowed money from the rent collector, as well as from other tenants.[30]

Personal charity such as Mrs. Robinson accepted was controversial among working-class women, especially when it was associated with religion. "Hypocrisy" was one term that had precisely the same meaning for rich and poor: taking the goods while faking either religion or gratitude. A Finsbury doctor active in the COS spoke with feeling in 1904 of the "hypocrisy of these people and the awful way in which they lie about things" and admitted that "in a large number of our cases we are absolutely and deliberately deceived."[31] A middle-class Ranyard superintendent reporting on a well-attended mothers' meeting in the Mint district in 1870 was comfortable neither with the "apathy" nor with the "hypocrisy" of some of the members. Poor women, too, found hypocrisy easy to spot. Women who attended the Ranyard mothers' meetings in the Whitecross Street area in 1870 were persecuted and ridiculed by their neighbors, who sang parodies of their hymns, locked them out of their houses, and called them hypocrites. A Biblewoman going door to door in Stepney in 1883 was told sharply that "they were all honest people in that house, not hypocrites, and did not want any of our rubbish."[32] The epithet signaled that a woman had violated neighborhood norms governing the use of charity, which, though varied and shifting, were forcefully asserted.

Philanthropy was obviously not a substitute for wages as the basis of family survival. Also, neighborhood-based help, the pawnshop, and the landlord's indulgence on rent arrears were, in general, more important sources of income than formal charity. But at certain moments in a household's life cycle the formal charities were crucial and wives worked actively to procure and maintain their offerings.

Charity is nearly invisible in the household budget studies that proliferated from the 1880s. In a study conducted by the Paddington and Marylebone District Nursing Association in 1887 of 923 local families in which a main earner was ill, 829 had survived on the earnings of other family members, only a few on charitable donations. (Of course, all of the families were getting free nursing care and sickroom equipment from the district nurses.) Of the 8,008 unemployed London men uncovered in a different 1887 survey, only 1,132 received parish, club, or charitable relief, while a much larger number, 2,288, were surviving on the earnings of other family members. The rest, apparently, were living "upon savings, a supposition which, if not absolutely impossible, seems in the highest degree improbable," in the words of statistician William Ogle, commenting on these figures from the Registrar General's Office. More realistically, in the West London budgets Arthur Sherwell collected in the 1890s, pawning over and over again made up the deficit between income and expenses at the end of the week.[33]

But household budgets surely underrate the value of charity to families. Some services, like children's meals, were often accepted as a right connected with school attendance and not noted as income. Others, like fuel or food from individual benefactors contacted by teachers, parish visitors, or settlement workers, may have been covered up to preserve respectability before the investigators. Certainly such sources were hidden as well as possible by applicants for poor law or COS aid. Investigators usually asked only about earnings in the form of wages, but charities (and neighbors, relatives, and friends) generally doled out goods in kind. Finally, many people would never have considered such things as the use of the poor law schools for "extra" children or hospital outpatient services as charity, though for our purposes they are.

To the extent that we can reconstruct family budgets for London households living on 31s. a week or less (the median for men in regular employment in 1893, a figure that did not change appreciably before the war) we would surely find public and private charity nearly universal as sources of household goods and cash.[34] Examples of household thrift recalled by the children of these generations suggest the range of charitable help which housewives used. A Tottenham woman remembers the pints of soup, milk, and bread tickets her mother was granted by a local Congregational church, as well as the regular loan of "maternity bags" of linens for new mothers and new Christmas outfits made by the church's needlework guild. Children's boots, an expensive item, were received with gratitude by parents, if not always by children, from parish sources or via the Londonwide Peek Fund for schoolchildren. One housewife sent her daughter weekly to pick up free disinfectant, probably from the office of a local medical officer of health. Another bought cheap, sturdy dresses made by a local order of nuns for her many daughters, which—unlike many charity garments—the daughter remembered with pleasure.[35]

When earning full wages, even modest ones, households had only a limited amount of contact with the charities; the working-class family cycle with its points of poverty and plenty drew some more than others into such contact. Widows, the elderly, and the handicapped were not only attractive as recipients of charity but also needed aid for longer periods than other households. Half of the children in poor law schools in England and Wales, for example, were those of widows. A study of children getting school meals in 1915 found 45 percent whose fathers were either dead or invalids.[36] Old people, especially old women, used charities to carry themselves along, keeping the workhouse at bay with a combination of expedients that included parish aid, visits by district nurses, care by neighbors and landladies, and earnings as laundresses and childminders. The old age pensions which, from 1909, provided 5s. a week for single people over age seventy, or half again as much for couples, merely injected one more source of income into those delicate systems without transforming them.[37]

All of the seven Lambeth households hit by long periods of unemployment whose budgets were recorded in *Round About a Pound a Week* (1913) had recourse to occasional contributions by public and private charitable agencies. One man had used a poor law infirmary for a month; a deserted wife got parish relief during an illness that prevented her from working; and the school-aged children of four of the households had had school dinners daily during the difficult weeks. All of the infants were receiving free milk as a part of the Fabian Women's Group project in which they were participating.[38] Another South London couple with three small children, the man an unemployed plumber, the wife too ill to carry on charring or homework, exhibited a different pattern. Economics Club members who "collected" their household budget noted their heavy use of charity during their very difficult months, which contrasts with the Lambeth households' far sparser reliance on charity. The Lambeth husbands and wives, however, were well established in their district, with kin, neighbors, and landladies close by and available to help, whereas the other South London couple "receives no visits and conceals its privations." The husband had spent a month at St. Thomas's Hospital, during which time the woman, after much cruel delay, received home relief. The woman's doctor had contacted a "charitable lady," who supplied them once with coal, and they used a free dispensary when they were ill. The sister of another doctor with whom they came into contact had also been helping them, as had the wife's former employer.[39]

A woman who was chronically short of money because her husband was a heavy drinker had a slightly different pattern of charity use. The COS was one of a great many expedients to which Violet Dawes, of Hornsey Street in North London, had recourse when she applied to that agency in 1908 to "place" her three children so that she could leave her violent husband and take a position as a servant. At that point she owed several weeks' rent, had a "great many pawn tickets," and had debts to a draper's club. Mrs. Dawes had applied to and been rejected by the guardians but had had help from the Salvation Army. Her husband's parents also "have helped till they are sick and tired." The COS denied her request because she was reported to have slept away from home several times.[40] When people were in trouble—illness, unemployment, or marriages as bad as Violet Dawes's, utterly routine disasters among working-class households—they were likely to call on charities for aid.

To dispel the suspicion of "charity mongering" attached to anyone seeking relief, many charities invested endless extra casework—though middle-class female time, the foundation on which "thorough investigation" of cases was built, was plentiful in the nineteenth century. Yet charity was (and still is) based on two fundamental dilemmas which made cheating on the part of the users and distrust on the givers' side inevitable. First, the rich would not often give the poor what they most wanted: cash to use as they pleased—to pay the rent, redeem the bedding from pawn, buy the "pieces" from the butcher for dinner, or even send for a pint of stout from the pub. Second, charities frequently gave to individuals, but most working-class individuals had powerful family obligations, and resources flowed in the direction of those obligations. Thus gifts from rich to poor were, as a matter of course, "deformed" (to use Stedman Jones's useful misreading of Marcel Mauss). Meant to bridge the chasm between the classes, charity was invariably distorted as it traveled from one side to the other.

Charity mongers are both stock literary figures[41] and the bête noire of the whole charity world. Working charities as a way of life, however, required time, considerable dramatic skill, information, and luck. Individuals who supported themselves this way were rare, and households rarer still, though charity mongers received considerable sensationalized attention in the press. In fact, they were small-scale operators indeed. City missionaries thought they spotted one in one of the little streets (colored "black" by Charles Booth) running out of Drury Lane, half demolished in a slum clearance project by the end of the nineteenth century. The husband, an old soldier and semi-invalid, made only a small contribution to the household. (One assumes that the writer's reference to the mother's "hard work" is facetious.)

> The mother works hard for her children and attends every mothers' meeting she can, as well as every mission hall if possible. This brings her soup three or four times a week and sometimes a loaf of bread, and so the poor woman keeps her little room, and the children with bread. At Christmas she may contrive to get two or three Christmas dinners from different places.[42]

The Hardings of the Old Nicol in the 1880s and 1890s were also genuine charity mongers, according to their son Arthur's detailed account. Arthur Harding's father, having lost or disqualified himself from a number of livelihoods, spent his last "working" years collecting surplus food from restaurants. The mother did not so much cheat local charities as display herself and her children to best advantage—a technique described with sympathy by the son when in his late eighties:

> My mother was a forager. God bless her, she foraged all her life, that's how she brought us up. She got a few bob off the people in the [Shaftesbury Society's Ragged School] Mission. She would tell the hard-luck story so as to get herself in. Well it was a true story. The whole thing was having your poverty well known to the people who had the giving of charity. They noticed that mother was a dead cripple, and that father was a loafer, and that she had children to bring up. . . . If you wasn't poor you had to look poor. . . . But you had to be clean and that was easy—soap and water didn't cost a lot of money.

Mrs. Harding sent her children to daily bread and milk breakfasts at the mission in exchange for which the children had to go to the mission's Sunday school. She also—and this was her only real racket—went to church rummage sales, about whose existence she was told by a male friend, stole rather large quantities of used clothing, and sold it to wardrobe dealers in nearby Petticoat Lane.[43] (That this practice was viewed as quasi-legitimate by poor women is suggested by a slightly later incident at a Bermondsey Settlement rummage sale in which none of the local woman would come forward to report the person who had stolen things from that sale.[44])

Charity seekers seem to have gravitated toward the churches. Clergymen canvassed by Charles Booth's investigators complained bitterly of people who expected that they would bring "tickets" whenever they called or who seemed to make a living out of cadging for relief. The 1887–92 diary of the Reverend James Woodruffe, curate of St. Matthews, Bethnal Green, reveals a man plagued by charity applicants who expected help as a matter of course and were abusive if turned down.[45]

Recipients of charity seldom used it in the ways they were intended to; the offerings were not necessarily used by the people to whom they had been given, nor in the form in which they were offered. Relief given to children in the shape of clothes or boots, indeed even school prizes like books or cricket bats, often went to the pawnshop for food money, for working-class schoolchildren did not have private possessions. School-teachers who brought secondhand clothes to distribute to their pupils noticed how few of them they ever saw the children wearing; the sturdy middle-class clothing donated was obviously too valuable to wear (and was often too dressy and fussy for comfort) and was placed in pawn or sold to secondhand shops.[46] Tickets for children's meals distributed at the schools were regularly sold by the children or their parents for the penny or half-penny they could bring in. And children given charity meals also pocketed bread and butter or bread and meat to be "relished by the parents" later on.[47] Grace Foakes and her sister, in early twentieth-century Wapping, regularly sat through hours of Sunday church services so they could attend the tea that followed and stock up on scones and rolls for their family's Monday meal. Mothers sent "excess" children to poor-law schools for periods of months, even years, and retrieved them when their circum-stances improved.[48] Elderly people might, after 1909, check into the work-house or infirmary while drawing and saving their old age pensions (tech-nically illegal) so as to donate it to a needier married son or daughter.[49]

"Duplication of services," a term that crops up in the charity world in the 1890s as a horror to be avoided at all costs by "Mutual Registration" among the charities, was obviously a way of life for the poor, as charitable donations from multiple sources mingled with other resources in the homes and on the dinner tables of the poor. A woman who asked a charity worker for coal tickets around the turn of the century, for example, had an unemployed husband and six children, for whom she had obviously rounded up a great many charitable goods. She was already receiving, the charity worker said with disapproval, bread and soup tickets from "a lady," coal tickets from "a gentleman," soup from mission halls, beef and cocoa from one of the children's schoolmistresses, and boots from another "gentleman," who had seen one of the children in a worn-out pair.[50] By taking advantage of so many different sources of largess the "coal tickets" wife indicated her lack of gratitude—none was generous enough to sustain her. She, not her benefactors, was in charge of whatever household she could keep together. She had obviously rejected a proper client relationship with the donors. The elementary survival needs of the poor were bound to destroy the "spiritual beauty" of the act of giving charity.

Schoolchildren's Meals

Schoolchildren's breakfasts and noon dinners are a deceptively mundane form of London charity. No one who has read Charles Morley's vivid account of hundreds of hungry children in the Borough sitting down to rapidly devoured hot meals supplied by the Referee Free Dinners Fund will dismiss the school feeding projects as bland exercises of upper-class benevolence.[51] Because they invoked the highly charged issue of feeding hungry children—a mother's job, after all—school meals were the object of hopes, fears, accusations, and fantasies for both the givers and the receivers. Classes and interests came into contact and opposition over the meals, and it was wives at the doorstep or in the committee room rather than husbands in the trade-union hall or street demonstration who negotiated these relationships. For the student of charity as a social issue, the London meals provide a striking case study in the gift relationship, its meaning for both parties, and its concrete results for children's bellies, mothers' budgets, and party politics. Throughout the period 1870–1918, the providers of the meals were volunteers (the kitchen staff and a few administrators were paid after 1907), whose impulses were on the whole generous, even loving, toward the poor, especially toward their children. Their soaring hopes for the feeding had sacramental overtones; volunteers spoke of the "spiritual beauty" of the feeding and of the meals as moments of "human communion."[52] But these ideals came into thudding contact with the routine ideological boundaries of Victorian charity with its suspicions of charity mongering, obsessive fears of "demoralizing" the poor, and nasty "means tests." The caregivers' colorful fantasies also clashed with the gray, instrumental hues of the mothers' (and occasionally fathers') approach to the meals; the parents simply wanted decent food for their offspring at some saving to themselves. To them, the meals represented no sacramental linking of the classes invoking reverence and gratitude but a household resource.

Feeding hungry children, seemingly the most compelling of benevolent gestures, has, of course, a long history among charities. In early nineteenth-century London, missions and ragged schools had provided meals for some of the poorest children,[53] and by about 1870 there were fifty-eight dining rooms for children there, open for various periods. But it was compulsory education, exposing hundreds of thousands of children, many ragged, barefoot, and hungry, daily to public view, that generated the charitable offering of children's meals on a massive scale years before the 1906 Education (Provision of Meals) Act regularized and funded these proceedings.

The meals themselves were supplied by volunteer organizations such as the Referee Fund (founded in the 1870s and organized through journalist George Sims's newspaper), the London Schools Dinner Association, the Jewish Penny Dinner Society, and the London Vegetarian Association. These organizations worked with subcommittees of school managers, groups of mostly middle-class volunteers who did charity work in association with the public schools in poor districts.[54] In the winter of 1904–5, at least thirty different associations were supplying funds or goods for these volunteers to use, as were countless private individuals contacted by the school managers. The feeding was carried out on a large scale, though the schools differed greatly in the number and quality of meals offered. During one week of cold weather and high unemployment in February 1895, about a tenth of the children on the London School Board rolls were being fed (52,000 out of 490,000 children) an average of two and one-third meals each week.[55] The London County Council (LCC) gave nearly 19,000 as the average number of children being fed in the board or council schools per week in the winter of 1900–1901, about 38,000 in 1908, and about 41,500 in 1912–13. Over the course of a given ordinary year, such as 1903, about a sixth of London's board school population was served meals for some period. In the year ending March 31, 1909, the LCC supplied over four and a half million meals; in the entire remainder of the country, only about 7 million meals were served.[56]

In the early 1900s, as efforts to regularize and expand the feeding proceeded, it was handled by health subcommittees of the managers—suggesting the way the language of public hygiene was supplanting that of charity in the meals operation. After the partial financing of meals out of local taxes was permitted nationally with the act of 1906, the subcommittees were renamed care committees and their duties were expanded beyond the feeding to include finding apprenticeships for school leavers, and getting parents to seek medical treatment for children whose health problems had been diagnosed in school medical inspections. By the 1890s, or even earlier, working-class London's school districts were obviously buzzing with charities. By 1914 there were eight thousand school care committee members, and more were being called for to carry on the massive amount of work they did.[57]

Meals for schoolchildren had long been a priority of the British Left. From at least the 1880s, trades councils in several large cities campaigned for publicly supported school meals offered as a right. Both Annie Besant and Stewart Headlam made the provision of meals a central plank in their platforms during their campaigns for the London School Board in 1888, and Besant herself served thousands of meals during the late 1880s, advertising for funds among the freethinking readers of the *National Reformer*. The Social Democratic Federation's (SDF) founding platform advocated free school dinners, and throughout the 1880s and 1890s its many London branches were active in serving children's meals. Marches, demonstrations, and even a deputation to Whitehall in 1893 demanded public feeding of schoolchildren. Prodded by Margaret McMillan, the Bradford Independent Labour party (ILP) came out for school feeding in 1903, and in the next year or two the Trades Union Congress (TUC), the London Trades Council, and the Labour Representation Committee were campaigning for free school meals. The bill to supply them to "necessitous school children" was introduced by a new Labour MP in the 1905 session of the new Liberal-dominated Parliament, and though chewed up with amendments, it became law at the end of 1906.[58]

The Left, however, shared its commitment to feeding children with many others across the political spectrum, ranging from the Ragged School Union, to the Women's Total Abstinence Union, to hundreds of churches and missions. When the TUC and the London Trades Council jointly organized a large London meeting in 1905 in support of school feeding, John Gorst, an Independent MP from Cambridge, chaired the meeting. Matilda Hyndman, a leading light in SDF meals, was doing exactly what her peers among Tory and Liberal women were doing.

Although all involved agreed on the rightness of feeding the children, political chasms divided their sense of the meaning of the meals. For the Left, school meals were a foot in the door of state-funded universal social services available as entitlements. Nonleftists active in school feeding, on the other hand, responded warmly to the obvious hunger of the children but worried endlessly about the implications of feeding them: were they not taking on a responsibility that properly belonged to parents—to fathers to find the cash and mothers to prepare the food?[59] The issues were clearest for the hundreds of COS members who participated in meals programs, usually as school managers or members of care committees. As an organization, the COS always opposed free feeding and maintained that position well past the point when the meals had begun to be paid out of rates. The COS believed that to feed working-class children was to "weaken parental responsibility and discourage effort." When Mary Brinton (later Mary Stocks) left school at seventeen in 1908 and took a volunteer position as the secretary of the Saffron Hill Elementary School Care Committee, she was distressed to find that "several of its members did not approve of care-committees at all, or indeed of any extension of state provision for impecunious persons."[60] It was this ambivalence about the legitimacy of the feeding programs that generated so many of the obstacles the committees placed between the dinners and the children, obstacles we label, collectively, their stigma.

The meals most committees were prepared to offer were rather poor; they compared favorably only with bread and butter. (Yet bread with butter, jam, or dripping was sometimes the only food children got during the day, and schoolteachers could identify the "bread children," as they called them, among their pupils.) An experienced London soup kitchen volunteer testified in 1886 that the charity food was normally not generously supplied: "You cannot, as a rule, supply as much as they could eat, but [only] as much as doctors state to be necessary." In 1885, a meat pudding and vegetable meal, which cost the children a penny, contained about one and a half ounces of meat, which, as John Hurt's calculations demonstrate, supplied only 360 of the 2,000 calories which are today the recommended daily intake for children over age five. Christchurch School, Shadwell, in the

1880s, served five hundred children lentil soup, which cost only a pound in all to prepare. Astounded at the huge home-made sandwiches working-class London children could be found eating in schoolyards at the dinner hour in the 1890s, Gertrude Tuckwell wondered whether the official dinners were indeed too scanty.[61]

Although some of the committee members spoke of tablecloths and flowers, the meals were more commonly hurriedly dished out in a single bowl or mug, essential eating utensils were often scarce, and the food was often sparse and unattractive. The number of dinners rejected by thin, hungry children—always a worry and embarrassment for the meals committees—suggests more than the notoriously finicky appetites of the young. The smell of the food cooking could be nauseating. Mrs. Burgwin, the London schoolmistress who pioneered school dinners, spoke glowingly in 1895 of the fortitude of the teachers at a school where soup was prepared daily, emitting a smell so unpleasant that "it is wonderful how the teachers endure it."[62] Walworth children voted with their feet against a penny dinner program at the King and Queen Street Board School. "They called the macaroni lumps of fat, and said it made them sick, and they really were sick," the headmaster reported graphically in 1885. On macaroni days many of them took their pennies to a local coffee house where they could get a more appealing portion of pudding for the same price. The meals workers themselves were often distressed by the bad quality of the food or by its unappetizing and unedifying presentation. One care committee member who visited the Shoreditch dining center he was responsible for in June 1911 found the potatoes there "very bad." After many complaints about the food and its service, a committee in Islington tried unsuccessfully in 1909 to break its meals contract with the Alexandra Trust. Two years later, however, the children were still getting a dreary carbohydrate-heavy menu:

Monday and Thursday: rice pudding, two slices of bread and butter
Tuesday and Friday: stewed mince beef, vegetables and bread
Wednesday: hot bread and milk, fruit, jam roll[63]

For the mothers, of course, feeding children was not a voluntary activity but a desperate necessity. Settlement worker Anna Martin spoke for dozens of other observers in 1910 when she referred to the "skill and ingenuity with which [mothers] contrive to keep their families, on about half the weekly sum per head [1s. for a teenager] found necessary in the Poor Law schools for each child's food and clothing."[64] The health subcommittees and the care committees were thus sharing this burden of work and responsibility. And indeed, Anna Martin thought that some of the women who attended her "women's socials" at Beatrice House in Rotherhithe, a branch of the Bermondsey Settlement, were uneasy about the meals as a result: "Each of them knows perfectly well that the strength of her position in the home lies in the physical dependence of husband and children upon her, and she is suspicious of anything that would tend to undermine this."[65] Mothers' oppressive labor in the home and their domestic power were inextricably linked.

Just as they negotiated most of the contacts with the school bureaucracy in general, it was mothers who dealt with the meals committees "90 percent of the time."[66] Although the committee volunteers were obsessed with the possibility that feeding his children might destroy the working-class father's motivation to work, it was the mothers who paid the large price that getting charity usually exacted. By the early twentieth century, in many districts, mothers had to apply for meals in person or in writing and then to reapply at frequent intervals, as more, and more elaborate, casework was demanded by the school meals bureaucracy in the London County Council. In other districts, teachers or doctors selected "underfed" children, whose homes were then duly visited and inspected by subcommittee members.

Keeping the meals coming for one or more children could thus require considerable maternal vigilance, as demonstrated by the case of Mrs. U., a Lambeth wife, who was part of the Fabian Women's Group study described in *Round About a Pound a Week*. When her husband lost his job in the summer of 1910, she attempted to get school dinners for her three school-aged children, but despite her persistence she did not entirely succeed. Two children were granted meals "after weeks of application," but a third, at another school and thus under the jurisdiction of another committee, was rejected because the household did not appear poor enough. As Pember Reeves described Mrs. U.'s dilemma: "The mother's very virtues told against her. Her rooms were spotless, the decent furniture, the tidy clothes of better days inclined the school visitor to believe that food could be forthcoming did the mother choose."[67]

When every housekeeping penny counted, the meals were worth the trouble, many women obviously thought. Mrs. U. found the children's meals a considerable help as she tried to run her household on the small savings she had managed to collect while her husband, now unemployed, had been working, together with what he could bring in through odd jobs. In August 1910, she was spending under 2*d.* a day per person on food for her family of five children and two adults, a sum that was typical for the Rotherhithe women who lived near Beatrice House at about the same time. One of them got "fourteen hot dinners for 6 1/2*d.*," by combining onions, rice, potatoes, carrots and turnips in a stew.[68] School dinners, or breakfasts (which some committees offered in addition or instead), cost the suppliers between 3 farthings and 2 1/2*d.* each, according to the care committee minutes, and were, by 1910, often served four times a week. Certainly they made it possible for Mrs. U. to budget so little money for food and thus keep up the rent, insurance, and other expenses less flexible than food. As one of the Rotherhithe women commented: "If you spend a bit less on food there's a bit more for coals and boots; and if your big girl falls out of work you can feed her on what you save on the little ones." Mrs. Ball, a Walworth mother, testified, incredibly, in 1886 that she often had only 2*s.* 9*d.* for the week's food for her family of eight (and managed it).[69]

Given the precision and minuteness of these maternal calculations, "penny dinners" were decidedly impractical. One observer thought that even if only a halfpenny were charged for a school breakfast, mothers would not use them because they could feed their children more cheaply on "good bread and bad tea." Mrs. B., another Rotherhithe mother, explained that penny school dinners were far too expensive for her to use: "It's no good to us if they provide the children with dinners at the school for 1d. each. Four of mine are attending . . . school and I can do better for them at home. I make a stew of three-pennyworth of pot-herbs. If I've got it I throw in a handful of rice. This makes a good dinner for all of us, including myself."[70] Mrs. Ball and Mrs. Anderson, the latter from Kennington Park, had both sent some of their children to penny dinners, but their support for the meals was probably rather awkward for the COS-organized committee who heard their testimony because both admitted that their children's penny dinners allowed them to carry on paid work all day without worrying about their children. Many of the street sellers who lived hand-to-mouth existences in Walworth were completely unable to supply their children with pennies in the morning for any purpose; often the children went without breakfast while their parents were out at work trying to get the cash for a late breakfast, which they sometimes brought over to the school.[71]

For the givers, the meals meant, among other things, friendship and "communion" with the poor; for the mothers, the meals meant savings of pennies and halfpennies, hours and half-hours, and they raised the subject of bread and meat prices far more often than that of the fellowship of rich and poor.

The Charity Organization Society's technique of thorough investigation of home circumstances even when only small donations like boots or meals were at stake, and which was especially well entrenched in several East London districts, was one of many barriers between the child and the meals. In these procedures, as in those of hundreds of other charities, we can see the mundane and very concrete meanings of stigmatization, a process by which charity was offered with the right hand but taken back with the left. "The stigma of charity" says little about how working-class communities viewed resources that originated with public or private charities but a great deal about techniques with which they diminished and compromised the gift they were offering. An ILP pamphlet correctly pointed in 1909 to the prevailing "system of investigation on charity organisation lines" as expressly "calculated to deter all self-respecting parents from making an application on behalf of their children."[72] The meals workers, who were generally influenced by COS principles, thus offered the dinners in most unpalatable forms, both socially and gastronomically. Even with the more formal and publicly financed operation of the school dinner machinery in the 1900s, at least some of the basic structures of stigma were enforced by most of the committees: careful investigation of the receivers; unattractive food or surroundings for the meals; public identification of the children in their classrooms; and/or attempts to extract payment from parents.[73]

The committees' formal rejection of many applications, combined with their efforts to stigmatize others, kept the numbers at the dinners down, as they were designed to do. In a suburban South London board school in the 1900s the meals program "was conducted in so condescending a way that the snobbery of the other children was invoked, and the recipients of the charity were made to feel their lowliness," as Ethel Mannin, a schoolgirl from a socialist household, remembered with distaste.[74] A Shadwell woman refused to ask for school dinners on behalf of her children after her request for milk for a sick husband had been humiliatingly rejected by a nearby church. Obviously recalling that experience, the woman, as well as her daughter, thought the school meals were "degrading."

On the other hand, meals committees that deliberately dispensed with many stigmatizing practices found their programs popular. In the late 1890s the Saffron Hill Board School experimented with serving its population of hawkers' children dinners in the classrooms rather than, as most schools did, renting a nearby mission hall for the purpose. The mission hall smacked of charity, but the schoolroom associated the feeding with the universal service that public education represented, the school managers reasoned. According to the headmaster, the popularity of the school in the neighborhood increased after the new plan began, and parent-teacher relations improved as well.[75]

The minutes of the children's care committees show sporadic attempts to get parents to justify themselves, to harass them for payment, and to cut the children off from the meals (from 1909, the LCC permitted an appeal in these cases). But the minutes also demonstrate the limits of the committees' capacity to compel gratitude, cooperation, and a sense of reverence for the charity they were receiving—even from these unorganized and relatively unsophisticated clients. The Popham-road (Islington) School Care Committee, for instance, was a rather liberal-minded group, as these went. In 1908–9 they fed an average of well over two hundred children each month in the peak poverty months of February and March; they tried to supply meals that the children liked; and they thoughtfully provided slippers for children to wear in school while their wet boots dried during the day. Yet the Popham committee regularly and harassingly summoned parents to come to their meetings to explain why the meals should not be terminated. (In 1910 only half of them actually appeared at first call.) In Shoreditch, the committee attached to the Curtain-road School which fed 107 children on a November day in 1910, a high number for one school, granted meals for periods of two or four weeks only, which meant that mothers had to reapply for them repeatedly. Not surprisingly, however, here too only half, sometimes far less, turned up at the scheduled hearing times. (The fiction was retained for record-keeping purposes that it was the fathers with whom the committee were dealing, though this was rarely the case. Curtain-road summoned six fathers in November 1909, but two mothers were the only people to attend the hearing.) When in the winter of 1909–10, a Mrs. O'Brien failed to come to two hearings to which she was summoned by the committee, they decided to demand that she repay the cost of the meals. A divisional officer sent to investigate, however, found that Mrs. O'Brien was an office cleaner whose evening work kept her from attending the hearings and recommended that the committee give up its plan to extract compensation from her. Obviously feeling that she had made her point, the mother ignored a third summons as well.[76]

One East London care committee, which deliberately set out to stigmatize its users, was met with popular surprise, hostility, and rejection. The committee was so wedded to COS methods of case investigation and so wary of demoralizing workers that it deliberately offered its children break-fasts of "an unvaried diet of porridge and milk." As one member, the Reverend Henry Iselin, stated without embarrassment, "This food was distributed at such an hour [between 8:15 and 8:45 A.M., though school did not start until 9:15] and was of such a character as to constitute in itself a definite test of need. . . . This policy has restricted the number consider-ably." Many potential users would have nothing to do with the meals. "I can give them better at home than what you gives them," one woman hissed. "It ain't worth while to tell lies about a bit of porridge," said another.[77]

The experience of Henry Iselin's East London committee in those years suggests that even in the heart of COS country, the poor parents viewed school feeding as an entitlement. When the LCC began to levy a small rate to defray the feeding costs in 1909, Iselin found parents even less likely than before to feel any gratitude or "loss of prestige." One father, whose children had been assisted sporadically for a few years, simply sent a note to the care committee's secretary saying: "I am out of work, so will you do the need-ful?"[78] Committee members elsewhere in London reported the same atti-tudes among the recipients. On Campbell Street in Islington, "the vilest road in London," the care committee in 1909 had a great deal of trouble with the rough one-room dwellers who inhabited the furnished rooms on the street. "Sometimes the parents are most abusive, and seem to take it for granted that they are entitled to Free Meals." In another district, "the poor generally regard the whole affair as a kind of food lottery without an entrance subscription." The only way the committee there could convince people that meals were not available for the asking was to promote "the prevalent idea that every child sent is keeping another out." (Although this was not technically true, it spoke to the way poor people actually did collectively ration scarce resources and was an effective alternative to stig-matization as a way of keeping the numbers down.) A care committee worker reported a 1912 conversation between a committee member and a Fulham "Artizan." The man, though employed, applied for school meals because his workmates' children were getting them. When his request was rejected, the man responded: "You people don't do the work properly, what you're paid for."[79]

Though their own correspondence registers distress at being taken for granted by recipients and confidence in the value of stigmatizing them, the logic of the food charities' situation—they did want to feed poor children and were judged to some degree on their effectiveness in doing so— demanded that they adapt their offerings to pressures from the recipients. The committees' practices, which varied enormously with the members' politics and with the neediness and sophistication of the applicants, were the product of a delicate and usually unspoken series of arrangements between givers and receivers. Like the school officials, for example, the school-centered charities became resigned to the fact that, despite their anomalous civic status, it was the mothers who were the "heads" of families when children were the issue, and they would be the ones to conduct the family's public business. The committees also offered the meals at the times when London's poor were usually most hungry and wanted them most: in the winter and early spring months, when work was short or nonexistent in many male trades, and on Tuesdays through Fridays, when the wages brought home on Saturday began to dwindle. As far as the food itself was concerned, vegetarians, oatmeal devotees, and other food faddists who gravitated to the world of school meals were, mostly, eventually overruled by those more observant of the tastes of the children (though oatmeal exponents were most tenacious). Determined to "summon" parents fort- nightly to justify their continued participation in the program, some com- mittees, however reluctantly, accepted that a great many would never come, grumbled, but continued to feed the children.[80] Thus the mothers were, at least to some degree, getting the meals for their children on their own terms.

After the Education (Provision of Meals) Act went into effect in 1907, the number of London consumers both in LCC and voluntary schools began to climb. According to Sir Charles Elliott, who had served before 1907 as head of the Joint Committee on Underfed Children ("more soup than joint," quipped school headmistress Clara Grant), the average number of children fed per month rose dramatically. The 1909 annual average was double the figure for 1906. Elliott's explanation for the sudden increase was that the money granted by the act, which provided better food, paid kitchen staff, and some salaried officials for the program, inspired the local committee, still volunteers, to undertake more meals, for which there was no shortage of hungry children—a development Sir Charles found "insid- ious."[81] Although taking school meals, the 1906 act explicitly stated, did not carry any of the legal consequences of pauperization, the donors and most non-Labour legislators continued to find it impossible to offer the food as the routine entitlement that primary education itself had become and as the parents were also increasingly inclined to see the meals. Investigation methods prevailed in London; nationally, also, considerably less than a third of education authorities were actually offering rate-financed free school meals in the prewar years, though they had a right to do so.

On the eve of World War I, Sir George Newman, the chief medical officer for the Board of Education, eager to get Parliament to support a bill authorizing more local tax money for school feeding, offered an argument hitherto unheard among those supporting school dinners, and one of the few likely to succeed in Parliament: "Experience shows that food riots are inspired largely by the hunger of children; and if that problem can be met, a large operating factor in the causation of riots is removed." The bill became law with unusual speed, and a record number of children were fed during the school year 1914–15, a year of enormous unemployment and social dislocation. The next year, however, the number of meals supplied declined drastically, in London by about three-fourths.[82] Though war work and wives' allowances improved living standards for a large minority of London households, the children's meals would have been very helpful for wartime working wives. But their social price was too high, as indeed it continued to be until World War II. With the edge of desperation temporarily blunted by full employment or separation allowances, the London mothers withdrew their children, or saw them ejected wholesale, from the dining centers.

Conclusion

Despite their mundane function, the school dinners provide a pageant dramatizing the meanings of charity in the late Victorian and Edwardian (adult) class system. The Thatcher regime's inroads on the huge school meals system that had been in place since early in World War II suggest that these issues are far from dead today. With all the interested parties gathered, a century ago, at the tables, we hear the acid comments of the mothers confidently telling the ladies and gentlemen of the meals committees, "I can give them better at home." A chorus of more cultivated voices, in turn, outlined the spiritual, medical, and military benefits to which the children's dinners would likely lead. The children, too, spoke, though they are not part of the story I have told here, about their loathing for porridge and pea soup and their fondness for cocoa and buns. For some of them, I think, the meals were indeed a kind of sacrament, promising care and love outside their homes from those with apparently more to give than their own parents.[83]

My general purpose has been to urge a view of London charity as wives and mothers, who were among its main objects, found it. Making them actors in this drama of giving and receiving gifts provides a fresh way of evaluating the charities beyond the analysis of their own sense of their mission—though this is interesting and complex enough. By watching the charities in their daily work with their clients, we can begin to judge their effectiveness, both in helping people materially and in shaping lives in the philanthropists' image. Obviously, charities did, and wanted to do, both. Theories of charities in which social control is the only dimension are obviously unsatisfactory, given the concrete and actively pursued help charity provided wives in London's chronic hard times, help the women worked hard to get while negotiating the barriers of harassment and humiliation that so often surrounded it.

Notes

The research in London on which much of this paper is based was funded by the American Council of Learned Societies and Ramapo College of New Jersey's sabbatical leave program. At the writing stage, funding was provided by the Shelby Cullom Davis Center for Historical Studies, Princeton University, where I was a Fellow in spring 1986. The essay owes much to the encouragement and companionship of many members of the Princeton University History Department and to those who attended the Davis Center seminar at which the first draft was discussed.

ABBREVIATIONS

COS	Charity Organisation Society
GLRO	Greater London Record Office
LCC	London County Council
LGB	Local Government Board
PP	*Parliamentary Papers*
TR	*Toynbee Record*

1. That wives and mothers were their main clients was a part of the shoptalk of Victorian and Edwardian social workers, though the point was seldom made statistically. A 1908 random investigation of 1,218 London homes with "necessitous" children who were getting school dinners in 1908 put investigators in contact with the wives in the great majority of cases, to judge from the eighteen sample case papers appended to the report in which the investigators spoke

with thirteen women, two men, and three couples (LCC, *Report by Miss T. M. Morton and Mr. H. D. C. Pepler on the Home Circumstances of "Necessitous" Children*, 1908, Appendix A).

2. David Owen, *English Philanthropy, 1660–1960* (Cambridge, Mass.: Harvard University Press, 1964), pts. 3 and 4; Maurice Bruce, *The Coming of the Welfare State* (London: B. T. Batsford, 1961); A. F. Young and E. T. Ashton, *British Social Work in the Nineteenth Century* (Routledge & Kegan Paul, 1956); F. K. Prochaska, *Women and Philanthropy in Nineteenth-Century England* (Oxford: Clarendon Press, 1980); Gareth Stedman Jones, *Outcast London: A Study in the Relationship between Classes in Victorian Society* (Harmondsworth: Penguin Books, 1971); Brian Harrison, "Philanthropy and the Victorians," in *Peaceable Kingdom: Stability and Change in Modern Britain* (Oxford: Clarendon Press, 1982); Elizabeth Wilson, *Women and the Welfare State* (London: Tavistock, 1977).

   The "consumers' side" is stressed in Jane Lewis, *The Politics of Motherhood* (London: Croom Helm, 1980), and in her "The Working-Class Wife and Mother and State Intervention, 1870–1918," in Jane Lewis, ed., *Labour and Love: Women's Experience of Home and Family, 1850–1940* (Oxford: Basil Blackwell, 1986); also by Lynn Lees in "The Survival of the Unfit," this volume. David Rubinstein's excellent *School Attendance in London, 1870–1904: A Social History* (Hull: University of Hull Publications, 1969), also stresses the users of education, both parents and children. A convincing argument about the limits of charities and other agencies in shaping working-class culture is Gareth Stedman Jones, "Working-Class Culture and Working-Class Politics in London, 1870–1900: Notes on the Remaking of a Working Class," *Journal of Social History* 7 (Summer 1974), 460–508.

3. Henry Pelling discusses the unpopularity of much early welfare legislation in "The Working Class and the Origins of the Welfare State," in his *Popular Politics and Society in Late Victorian Britain* (New York: St. Martin's Press, 1968).

4. See A. P. Donajgrodzki, ed., *Social Control in Nineteenth Century Britain* (London: Croom Helm, 1977). Most of the essays in the volume are thoughtful and detailed, and indeed social control seldom appears as a simplistic explanation for this period or for the early nineteenth century in Britain. It is more often a strand intertwined with other arguments, as, for example, in Stedman Jones, *Outcast London*. Robert Storch's "The Policeman as Domestic Missionary: Urban Discipline and Popular Culture in Northern England, 1850–1880," *Journal of Social History* 9 (Summer 1976), 481–509, based on a social control model, is in fact an exemplary piece of social history.

5. The distinction between private philanthropic effort and state or municipal welfare measures is not very important for the purposes of this essay. In any case, this distinction cannot be made for Victorian and Edwardian Britain, where so much public work was carried out by private philanthropies. Volunteer "managers" were attached to board schools; ladies from the volunteer Workhouse Visiting Society helped care for inmates; private effort was heavily involved in the job placement of children leaving the workhouse schools in their early teens. Even massive public programs like national insurance in 1911

were undertaken in close conjunction with private providers, in this case the gigantic Friendly Societies. A private charity, the Soldiers' and Sailors' Families' Association, was designated to administer state-legislated pensions for soldiers' dependents during the initial months of World War I, using, to a large extent, private money provided by the Prince of Wales Fund. Charity volunteers were important parliamentary lobbyists and witnesses; and, of course, twentieth-century British politics is dotted with men and women whose political careers began with charity work. Harrison's "Philanthropy and the Victorians" has a useful discussion of the pattern by which charity led to social legislation (pp. 234–37). On the delicate negotiations between private agency and state activity in early welfare legislation, see Pat Thane, "Non-Contributory versus Insurance Pensions, 1878–1908," in Pat Thane, ed., *The Origins of British Social Policy* (London: Croom Helm, 1978); and Bentley B. Gilbert, *The Evolution of National Insurance in Great Britain: The Origins of the Welfare State* (London: Michael Joseph, 1977). On school dinners in particular, John Hurt, "Feeding the Hungry Schoolchild in the First Half of the Twentieth Century," in Derek J. Oddy and Derek S. Miller, eds., *Diet and Health in Modern Britain* (London: Croon Helm, 1985), is invaluable.

6. A model for this way of looking at philanthropy is Linda Gordon's *Heroes of their Own Lives: The Politics and History of Family Violence* (New York: Penguin Books, 1988).

7. Paul Thompson, *Socialists, Liberals and Labour: The Struggle for London, 1885–1914* (London: Routledge, 1967), 12; Rubinstein, *School Attendance in London*, 57. For good figures on London overcrowding by borough, see *PP*, 1904, vol. 32, Appendix, p. 51.

8. I discuss gender divisions and the working-class family economy more fully in "'Fierce Questions and Taunts': Married Life in Working-Class London, 1870–1914," *Feminist Studies* 8 (Fall 1982), 575–602. The most comprehensive studies of gender and family budgets are Laura Oren, "The Welfare of Women in Labouring Families: England, 1860–1950," *Feminist Studies* 1 (Winter–Spring 1973), 107–25; and Melanie Tebbutt, *Making Ends Meet: Pawnbroking and Working-Class Credit* (London: Methuen, 1983), esp. ch. 2. A lively and convincing rereading of the husband-wife exchange is Pat Ayers and Jan Lambertz, "Marriage Relations, Money and Domestic Violence in Working-Class Liverpool, 1919–39," in Lewis, ed., *Labour and Love*.

9. Pat Thane, *The Foundations of the Welfare State* (London: Longman, 1982), 32–38. The LGB reported in its 1914–15 Annual Report that in London about twenty thousand children were getting outdoor, twelve thousand indoor relief. In the rest of the country outdoor relief for children (and their mothers) was far more common than relief through workhouse schools (LGB, *44th Annual Report, Part I* [1914–15]).

10. Thane, *Foundations*, 81–96; Gilbert, *Evolution of National Insurance*, chs. 4–7.

11. *LCC Annual Report for 1910*, Vol. 3, *Public Health*, Report of the Medical Officer of Health of the County, p. 12; Ellen Ross, "Labour and Love: Rediscovering London's Working-Class Mothers, 1870–1918," in Lewis, ed., *Labour and Love*, Table 3.1, p. 76.

12. Owen, *English Philanthropy*, 469; Prochaska, *Women and Philanthropy*, 21; Brian Harrison, "Philanthropy and the Victorians," *Victorian Studies* 9 (June 1966), 354. J. M. Winter points out, though, how backward many other London boroughs remained into wartime (*The Great War and the British People* [London: Macmillan, 1985], 193–204).

13. Owen, *English Philanthropy*, 479, and, on charitable support for hospitals more generally, 483–89.

14. Lt. Col. Montefiore, "Uses and Abuses of Medical Charities," *Charity Organisation Review*, n.s., 14 (July 1903), 18. Another 12,137 used poor law infirmaries, or Metropolitan Asylums Board hospitals according to 1884 figures (R. Thorne Thorne, *The Progress of Preventive Medicine in the Victorian Era* [London: Shaw & Sons, 1888], 262).

15. Children's Country Holiday Fund, *Report for 1899*; "The Children's Country Holiday Fund," *TR*, December 1908, p. 45.

16. Jeffrey Cox, *The English Churches in a Secular Society, Lambeth, 1870–1930* (New York: Oxford University Press, 1982), 58–59. Also see Hugh McLeod's splendid *Class and Religion in the Late Victorian City* (London: Croom Helm, 1974).

17. F. C. Smith, *The People's Health, 1830–1910* (New York: Holmes and Meier, 1979), 251.

18. Margaret Nevinson, *Life's Fitful Fever* (London: A. & C. Black, 1926), 96; "Record of the Inhabitants [of Katherine Buildings] during the years 1885–1900, Begun by Mrs. Sidney Webb (Beatrice Potter); Continued by Miss E. Pycroft," Coll. Misc. 43 R., London School of Economics Manuscript Collection.

19. "Testimony of Robert B. Williams, Second Report of Royal Commission Appointed to Inquire into the Working of the Elementary Education Acts, England and Wales," *PP*, 1887, vol. 29, Qq 40, 943; *Missing Link*, December 2, 1878; *Bible Women and Nurses*, May 1906, p. 94. State entitlements, such as the old age pension or the maternity benefit, had the enormous advantage of being applicable to many millions of recipients, and their existence could be far better publicized than the offerings of private charities. One of the real services the Charity Organization Society could provide for its carefully selected client households was referral to other charities nearly inaccessible to them otherwise: convalescent homes; schools for the blind; organizations providing free spectacles, trusses, orthopedic shoes, or whatever.

20. City of Westminster Health Society, *Annual Report for 1913*, p. 20; Westminster City Archive, London.

21. I have written about the female, neighborhood-based form of this "charity" in "Survival Networks: Women's Neighbourhood Sharing in London before World War One," *History Workshop* 15 (Spring 1983), 4–27. Journalist George Sims rhetorically connected his own experience of middle-class isolation with the openness of life among the poor in *Horrible London*: "The poor are kinder to each other than the rich; they are bound by stronger ties of sympathy; their hearts respond more readily to generous impulses. They have greater opportunities of helping each other, and there are no barriers of pride between them. They live their lives before each others' eyes, and their joys and sorrows are the

common property of the entire community. The rich man wraps his mantle about him and breaks his heart, locked in the darkest room of his house; the poor man bares his breast to the light of day, and has not a neighbour but knows the nature of this woe and has seen every link in the chain of circumstances that brought his trouble about" (*How the Poor Live* and *Horrible London*, combined ed. [London: Chatto & Windus, 1889], 144).

22. "Testimony of Mr. J. Rose, Royal Commission on Divorce and Matrimonial Causes," *PP*, 1912–13, vol. 18, Q 1931.

23. Arthur Jephson, *My Work in London* (London: Isaac Pitman & Sons, 1910), 21; Helen Dendy [Bosanquet], "The Industrial Residuum," *Economic Journal* 3 (1893), 612–13; Prochaska, *Women and Philanthropy*, viii.

24. Margaret Loane, *The Queen's Poor* (London: Edward Arnold, 1909), 159; V. de Vesselitsky, *Expenditure and Waste* (London: G. Bell & Sons, 1917), 16–17. See also E. J. Russell's study of Manchester budgets in *TR*, November 1903, 23.

25. E. Robinson, "I Remember," p. 9, typescript written between 1960 and 1970, Brunel University Library, Uxbridge. Brunel University's library has collected this and dozens of other unpublished autobiographies (see *The Autobiography of the Working Class: An Annotated, Critical Bibliography*, comp. John Burnett, David Vincent, and David Mayall, 2 vols. [Brighton: Harvester Press, 1984, 1986]). My thanks to Professor Burnett for his hospitality and archival help with the Brunel collection.

26. Maud Pember Reeves, *Round About a Pound a Week* (1913, rpt. London: Virago Books, 1979), 16. See also Peter Bailey, " 'Will the Real Bill Banks Please Stand Up?': Towards a Role Analysis of Mid-Victorian Working-Class Respectability," *Journal of Social History* 7 (1979), 336–53.

27. See Mrs. Benjamin's portrayal of a Hoxton childhood of grim poverty in the years before and during World War I in the Hackney People's Autobiography's office at Centerprise in London, ms. transcript, p. 2: "We were threatened with the RSPCC [sic], and when they came round we were told to say yes if they asked us if we'd had our breakfast. That was drummed into us. These people came round and they said 'have you had any dinner today?' and one of us said yes. Then they said, 'well what did you have?' and I had to think of something, though I couldn't think of a dinner, really."

Psychiatrist James Crichton-Browne, investigating the effects of "over-pressure" on board school children in the early 1880s, was struck that girls whose teachers were convinced they were hungry remained silent when asked about their morning meal, while "the boys blurted out their privations at once." See *Report of Dr. Crichton-Browne to the Education Department upon the Alleged Over Pressure of Work in Public Elementary Schools* (London: Hansard, 1884), 8–9.

28. Snell, sanitary reformer, founder of the Woolwich Labour party, MP, and member of the LCC, was, as a COS worker, sympathetic to his clients though he knew that they regularly deceived him. He parted company with the COS when his dissident Woolwich branch was brought into line with COS orthodoxy. His autobiography is *Men, Movements and Myself* (London: J. M. Dent, 1936). The account of his casework is on p. 72. Clara Grant, *Farthing Bundles* (London: Fern St. Settlement, [1930]), 83.

29. Robinson, "I Remember," 10–11. For a similar relationship, this one between a young widow with a large family and a group of Anglo-Catholic curates, see *Father Joe: The Autobiography of Joseph Williamson of Poplar and Stepney* (London: Hodder & Stoughton, 1963).

30. This habit, and her "evil tongue," eventually made the constable's wife many enemies, including the young rent collector (Potter, "Record of the Inhabitants," Room 110, Thomas Robbins).

31. "Testimony of Dr. Lewis A. Hawkes, Report of the Interdepartmental Committee on Physical Deterioration," *PP*, 1904, vol. 32, Qq 13050, 13195.

32. *Missing Link*, March 1870, p. 86; May 1870, pp. 130, 133–34; and June 1883, p. 167.

33. Paddington and Marylebone District Nursing Association, *Report for 1887*, 20; "Men Living in Certain Selected Districts of London in March 1887," *PP*, 1887, 71:viii; Arthur Sherwell, *Life in West London* (London: Methuen, 1897), 111–14. See also Metropolitan and National Nursing Association, *Second Report for the Year Ending January 1, 1878*, Appendix D, p. 40, Guildhall Library, London.

34. A. L. Bowley, *Wage and Income in the U.K. since 1860* (Cambridge., Eng.: Cambridge University Press, 1937), xiii, 9–10, 35–36, 43. On recourse to poor law institutions, see Lees, "Survival of the Unfit."

35. Tottenham History Workshop, *How Things Were: Growing-Up in Tottenham, 1890–1920* (n.p., n.d.), 21; Lillian Hine, "A Poplar Childhood," *East London Record* 3 (1980), 40; Grace Foakes, *Between High Walls: A London Childhood* (Oxford: Pergamon Press, 1972), 22.

36. Sidney Webb, *The Decline of the Birthrate* (London: Fabian Society, 1907), 18; *School Child* 6 (January 1916), 1.

37. W. A. Bailward, "Some Recent Developments of Poor Relief," *Economic Journal* 22 (1912), 548.

38. Pember Reeves, *Round About a Pound a Week*, ch. 14.

39. E. Collet and M. Robertson, *Family Budgets: Being the Income and Expenses of 28 British Households, 1891–1894* (London: P. S. King & Son, 1896), 19–20.

40. Case records of the COS (now Family Welfare Association), Area 4, St. Pancras North, held by the GLRO, A/FWA/TH/B2/ no. 22478. I am grateful to the Family Welfare Association for giving me permission to examine these records and have used a pseudonym as promised. This woman remained an active case through 1946.

41. As in Edwin Pugh's sketch, "The Charity Mongers," a conversation between two old women complaining about the poor quality of the multiple offerings available through the churches at Christmas (*The Cockney at Home* [London: Chapman & Hall, 1914]).

42. Charles Booth, *Life and Labour of the People in London*, 1st ser.: *Poverty*, vol. 2 (1902–4; rpt. New York: Augustus M. Kelley, 1969), 54.

43. Raphael Samuel, *East End Underworld: Chapters in the Life of Arthur Harding* (London: Routledge, 1981), 24–25.

44. Anna Martin, *The Married Working Woman: A Study* (London: National Union of Women's Suffrage Societies, 1911), 10–11. For other examples of charity cheaters see *Missing Link*, December 1878, p. 377; and Olive Christian Malvery, *Baby Toilers* (London: Hutchinson, 1907), 93.

45. Charles Booth, *Life and Labour of the People in London*, 3d ser.: *Religious Influences*, vol. 7 (1902–4; rpt. New York: AMS Press, 1970), 408–9; the trials of the Reverend Woodruffe are described in McLeod, *Class and Religion*, 112–13.

46. Elizabeth Rignall, "All So Long Ago," typescript, ch. 10, Brunel University Library; School Board for London, *Report of the Special Sub-Committee of the General Purposes Committee on Underfed Children, 1898–99*, Appendix I: Evidence of Witnesses, testimony of Mr. J. Morant, February 27, 1899, p. 17, GLRO, SBL/1469.

47. M. E. Bulkley, *The Feeding of School Children* (London: G. Bell and Sons, 1914), 16; Richard Free, *On the Wall: Joan and I in the East End of London* (London: John Lane, 1907), 142.

48. Foakes, *My Part of the River* and *Between High Walls*, combined ed. (London: Futura, 1976), 128. The practice of parking children temporarily in poor law homes can be noted in the records of any of the children's schools run by London poor law unions and is discussed widely by officials at their annual Poor Law Conference.

49. Bailward, "Some Recent Developments," 552; S.J.F., "The New Pensioner in the East End," *TR*, February 1911, p. 72.

50. Agencies interested in mutual registration passed lists of their clients and what they were receiving to a central office, usually staffed by COS workers, in each district. The COS, as its case records indicate, always checked each applicant this way as well as through interviews with landladies, neighbors, clergymen, and employers ("Coal Tickets," *Charity Organisation Review*, n.s., 14 [October 1903], 206; S. G. Tallents, "Inquiry into the State Feeding of School Children," *TR*, March 1909, p. 97).

51. "A Little Dinner in the Borough," in *Studies in Board Schools* (London: Smith, Elder & Co., 1897). Also see "One Dinner a Week," reprinted from *All the Year Round*, in *One Dinner a Week and Travels in the East* (High Wycombe: Peter Marcan Publications, 1987).

52. Sir Charles Elliott, "State Feeding of School Children in London," *Nineteenth Century and After* 65 (May 1909), 869; Margaret McMillan and A. Cobden Sanderson, *London's Children: How to Feed Them and How Not to Feed Them* (London: Independent Labour Party, [1909]), 2. Another rhapsodic account, this one of a successful administrator of oatmeal (sensibly accompanied by milk and sugar to suit each child's taste), is A. R. Price, "Meals for School Children," *TR*, January 1893, p. 43.

53. For all that one might want to know about school meals in this early period, and later, see Bulkley, *Feeding of School Children*.

54. See Peter Gordon, *The Victorian School Manager: A Study in the Management of Education, 1800–1902* (London: Woburn Press, 1974).

55. LCC, *Report of the Joint Committee on Underfed Children for 1904–05* (London: King, 1905), 15–21; School Board for London, *Report of the Special Sub-Committee, 1898–99*, iii; see the discussion in J. S. Hurt, *Elementary Schooling and the Working Classes 1860–1918* (London: Routledge, 1979), 121.

56. The meals tended to be discontinued in March or April and resumed about November because unemployment rates were higher during the winter in

London. See Bulkley, *Feeding of School Children*, 143; Rubinstein, *School Attendance in London*, 82; Board of Education, "Report on the Working of the Education (Provision of Meals) Act 1906 up to 31 March 1909," *PP*, 1910, 23:24.

57. James Kerr, ed., *The Care of the School Child* (London: National League for Physical Education and Improvement, 1916), 4; Clara Grant, *From "Me" to "We": Forty Years on Bow Common* (London: Fern St. Settlement, [1940]), 71; and Grant, *Farthing Bundles*, 80.

58. Pat Thane, "The Working Class and State 'Welfare' in Britain, 1880–1914," *Historical Journal* 27 (1984), 877–900; Brian Simon, *Education and the Labour Movement, 1870–1920* (London: Lawrence & Wishart, 1974), 134–37, 278–79, 282–83. Annie Besant's columns on school meals and the proceedings of the School Board are in the *National Reformer*, December 1888 through July 1890.

59. The gradual appearance of a more scientific discourse on the meals—the need for "proteid matter" in the diet, caloric standards of physical efficiency, and so on—provided something of a solution to these political dilemmas. A good discussion of medical and nutritionist views is found in Deborah Dwork, *War Is Good for Babies and Other Young Children: A History of the Infant and Child Welfare Movement in England, 1898–1918* (London: Tavistock, 1987), 171–74.

60. *The Feeding of School Children* (London: COS, 1907); see also Helen Bosanquet, *Social Work in London, 1869 to 1912* (London: John Murray, 1914), ch. 12 (a restrained attack on free, as opposed to penny, meals for children, written just before World War I). The statement quoted was made by a COS representative at a 1900 conference, reprinted in *TR*, January 1901, p. 43; Mary Stocks, *My Commonplace Book* (London: Peter Davies, 1970), 60. Other opinions from care committee members hostile to the programs are cited in Dwork, *War Is Good for Babies*, 173. For the results when two COS activists became managers at a school in the Seven Dials district, see Margaret Frere (who was one of them), "The Charitable Work of a Local Manager in a Board School," *Charity Organisation Review*, n.s., 75 (March 1903), 133. Frere, a charismatic and activist manager at the Tower Road "Special Difficulty" Board School, Seven Dials, later worked on the LCC Education Department's side of the schools charity bureaucracy.

61. *Charity and Food: Report of the Special Committee of the Charity Organisation Society upon Soup Kitchens, Children's Breakfasts and Dinners, and Cheap Food Supply* (London: Spottiswoode & Co., 1887), 55, 11; Hurt, *Elementary Schooling*, 118–25; Gertrude Tuckwell, *The State and Its Children* (London: Methuen, 1894), 74.

62. "Report on the Working of the Education (Provision of Meals) Act," *PP*, 1910, 23:17–20; Hurt, *Elementary Schooling*, 119.

63. *Charity and Food*, 33; Minutes of Children's Care Committees, Curtain-road School, EC2, June 20, 1911, GLRO, EO/WEL/2/15; Popham-road School, N1, October 1909, May 1911, EO/WEL/2/6.

64. Mothers' "auto-starvation" is discussed in Oren, "Welfare of Women," and Ross, "'Fierce Questions and Taunts.'" See also Derek J. Oddy, "A Nutritional Analysis of Historical Evidence: The Working-Class Diet, 1880–1913," in Derek Oddy and Derek Miller, eds., *The Making of the Modern British Diet* (London:

Croom Helm, 1976), 219–20. The quotation is from Anna Martin, "The Women's Socials at Beatrice House," *Bermondsey Settlement, Eighteenth Annual Report*, 1910, p. 14.

65. Martin, *Married Working Woman*, 14. Several London women told Margery Spring Rice in the 1930s that they refused school meals because they thought it "unnatural for the children to eat away from home" (Margery Spring Rice, *Working-Class Wives: Their Health and Conditions* [1939, rpt. London: Virago, 1981], 14n).

66. Evidence for this point is found in Rubinstein, *School Attendance in London*, 102; an anonymous letter to the editor by a care committee member, *School Child* 3 (March 1913), 14; and Jane Lewis, "Parents, Children, School Fees and the London School Board, 1870–1890," *History of Education* 11 (1982), 298; the quotation is in Henry Iselin, "The Story of a Children's Care Committee," *Economic Review* 22 (January 1912), 44; see also *School Attendance Gazette*, January 1901, pp. 164–65.

67. Pember Reeves, *Round About a Pound a Week*, 206.

68. Ibid., 204; Martin, *Married Working Woman*, 13–17; recipes for fourteen hot dinners are given, ibid., 15.

69. Martin, *Married Working Woman*, 31; the quotation is by a woman whose scruples kept her from applying for the meals despite the advantages she was so conscious of: *Charity and Food*, 38.

70. Price, "Meals for School Children," 43; Martin, *Married Working Woman*, 14.

71. *Charity and Food*, 36–41, 33, 35, 52; Crichton-Browne, *Report*, 9. Even in the lengthy hearings the COS organized in 1886, apparently to advocate penny dinners, much of the testimony did not support the idea. By the 1890s, penny dinner schemes had mostly been abandoned; only about 10 percent of the meals that had been offered at a penny, it was estimated, had actually been paid for (*Charity and Food*, passim; Bosanquet, *Social Work in London*, 24–46; Bulkley, *Feeding of School Children*, 18).

72. The authors, like most socialists, supported free breakfasts open to all (McMillan and Sanderson, *London's Children*, 1).

73. Those who spoke of the shame of applying to the poor law for relief similarly often mentioned the humiliating experience of the relieving officer's home visit, when he assessed the household belongings and refused help unless the piano, mantel ornaments, extra clothes, and other items were sold or pawned away. Autobiographical accounts suggest that knowledge of this routine was widespread in working-class neighborhoods.

74. Ethel Mannin, *Confessions and Impressions* (Garden City, N.Y.: Doubleday Doran, 1930), 34.

75. Family Life and Work Experience Archive, collected by Paul Thompson and Thea Vigne, housed at the University of Essex, transcript no. 331, p. 42; see also ibid., no. 368, p. 58. My thanks to Paul Thompson for permission to work with this archive. Testimony of Mr. J. Morant, School Board for London, *Report of the Special Subcommittee, 1898–99*, 16.

76. Popham Road, EO/WEL/2/6, GLRO; Curtain-road, March 8, 1910, EO/WEL/2/15.

77. Iselin, "Story of a Children's Care Committee," 43. Samuel Barnett, who had by this time broken decisively with the COS, also favored very early hours for breakfasts as a test of need. See *PP*, 1906, vol. 8, Q 2408.

78. Iselin, "Story of a Children's Care Committee," 59–60.

79. The Secretary of an Islington Care Committee, "Difficulties in a Very Poor District," *School Child* 2 (February 1912), 7; Tallents, "Inquiry into the State Feeding of School Children," 97; "Saturday Afternoon in Fulham," *School Child* 2 (April 1912), 13. See also J. T. Mustard, "Investigation and Coordination," *School Child* 2 (June 1912), 6.

80. This discussion is based on a study of the minutes of several of the London children's care committees, most of which begin in 1909: Curtain-road school, EC2; Popham-road school, N1; Wood Close school, E2; Bay Street school, Central Hackney; St. Matthews N. School, NW, all in GLRO.

81. Grant, *From "Me" to "We,"* 71; Elliott, "State Feeding of School Children," 865.

82. Thane, *Foundations*, 75–76; Hurt, "Feeding the Hungry Schoolchild," 182; *Women's Dreadnought*, September 29, 1917, summarizing Newman's annual reports; Sir William Beveridge, *British Food Control* (Oxford: Oxford University Press, 1928), 327.

83. Some autobiographical accounts of school meals are George Acorn, *One of the Multitude* (London: Heinemann, 1911), 28; Samuel, *East End Underworld*, 26; W. J. Bennett, *I Was a Walworth Boy* (London: Peckham Publishing Project, 1980), 4; Mrs. Benjamin, Hackney People's Autobiography, 1; and most remarkably, *Autobiography of Joseph Williamson*, 28.

7. To Give and to Receive: Philanthropy and Collective Responsibility Among Jews in Paris, 1880–1914

TSEDAKAH, THE HEBREW WORD FOR CHARITY, also means justice. According to religious precepts, giving is the duty of the rich to provide for the poor. On an individual level, this can create a symbiotic relationship between donor and recipient, as incarnated in the legendary beggar of eastern European Jewish tales. As the well-known joke goes: Beggar complaining to rich man: What's the matter? Last year you gave me twice as much. Rich man to beggar, sighing: Ah, but business has been bad this year. Beggar: So just because your business is bad, mine should be too?

More globally, philanthropy, particularly among Jews, is a community affair. It is a form of intracommunal solidarity. The collective responsibility it implies is both externally and internally imposed. Yet, as we shall see, such responsibility is not interpreted by everyone within the Jewish community in the same manner.

Over the last fifteen years, the modern Jewish "community" has come under scrutiny by historians looking at divisions within it. Although the notion of "community" remains particularly pertinent for the Jews, the divisions within have nonetheless been very real. The first wave of mass migration of eastern European Jews to the West, from the 1880s to World War I, resulted in differences between native and immigrant Jews that were socioeconomic and cultural as well as ritual. Conflicts occurred over community institutions.[1] Yet, on reflection, we can see that there were also basic differences in attitudes between western and eastern Jews over the very concept of community and the collective responsibility of the group toward its individual members.

The realm of philanthropy is a particularly good starting place for examining this issue. It was one of the very real "intersection points" at which native and immigrant Jews met and collective responsibility was enacted, though not without difficulties. Attitudes toward charity, and indeed toward the responsibility of the Jewish community for its members, varied. At one level, non-Jews, French Jews, and eastern European immigrants in Paris at the end of the nineteenth century all assumed the working of a certain intracommunal Jewish solidarity, yet at another level interpretations over the nature of philanthropy varied greatly. It is these different expectations, particularly between donors and recipients, upon which I will focus.

Church and State: The Role of Jewish Philanthropy

The specific nature of Jewish philanthropy may be situated within what could be called the macrohistory of church-state relations. Recent works on charity and welfare have placed giving within the history of the secularization of society over the last two centuries, showing the increasing shift of certain functions, notably education and welfare, away from the church to the state. In France this change was concretized through important welfare legislation in 1892 and in 1905, the year of the official separation of church and state. From 1871 to 1912, the number of state welfare bureaus grew by 45 percent. In the same period, workers' protective legislation was passed as the state increasingly intervened for the general welfare of its inhabitants.[2]

Private welfare continued, of course, indeed becoming, in many ways, a refuge for the declining aristocracy. The list of those participating in the annual fund-raising event called the Bazar de la charité looked like the Annuaire des châteaux, while the ideal of noblesse oblige permeated the French bourgeoisie as well.[3] Although this private philanthropy remained Catholic in tone, it too was moving away from formal ties to the church.

Jewish charities, however, played a somewhat different role. In spite of the increasing secularization of welfare, the Jews were not only allowed but expected to continue to carry the burden of their own poor. There were two reasons for this situation. First, in the move toward separation of church and state, it was the more powerful Catholic church, not the Jews, that was perceived as the major threat and whose functions were to be "nationalized." Second, the relegation of Jewish philanthropy to the Jewish community corresponded to perceptions of the semiautonomous nature of that community in spite of a century of emancipation.

When in August 1892, 120 eastern European Jewish refugees camped for three nights at the Gare de Lyon train station, the Parisian press chided city authorities, but also the Jewish community, for not having taken care of them. *Le Figaro* spoke assuredly of a Rothschild or the Baron de Hirsch coming to the emigrants' aid.[4] A year later, after a similar incident, other newspapers blamed the French Jewish community more explicitly: "The Consistory [official body of the Jewish community in France] should wake up and not allow these unfortunates to become a burden on the city when it is rich enough to take care of them itself."[5] The anti-Semitic press was harsher, assuming that some Rothschild would not only come to the poor immigrants' aid but would undoubtedly make "future barons" out of them.[6] In any case, the general non-Jewish attitude was one of expecting Jewish philanthropy to be operative, even while the Jewish community itself was struggling over what to do.

In fact, Jews did "take care of their own." Although the anti-Semite Edouard Drumont claimed that Jews were stingy and that he could not understand how the myth of their benevolence had arisen, a wide variety of Jewish philanthropic organizations existed in Paris at the turn of the century. From aid for unwed mothers to orphanages to rest homes for the elderly, the philanthropic structure extended from cradle to grave.[7] If the Jewish immigrants seem to have gone to the public welfare office in proportions roughly representative of their presence in Paris, they did not rely to excess on this form of aid. For the years 1883 and 1886, for example, eastern Europeans, who were respectively 3.5 and 4.2 percent of all foreigners in Paris, were 2.5 and 3.3 percent of the foreigners in the city welfare statistics. By contrast, the Germans were 19.0 and 16.8 percent of the foreign population in these years but 40.7 and 27.3 percent of the welfare-receiving foreigners.[8]

It was not that the Jewish immigrants were less needy. Abundant evidence points to the contrary. But they had other options. That the Jewish immigrants did not apparently have greater recourse to the city welfare facilities reflects the symbiotic relationship between French and immigrant Jews. Jewish philanthropy was both a response to external attitudes from French society concerning Jewish community responsibility and an internal desire, emanating from expectations on the part of native as well as immigrant Jews.

To Give: Motives and Policies

Individual gestures of giving can be motivated by anything from pure altruism to outright self-interest, but what I will examine here are collective attitudes toward philanthropy and its role for the community. A combination of Jewish tradition and the specific context of late nineteenth-century France informed the philanthropic offering of the French Jewish community. A century of emancipation, social and economic integration into French society, and increasing secularization all form the background to turn-of-the century attitudes. The Dreyfus Affair only doubled the French Jews' determination to prove their patriotism to the French state and to relegate religious identity to the private sphere.[9] In this context, it is not surprising that the Jewish press stressed not only the "Jewish duty" but also the "French duty" of giving.

Calls for donations and writings about philanthropy in the Jewish press and brochures combined a series of motifs, many of which appealed to the more general and generic repertoire of what W. K. Jordan has called the "literature of exhortation."[10] Two specifically Jewish themes, however, had to do with religious precepts and Jewish solidarity as motivations for giving. The religious reference seemed to provide above all a background of shared culture and belief to which adherence (if not active participation) could be assumed. Examples abound in ancient Jewish law establishing a structure of philanthropy: every seventh year all harvests shall belong to the poor; every fiftieth year, the jubilee year, slaves are freed, debts annulled, and all property reverts to its original owner. Even in nonsabbatical or nonjubilee years a part of the crop should always be left on the vines for the poor; at other times a tithe must be set aside for the less fortunate. In ancient times communities had rooms set aside for poor travelers, and the Talmud speaks of soup kitchens. Although there were means of avoiding such laws (as in placing the land in the name of a Christian during the sabbatical year), the appeal to these ancient (ideal) laws when urging modern-day charity served to reinforce the religious foundation of charity. Charity was seen as a "sacred duty . . . we cannot flee from it without dishonoring Judaism."[11] Such appeals implied that religious beliefs and, by extension, the Jewish community were the cause of giving. Even a rabbi could suggest an inverse causality. Commenting on the decline of the religious bond in the secularizing West, the head rabbi of France, Zadoc Kahn, argued that philanthropy could be the stimulant for community cohesiveness.[12]

The same could be said with regard to appeals to Jewish solidarity. Here, too, we can ask whether philanthropy was the cause or the effect. The late nineteenth-century essayist Maxim DuCamp, in his laudatory account of Jewish charity in *Paris bienfaisant*, suggested that Jewish giving was prompted by a shared memory of collective suffering.[13] Charity was indeed often described as the last bastion of Jewish solidarity (if not of Jewish identity); conversely, solidarity was invoked to stimulate the philanthropic imperative.

The arrival of their poor coreligionists from the East, fleeing the tsarist regime from the early 1880s on, reactivated the collective memory of suffering and called Jewish community philanthropy into action. Non-Jews, French Jews, and East European Jews all expected it to work. And to a certain extent, it did. The newcomers turned to the existing institutions (Hôpital Rothschild, Comité de bienfaisance, consistorial[14] religious schools), and a few new organizations were created. Individual efforts also were important. But in moving from appeals to giving to what can be called the administration of giving, one cannot help but be struck by the difficulties encountered and the disappointments engendered on all sides, indicative of differing attitudes about the philanthropic intersection.

The French Jews offered aid to the immigrants largely in three areas: educational programs, work relief, and general welfare. These can be described briefly, and I will focus first on the attitudes of the donors.

Although education for the poor is not an act of charity per se, it often performs many of the same functions, particularly with regard to "moralizing" the poor. The French Jews sought not only to assure the religious training of the immigrant children and to help the immigrants learn the French language and customs but also to moralize and above all Frenchify the immigrants.

Educational programs ranged from the Consistory's full-time but small-enrollment religious schools (which by 1906–7 were dominated by immigrant children), to after-school religious classes for children and evening French lessons for adults, to the Université populaire juive (UPJ). The UPJ, founded in 1902 (by the Zionist Marmorek) along the lines of other "popular" universities then current in France, was explicitly aimed at helping ease the culture shock of immigration: "tsu makhn heymish di fremde in Paris" or to make the foreign feel at home in Paris, as a Yiddish almanac described it. The object was to familiarize the immigrants with the French language and "esprit" and to offer practical information on life in France. Jewish subjects were taught as well.[15]

The Oeuvre française pour l'éducation morale de la jeunesse juive immigrée, launched in July 1914, expressed more clearly the worry that the eastern European immigrants, devoting all of their energy to surviving, had no time to supervise the moral education of their children. It was perceived as a patriotic, French, as well as Jewish, duty to fill this lacuna. At the same time, the aim was to make the immigrants over in the Parisian image: "[It is necessary to] coordinate all of the efforts . . . to give this population . . . a very suitable Parisian demeanor, to 'wash away' [*débarbouiller*] that which is exotic and too shocking. . . . We are not suggesting either makeup, nor a disguise, but a sort of material and moral adaptation."[16] Immigrant children had to be taught not only the rudiments of French but also of cleanliness ("don't forget that we are dealing with Russian-Polish children"[17]), and although community leaders hoped that the immigrants would become "refined by [mere] contact with [French] civilization," the educational efforts, although ultimately limited in scope, were to accelerate the process.[18]

The Université populaire juive had an even more ambitious task, that of functioning as a veritable melting pot of Russian Jewish, French Jewish, and French culture: "to make of the Parisian *kehilla* a homogeneous whole and in particular to incorporate . . . the foreign-born."[19] The fears and hopes of the French Jewish community as well as its own self-image were expressed by one of the community's organs in its praise for the UPJ:

> [The UPJ] first of all wards off the danger which could be created for the Parisian community by a Jewish population with a mentality that is sometimes so different from our own; it furthermore preserves for Judaism followers who are courageous and enlightened; and finally it shows, by making excellent patriots of these foreigners, that our particular duties as Jews, far from counteracting our duties as citizens, on the contrary, support, fortify and raise up the latter.[20]

Assimilation of the immigrants to the Jewish community was to parallel their integration into French society as a whole.

While these (limited) educational programs sought to integrate the immigrants into French society and culture, a small vocational training and work relief program attempted to integrate the poor into "the path of labor [to] figure honorably in the ranks of society."[21] Once at work, the immigrants would not only ease the burden on the charitable organizations but would also help counteract old myths. The "calloused hands with their tools" would prove that Jews could be productive, not merely parasitic.[22] In this respect the Ecole du travail and other apprenticeship programs set up during the nineteenth century sought to further one of the Consistory's original purposes: to promote "useful" trades as opposed to "traditional" (moneylending, peddling) occupations among the Jews.[23] With the arrival of the eastern European migrants, this concern was renewed, although ultimately the scope of the apprenticeship programs was much too limited to be very effective.

Other attempts at *assistance du travail* included individual placement efforts. A form letter from the Comité de bienfaisance (consistorial welfare bureau) addressed to the personnel officer at the Chemin de fer du Nord (train company), with a Russian "israélite"'s name to be filled in, seems to indicate that some individuals were able to find employment in this manner.[24] Others were put to work in the three paper goods workshops created in November 1882, which employed thirteen men and thirty-five women at two francs per day.[25]

Finally, a more successful employment program was the Atelier, begun in 1906 by a student and an artist who opened a workshop in the Marais, which eventually employed up to sixty-five immigrants making Parisian souvenirs (photo albums, postcards, and the like) and small furniture items. The founders were able to interest James A. de Rothschild and others in the project, and by 1909 they had an operating budget of 150,000 francs. The Atelier was lauded for developing those talents and "treasures of intelligence" which would otherwise be wasted in "exploitative trades and parasitical professions."[26]

Despite the minimal success of the programs aimed at the eradication of peddling and poverty, they are indicative of middle-class native Jews' attitudes toward poverty in general. In this respect the programs differed little from similar non-Jewish ventures. But the Jewish middle class was particularly worried about anti-Semitic accusations concerning the traditional, "parasitic," "Jewish" trades. Much of their philanthropic work was thus ultimately aimed at preventing the immigrants from flocking to such occupations.

Comité de bienfaisance

The one organization that was by far the most important in responding to the changing needs of the Jewish community, and which continues that role today, was the Comité de bienfaisance (Jewish Welfare Committee).[27] Founded in 1809 by the Consistory as the Comité consistorial de la Société israélite de secours et d'encouragement, the Welfare Committee had as its aim by the end of the century to take care of orphans, help poor workers, and take care of the ill, disabled, and aged.

Distribution of aid was based on a fundamental distinction between the permanent or hard-core poor and the temporarily needy, a distinction underlying philanthropic theory from ancient Judaism to nineteenth-century France. Ancient Jewish law provided for a *kuppah*, or community fund, to serve a fairly constant number of protégés and a *tamchui*—daily distribution "plate" or even soup kitchen—to help nonresidents or those in temporary distress. The French public welfare system of the late nineteenth century also differentiated between *indigents* (to whom annual aid was allocated) and *nécessiteux* (those receiving occasional aid). The Comité de bienfaisance distinguished between *pauvres inscrits* (registered poor) and *secours immédiats* (immediate aid). The registered poor, aided on a regular basis, were the elderly and infirm, widow(ers), and orphans, categories little represented among the immigrants. The *secours immédiats*, however, included *distributions quotidiennes* (daily hand-outs), which, along with soup kitchens, provided the most immediate aid available to the immigrant poor. With the arrival of the first wave of immigrants in 1882–83, lodging was found for some thirteen hundred Russian refugees, and 326,000 meals were served in the Welfare Committee's soup kitchens, almost double the number it distributed during the siege of 1870–71.[28]

Although I will return to some of the difficulties the committee had with its philanthropic work, it was the sole preexisting organization able to meet the material needs of the immigrants. The majority of the community's charitable institutions were simply not prepared to succor some thirty-five thousand immigrants who arrived between 1881 and 1914. The Oeuvre israélite de travail et de placement, founded in February 1881 just before the mass immigration began, closed three years later, unable to keep up with the Russian Jewish influx.[29] When the Refuge de Plessis Piquet, an orphanage founded in 1899, received a letter asking if it would accept some Russian orphans, it answered that out of a sentiment of "haute solidarité religieuse" it would, "à titre exceptionnel" (as an exception), make room for five children, who preferably already knew French.[30]

The Limits to Giving

Even with the best of intentions, French Jewish philanthropy was reticent, for a variety of reasons, when confronted with the challenge of immigration. In the first stage, there was a hesitancy even to accept the immigrants—for a long time they were referred to as *em*igrants, and it was hoped and assumed that they would move on (to America). Community resources were strained. The mass migration represented a crisis situation for which the French community was not prepared. The ever more frequent appeals for donations and the sometimes desperate or reproachful character of those appeals reveal the growing pressures on the community. More than once the Comité de bienfaisance wrote that it was necessary to "get rid of" (se débarrasser) the refugees because they "are frightfully expensive" (nous coûtent les yeux de la tête).[31]

As immigration increased, the Comité de bienfaisance asked the Alliance israélite universelle again and again to increase its subsidy, which reached 50 percent of the committee's budget in the 1905–6 crisis period. But the Alliance, founded in 1860 to aid Jewish communities abroad—particularly through its educational programs in the Levant—was besieged by requests from all sides and answered on at least two occasions by dissociating itself from the Parisian Jewish community and emphasizing its international identity: "The Alliance cannot do for the rich community in Paris what it cannot do for smaller and less well-off communities [around the world]."[32] The Alliance thus took somewhat of an outsider's view and, like much of the non-Jewish press, presumed the duty of solidarity and charity of the rich Parisian Jewish community for its poor immigrant coreligionists.

Not only did the French Jews feel the economic strain of giving to those who came their way, but they were afraid that their generosity would attract even more immigrants. Fears that charity encourages poverty and acts as a pull upon the wandering poor have caused donors worries from the oldest poor laws to the modern welfare state.[33] When it was reported in 1892 in the Parisian press that the Baron de Hirsch had paid for the immigrants to come to Paris on their way to America, the French Jewish community felt compelled to make a formal statement, which appeared in a Parisian daily, denying that the Consistory or the Alliance had had any role in bringing the immigrants there.[34]

The fear of encouraging immigration through a too liberal aid policy was neither the particular province of the French Jews nor specific to late nineteenth-century philanthropy. It explains the French state's desire to separate the indigents from the nécessiteux and to impose time limits for residence on most charitable offerings. A decree of August 12, 1886, provided that annual aid was available only to French citizens living in Paris; a subsequent law of November 15, 1895, further stipulated that the indigent must have resided for three years in the city to qualify. The government was cautious lest a too liberal policy attract vagabonds from the world over.[35]

Similarly, the Jewish community, since the early nineteenth century, was concerned that it might attract impoverished immigrants. Although migrant beggars had long been a tradition in eastern Europe, the Comité de bienfaisance at first limited aid to Paris residents. Soon, however, the wandering poor were accepted as well. Along with them, however, came those who begged habitually. In the constant struggle of the French Jewish community against *shnorers*, which ensued throughout the century, poverty was often no longer seen as an opportunity for doing a *mitzvah*, a good deed, but as a social plague. As the director of *L'Univers Israélite*, a French Jewish weekly, had expressed it in 1836: "It is generally recognized that, due to a misguided feeling of charity, the Jews maintain entire hordes of beggars who block the roads like the gypsy hordes of long ago, exposing their frightful features to everyone in sight and thereby creating a veritable scourge for themselves and for all society."[36] From that year on, the system of registering the poor (as *pauvres inscrits*) was instituted for the purpose of weeding out professional beggars.

Beyond distinguishing between the permanently poor and the temporarily needy, between the locals and the wandering beggars, was a further notion, also common to most charitable efforts, of weeding out the worthy from the unworthy poor. It was, as L. K. Amitai noted, "the eternal struggle between energy and inertia."[37] To recognize "true" misery, that which struggles energetically against its lot, as opposed to that which is the product of laziness and vice ("we strive to aid the one without encouraging the other") was a crucial function of the officials who administered the daily distributions.[38] Recidivists at the soup kitchens or at the distributions were regarded suspiciously as professional beggars, and the French Jewish weekly *Archives Israélites* wrote: "One of the inconveniences of the oppression [in eastern Europe], which drags along so much in its wake, is the creation of a class of parasites."[39] Finally, it was the "*shnorer* ambulant" who was blamed for distorting the philanthropic process. By abusing the donor's confidence with moving stories "told to elicit tears from your eyes— and the money from our wallets," it was above all the *vrai pauvre* who was thus wronged.[40]

To discourage those professional beggars who made the rounds of all philanthropic organizations and individuals in Paris, a system of centralized charity was organized by the Welfare Committee in 1893. Donors were requested to give money to the Comité de bienfaisance in exchange for tokens, to be handed out to the beggars and redeemable at the committee's office. It was then up to the committee, based on its experience in such matters, to decide whether the needy person was sincere or not. Ticket systems of this sort had been used by Jewish communities in central and eastern Europe, and similar plans had recently been organized by the local town halls of the fourth, twelfth, and nineteenth arrondissements in Paris.[41] The theory behind the centralization of philanthropic donations and distribution was everywhere the same: to counteract what has been described as "philanthropic anarchy,"[42] to make the most efficient use of funds, to maintain public order, and above all to allow a more thorough investigation into the worthiness of recipients. To enhance its powers of identification, the Welfare Committee created a central information bureau in 1900 to "démasquer le pauvre exploiteur," "ces éléments parasitaires," so as to be able to transfer them out of Paris.[43]

Finally, donors' attitudes were circumscribed by more general concerns over the mass migration. In France, as in the United States, England, and Germany, middle-class Jews greeted their "backward" and poor coreligionists with great reluctance, to say the least. Class and cultures clashed, disturbing everyone's notion of Jewish solidarity. In France, shaken by the Dreyfus Affair's challenge to Jewish integration, the Jewish community was particularly defensive with regard to anti-Semitism and anxious to reaffirm the gains of a century of emancipation. Its reaction to the immigrants was thus an inevitable expression of its insecurity and its own image of its status in France. It is no surprise that the French Jews' response was a projection of those values onto the immigrants just as it was their collective attempt at self-preservation as a minority community.

Self-preservation could mean increased giving to hide the shameful poor. The Jewish community sought to "remove [the immigrants] from the public eye," for their condition was "often" seen as an embarrassment for themselves, but "always" as one for the community.[44] The *Archives Israélites* complimented the poor Jews on their invisibility: "This anxious care put into hiding from the world the spectacle of misery"[45] helped form a protective shield for the Jewish community as a whole. Self-preservation, however, also meant a certain filtering function at the frontiers of the community, just as attempts to restrict the size and ensure the financial solvency of medieval Jewish communities had been regulated through the much more stringent immigration restrictions of the *herem hayyishub*.[46] Unmasking the unworthy wandering poor and worrying about encouraging immigration through too much generosity were not new phenomena in this context.

Jewish philanthropy must thus be understood on three levels. Its origins, like the Braudelian triptych, may be found in the "longue durée" of Jewish philanthropy, the structural constraints of (nondenominational) giving, and the specific context of late nineteenth-century France.

The triple background informed donors' attitudes and expectations, leading the French Jewish community to approve the immigrants at times for their discretion but to be disappointed in other ways. The French Jews complained that their efforts did not meet with greater success. The more established and well-off immigrants were reproached, for example, for not recognizing their debt to the Parisian community by coming to the Université populaire juive's aid. (Of the 201 members in 1904 who had paid their six-franc yearly dues, only 35 have clearly eastern European names.) When an 1883 attempt at adult French classes had to be discontinued, the French Jews criticized the immigrants' disaffection, postulating that either they were speedy learners (quitting after only a few weeks), had left because they were "enamored with risk and the idea of self-government," or were simply lazy or indifferent.[47] In more serious cases disillusionment turned to bitterness and an appeal to outside help. The police were even called in when the beggars at the donors' doors proved too unruly. As we will see, such incidents expressed very different attitudes about the charitable gesture on the part of the recipients.

To Receive: From Gratitude to Demands

If French Jewish donors were often disappointed with their immigrant recipients, immigrants were often disappointed with their benefactors. That which the donors offered as a magnanimous gesture, the immigrants often felt to be their due. This basic misunderstanding over the nature of the philanthropic act explains many of the conflicts that occurred and why the immigrants turned to their own sources of aid in getting settled in Paris.

Although data are much more sparse concerning immigrants' ideas about receiving than donor attitudes toward giving, moments of conflict between the two groups provide insight into differing interpretations of solidarity and collective responsibility. This does not mean that common attitudes did not exist or that there were not happy donors and contented recipients. One daughter of immigrants gratefully remembered until late in life her "dame patronnesse," to whom she was announced by the maid, at her weekly visit, as "une petite protégée de Madame."[48]

Immigrants' expectations could predate departure. Immigrants headed for Paris not only because of the existence of a large and comfortable Jewish community—the myth of the Rothschilds' wealth was operative for Jews as well as non-Jews—but also because of the renown of its organizations. The Alliance israélite universelle, for example, founded in 1860 to help poor Jews abroad, had a reputation well beyond French borders. The Consistory's Welfare Committee also became known in eastern Europe through the immigrant grapevine; immigrant aid publications such as the Yiddish calendar by Wolf Speiser, printed in Paris in 1910, listed, among other things, the Paris Jewish welfare organizations. Whether such knowledge was a direct incentive to migrate is difficult to evaluate. The *Univers Israélite* once denied the logic of such an attraction, arguing (when the Jewish community was criticized for attracting the poor to Paris): "Anyway, who would believe that a father would leave Russia with his wife and children to cross Germany and France, knowing all of the difficulties before them, in order to come to Paris because there is a refuge where he can spend five nights."[49] It had a point, but the very existence of a strong Jewish community, with world-renowned institutions, was undoubtedly perceived by the emigrants as a safety net in the event of trouble in resettlement

Upon arrival, that safety net could be called into action, with insistence. It is within this realm that the immigrants' responses to native charity are telling. Demonstrations of discontent reveal the point at which the poor no longer merely accept charity but demand it as their due. Although unacceptable and even an outrage to the philanthropist, this attitude manifests a turn to active intervention by the poor. From individual acts of desperation to collective rowdiness, to the creation of their own shelter, the immigrants were often inventive in their alternatives to the native handout.

The most extreme example of a desperate vote of discontent occurred in 1887, when a man came to the Comité de bienfaisance asking for passage money to America. He threatened to commit suicide if his request was not granted. The Welfare Committee took no heed, believing him to be a professional in such tactics. Yet the next day he threw himself into the Seine. Luckily, he was rescued, although we do not know if he ever made it to America.[50]

The committee's skepticism with regard to urgent requests was not entirely unfounded. A certain amount of fraud indeed existed and was a strategy on the part of some to make the utmost of community philanthropy. Deceit was discovered in the annual matzoh distribution in 1889 with some people receiving unfair portions.[51] A more elaborate scheme for taking advantage of the Welfare Committee's generosity was described in an autobiographical novel about the period. If a migrant presented him or herself as a candidate for repatriation to Russia, the committee, more than happy to see "the incorrigible loafers disappear," would purchase a ticket to Cologne or Berlin. The returnee would be accompanied to the train station by a committee official to be sure that the ticket was put to its intended use. But the "repatriate," once on board, would find someone who really wanted to go to the prescribed destination and who would agree to buy a cheap ticket for the next stop after Paris. They would exchange tickets and, after a short trip out of town, the "repatriate" would be back in Paris, richer by the difference of the two tickets.[52]

In the same novel a colorful character, Baruch, a hub of immigrant installation information (where to locate an apartment, how to find a job) was also a veritable data base of charitable opportunities. For a fee, he would consult his file cards on philanthropists' preferences to steer the newcomer to the most sympathetic source. Baruch gives a modern look to the "professional beggar." Did the *shnorers'* assiduity imply fraud, as was sometimes suspected? Or was welfare a method of earning a living?

Instances in which the immigrants vociferously and sometimes violently—from the unruly individual beggar to minor food riots—demanded their rights to aid are perhaps the most indicative of attitudes differing starkly from those of the French donors. Fights broke out repeatedly at the Jewish welfare office on rue du Vertbois, and the "growing audacity" of the poor necessitated police protection for the Comité de bienfaisance on several occasions.[53] A demonstration took place in front of the Welfare Committee's soup kitchen in March 1894 during which one of the administrators was grossly insulted and roughed up. In 1905, at the time of an important immigrant wave resulting from the repression after the Russian Revolution of that year, a Groupe des émigrés juifs repeatedly sent letters to the Welfare Committee asking for help. When they received no response, sixty-three immigrants demonstrated in front of the committee's office in early August, crying "bread, lodging, and food." Another thirty people gathered in protest on August 9. The Welfare Committee was both disappointed and outraged at the ingratitude of the immigrants in not appreciating the generosity of "our" (not their) opulent coreligionists. But it eventually handed out food coupons, later complaining about the "noisy and brutal demands of several poorly counseled unfortunates, poorly warned as to the nature of our work."[54]

In some instances the immigrants' answer was simply to go home. In at least one case the issue was not just a demand for what they considered to be their due but resentment at the way the charity was distributed. The paper workshops experiment of 1882 is one example. The immigrants complained to the grand rabbi about the contemptuous way they were being treated, and a delegation went to see Rothschild. When no satisfaction was reached, twenty of the forty-eight workers eventually returned to Russia. The workshops closed after only six months.[55]

Finally, however, like immigrants the world over, the eastern European Jewish poor relied on each other. The disillusionment of both philanthropists and recipients with regard to assumed reciprocal patterns of behavior resulted in an immigrant philanthropy lauded on both sides. Commenting that such efforts "will singularly diminish the expenses of our Comité de bienfaisance,"[56] the French Jews warmly praised the immigrants' resourcefulness and self-sufficiency. Yet immigrant networks were the implicit and at times explicit response to disappointment over the French Jewish community's aid, in content or form.

Immigrant Self-help

Immigrant philanthropy paralleled native charity in a number of ways. The immigrants organized their own French classes and set up employment bureaus. The Table d'hôte des émigrés, a subsidized restaurant, was established, offering cheap meals to all comers and serving up to two hundred people daily. A six-month vocational training course was started, specializing in machinery mounting.[57] More important was the Bureau russe du travail for which we have reports for 1911 and 1912. In 1911 the bureau found employment for 546 immigrants and in 1912 for 309. A breakdown for 1912 shows that 34 percent of those jobs were for skilled workers, 29 percent for day laborers, 17 percent for domestic servants, and 20 percent for intellectuals. The numerous out-of-work writers and journalists eventually got their own job placement service: the Association des travailleurs intellectuels.[58] These organizations were more than just labor market clearinghouses, however. Like the French Bourses du travail, they combined educational, fraternal, and practical functions. Reading rooms were central features of the premises; lectures were held periodically, French classes organized, and legal and medical aid provided.

More generally, immigrant networks acted as information centers for finding skilled or unskilled work. Speiser's *Kalendar* (1910) was the printed form of the immigrant information exchange. In addition to describing existing community institutions and warning about unscrupulous lawyers who would offer newcomers unneeded services, the almanac gave hints for job-hunting which included, for example, mention of specific restaurants where capmakers, furworkers, or jewelers could find employment.

Speiser's calendar, like immigrant letters, must have circulated in eastern Europe because immigrants knew where to head the minute they got off the train. Léon Novochelski, a secondhand clothes dealer by vocation and founder of the first immigrant philanthropic organization, the Société de bienfaisance et d'humanité (in 1886), by avocation, described how immigrants often came directly from the train station to the small St. Paul *shul* connected to the society.[59] Another organization, the Prévoyante israélite, was founded by immigrant Jews in 1893 with the aid of the French rabbi Zadoc Kahn. Its double purpose was to help immigrants find work and especially to help them learn French.[60]

The various mutual aid societies (*landsmanshaftn*) founded by the immigrants were multifunctional. Organized primarily for religious or fraternal purposes, these societies had a particularly important function, which, as one immigrant later recounted, could best be handled among one's own: burials. Not only was a *landsmanshaft* burial less costly than a consistorial one, it ensured a Russian-Polish ceremony more comforting than the French rituals.[61] Most important, attendance at the funeral was required of all members (under pain of fine), and the remembrance of one's fellow member was statutorily ensured each *yortsayt* (anniversary of the death). Finally, these societies also provided a form of health insurance. Payment into the fund meant help with doctors' bills, sick pay, and other benefits. Some of the societies were organized by trade affiliation and ultimately transformed into unions.[62]

The most important immigrant welfare organization was the Société (later Association) philanthropique de l'Asile israélite de Paris, founded in 1900, as it said proudly on the cover of its annual reports, "par l'initiative des Israélites russes et roumains."[63] Moïse Fleischer (who was in the hosiery and cotton print business), the founder and "soul" of the Asile, was its president until his death in 1905, when Salomon Novochelski, son of Léon, took over. The organization began with forty members in 1900 and grew to seven hundred by 1909. In 1910 it moved from small rented quarters in the Marais to its own building on Montmartre. The following year the Asile innovated by opening a workshop for women (*ouvroir*), pointing out that the Atelier, which employed mostly men, needed a women's counterpart. A day care center was opened simultaneously, and after World War I ended, the combined Asile de nuit, Asile de jour et crèche israélite moved to 16, rue Lamarck, where a center still exists today.

In 1901 the Asile had thirty beds; by 1909 it had one hundred. People stayed an average of six to nine nights, and the number of daily visitors ranged from thirty-four to forty. Shelter as well as tea, bread, soup, and clothing were offered free to those in need (regardless of religion or nationality). When necessary, the five- to fifteen-night limit was extended for those who needed to stay longer while looking for work.

The Asile's revenue came from membership dues, donations, and fund-raising balls. A major source of financing was a group of immigrant diamond merchants, but yearly dues (twenty francs per member) represented a significant 34 percent of the total revenue in 1905–6, for example.[64] The Asile was not entirely isolated from the Parisian Jewish community, however. Like most immigrant organizations, it turned expectantly to the latter for aid.[65] And, indeed, the Asile had the French community's moral and financial backing: *L'Univers Israélite* admired its "discreet and quiet" work, and the *Archives Israélites* complimented its efforts as doing honor to the Parisian Jewish community; the grand rabbis gave the Asile their spiritual patronage; and generous financial support was forthcoming from the Alliance israélite universelle, the Merzbach family, the Rothschilds, and others. Even the chief commissioner of the Paris police, Louis Lépine, was listed as a benefactor.

Though it was specific in origin, content, and purpose, the Asile paralleled other French and French Jewish philanthropic organizations in many respects. There were "dames patronnessses" for the day care center, annual charity balls to raise money, and endowed beds inscribed with the donor's name. There was also a similarity of discourse between French and immigrant philanthropy. The annual reports of the Asile echoed familiar themes: the struggle against begging, the "scourge of pauperism," the problem of "faux pauvres" alongside "vrai" ones, and the importance of working because it "ennobles humanity." Furthermore, praise of France, such as found in the French Jewish press—"our beautiful France" (showing to what extent the more established immigrants felt at home)—was expressed with a special emphasis on France's hospitality, the most generous in all Europe.

Just as the French Jewish community often had to respond to anti-Semitic arguments, the speakers at the annual Asile meetings also found it necessary to ward off criticisms. Thus one report emphasized hygiene so as explicitly to refute a rumor that the immigrants in the fourth arrondissement had caused a conjunctivitis (eye disease) epidemic. On several occasions the Asile, like the French Jewish institutions, had to refute accusations that the very knowledge of its existence enticed refugees to come to Paris. It also countered the idea that the Asile would become the refuge of professional beggars. The Asile board members repeated over and over that many of their visitors were merely en route to another country and defended the far larger numbers who stayed on as "honest workers" looking for employment.

If the Asile was similar to French Jewish philanthropy in many respects, it was also dissimilar in ways that were made explicit in its annual reports. First, pride in the humble origins of the organization was stressed. It was often repeated how the Asile de nuit had been started with less than 150 francs by the Russian and Romanian Jews themselves. Second, the self-help character of the immigrant initiative was made explicit. Asile representatives frequently referred to the "collective character" of their philanthropic effort and how it devolved from the mutual aid tradition.

Third, the frame of reference was eastern European norms. The Asile's immigrant leaders had recognized a specific need which the Parisian community never furnished (for fear of encouragement?): a shelter. The tradition of *ha'keneset orkhim*—a guesthouse for travelers—was referred to as the raison d'être of the Asile. An implicit if not explicit criticism of this lacuna in Paris was expressed in the annual report for 1905–6:

> The Parisian [Jewish] Community, so rich in charitable works, yet lacked that which would have given a provisional hospitality to unfortunate emigrants, to permit them to learn how to become oriented in the labyrinth of the capital. . . . *But we have to practice hospitality such as it was practiced by our forefathers, such as it was practiced in our homelands.*[66]

Hospitality rather than welfare was the key to immigrant philanthropy. Psalms and Talmudic passages were often quoted in the Asile's reports, from "Enlarge the space in your tent" to, during the Pesach matzoh distribution, "Let he who has hunger come and eat; let he who is needy come and celebrate Pesach."[67]

Finally, the importance of giving refuge to newcomers or those just passing through Paris was felt keenly by people who had had the same experience: "We who know the anguish of the poor in a foreign country, where he knows not the language, has no friend or acquaintance, we, who have all more or less gone through this critical stage ourselves, we must

raise high the banner of hospitality."[68] The term "our unfortunate brethren"—also used by the French Jews—seemed to reflect a more immediate
solidarity of suffering among the immigrants. And expressions of specific
immigrant needs could read like implicit criticisms of that which the French
Jewish welfare efforts lacked: "We have thus wanted to come to their [*nos
malheureux frères*] aid, in offering them a refuge, their own home, where
they will be considered, not as beggars, but as wounded brothers whose
bleeding sores demand consideration and respect."[69] In the idealized form
of immigrant philanthropy, then, immigrant recipients were brothers, not
beggars.

Collective Responsibility

Different conceptions of hospitality perhaps meant somewhat different
interpretations of community, based on differing experiences in the East
and in the West by the end of the nineteenth century. The classic notion of
collective responsibility and traditional norms of welfare had been forged
since ancient times as a result of both internal cohesion and external stric-
tures regarding the Jewish communities. Charity was assumed as a form of
justice and had what we could call its everyday and its crisis functions.
Everyday welfare was instituted through community funds, via internal
taxation and traditional practices of extending invitations to poor strangers.
Crisis welfare had to be called into action at the time of the expulsion from
Spain or the Chmielnicki massacres and now the mass emigration from
Russia.[70]

Ideal philanthropy never wholly existed, but the image of this traditional
norm remained present as both French and immigrant Jews looked to each
other to ease their respective migration pains. The strong internal ethic of
collective aid was activated. Statements referring to the ideal type of solidarity abound, and, as we have seen, the French Jews did assume certain
obligations toward the immigrants, and the immigrant poor did turn to
their agencies for help. But it is the dysfunctional moments that interest us.
The desperate demands of dissatisfied immigrants or the exasperation of
insulted social workers indicate that perhaps other factors were gnawing at
the community fabric and redefining notions of collective responsibility.

The legal emancipation of the Jews in France in 1790–91 ultimately
changed the very concept of Jewish community, along with the actual
functioning of community structures. This does not mean that the commu-

nity disappeared, but rather that it took on a more diffuse character. Before emancipation, the community was legally, and especially fiscally, responsible for each of its members. Afterward, in keeping with the anticorporatist ideology of the Revolution, the Jews had been emancipated as individuals, not as a nation.[71] Theoretically, each Jew was no longer responsible for the faults of all other Jews.

In practice, of course, this was not always the case. At the end of the nineteenth century, after a century of emancipation, the remembrance of things past and the fear of anti-Semitism could still lead to a "sort of *numerus clausus*, not imposed from without, by others, but by oneself," as André Spire expressed it.[72] Nevertheless, the differentiation of the individual from the collectivity and the consequent rejection of group self-censorship was increasingly seen as an inalienable right devolving from the French Revolution.

The concept of the Jew as an individual as opposed to a part of a nation was subscribed to by the Jews not only to promote their emancipation and integration into French society but also as a much needed defense against anti-Semitism or any other threat (the immigration of poor Jews?). Accusations against a Jewish race or a Jewish nation were rejected by strident affirmations of individual responsibility. For example, though statements concerning solidarity continued, an important editorial in the *Archives Israélites* in 1887 criticized the "injure collective," which held all Jews to blame for the actions of one.[73] Then, in 1894, one month after Dreyfus's arrest, the involvement of the Jewish community was disclaimed: "The Jews—as Jews—thus have nothing to do with this affair; the errors—if there are any—are and must always be considered individual errors. Neither a nation, nor a creed, nor any profession must bear the punishment for the unlawful acts of one of its members."[74]

The contradictions between collective and individual responsibility were best summarized in the first-page editorial of the *Archives Israélites* of May 1, 1913, entitled "Solidarité!":

> This solidarity, noble waif of that treasury of Jewish virtues which the century has swept away through its steamrace, we reclaim it with legitimate pride. It evokes for us that Jewish life of the past. . . .
>
> But, one must admit, the conditions of existence for the Jews in our modern era are considerably modified along with their customs as well. For the Jews, as for others, individualism has retrieved all of its rights. . . .
>
> Each man for himself, for better or for worse, such is the principle which must guide us in our understanding of the facts. . . .

This tunic of Nessus which is Jewish solidarity, in the sense in which these "Messieurs" [the anti-Semites who took the crime of one as the crime of all] understand it, has fallen from our shoulders ever since the day when, in right as in equity, collective responsibility ceded its place to individual responsibility.

Such a clear expression of independence from the notion of collective responsibility was possible only after more than a century had elapsed since Jewish emancipation, and this attitude necessarily underscored the way French Jews received the eastern European immigrants. Having spent almost one hundred years ridding themselves of the "Jewish disabilities" criticized before emancipation, the French Jews now found themselves in a double bind. Attacked, through Dreyfus, for their very success at assimilation, they did not dare risk, with the coming of the eastern European immigrants, renewed attacks on Jews as foreigners, parasites, or peddlers.

The immigrants, however, it could be argued, still perceived things through another form of Jewish community, and misunderstandings or conflicts over the responsibilities of donors and donees may be understood in this context. Immigrants initially turned to the French Jews because they expected certain forms of communal behavior as organized in eastern Europe. Even if, as historians Simon Dubnow, Salo Baron, and others have made abundantly clear, nineteenth-century Jewish Russia was no ideal type of a harmonious Jewish community—internal anarchy wrought by oligarchic mismanagement, religious conflicts (between *hassidim* and *mitnagdim*), and economic decline all affected Jewish communal life[75]—in contrast to French Jewry, the eastern European community was still conceived as a corporate body, joining its Jews for better or for worse.

Jewish population density was undoubtedly one reason for this. But just as important, the Jewish community as a whole still remained accountable to the state. Although Jewish autonomy had been formally abolished in Poland in 1821–22 and in Russia in 1844, this did not mean total equality—or "individuality"—for the Jews, as in the West. The newly formed "congregations" were still collectively responsible for providing special taxes and military recruits. Furthermore, with continued persecution, poor economic opportunities, and no real legal emancipation, the Jews in eastern Europe had less cause to change than their western brethren. They persisted in their old mode of life, clinging to the ideals of their worn-out community institutions. Finally, however, we might suggest that the "national awakening," through socialist and Zionist movements in eastern Europe at the end of the century, reflected yet another imagery of Jewish community which perhaps informed the attitudes even of nonmilitant, westward-bound Jews.

The immigrants imported expectations based on another form of communal experience. I would argue, however, that migration itself reinforced and redefined a microcommunity based on a shared experience. That experience not only created a nostalgia and perhaps idealization about mutual aid in eastern Europe, but it helped foster the immigrant networks on which many of them would rely.

The French donor and immigrant recipient roles were never absolute on either side. The immigrants both thanked the French Jews and criticized their own kind when need be. Immigrant self-help had its limits, too, as immigrant philanthropists chided those of their compatriots who did not respond to their fund-raising appeals:

> Much smaller communities than that of our Poles [Polish Jews] in Paris have magnificent hostels for travelers [*ha'keneset orkhim*] in the East; let it not be said that Russian and Romanian Jews, brought up with the sentiment of solidarity, raised with noble ideas of charity, refuse to contribute to a work so important for their brothers in misery once they have left their homeland.[76]

Within the French Jewish community, there were also at times differing perceptions concerning the philanthropic effort. The *Archives Israélites* complained when the Welfare Committee's rationalizing of the philanthropic process led to harsh results. After the suicide attempt mentioned above, the newspaper concluded that it was better to give, give always, and err in that sense than in the other. Although agreeing to the principle of more stringent measures, the paper at another time lamented that foreigners had arrived to find the welfare office closed: "*voilà* something which disturbs a little our traditional ideas about the practice of charity." Resorting to police measures to counter dishonesty only ended in wronging the truly needy, the editorialist concluded.[77] There were thus clasped hands across the French-immigrant divide, just as there were fissures in each camp concerning the administration of giving or disapproval of nongivers.

As Michael Walzer has emphasized, "spheres of justice" can best be interpreted in concrete historical situations.[78] The case of Jewish philanthropy is particularly interesting, given strong traditional notions of justice and charity and internally and externally imposed definitions of the sphere(s) involved. Charitable justice remains a Jewish strength and a testimony to Jewish solidarity. But it has been transformed since its ideal

Talmudic form. Certain assumptions concerning behavior on the part of donor and donee have persisted. Yet attitudes toward collective responsibility have undergone redefinition.

The notion of collective responsibility must thus also be understood historically. François Ewald, in his fascinating book *L'état providence*, has traced the evolution of the notion of responsibility within the nineteenth-century French state. The questions he asks are pertinent for private charity as well because the larger question, it seems to me, has to do with how groups define the boundaries within which they will accept responsibility. Mass migrations have brought these questions to the forefront for states as well as ethnic groups and immigrant communities. As the immigrant poor's expectations become demands, we can understand their use of charity in another way. Are they not seeking to redefine the boundaries of collective responsibility?

Notes

This essay is a considerably revised version of "Philanthropy and Intra-Communal Solidarity, Native and Immigrant Jews in Paris, 1880–1914," published in *Research in Social Policy: Historical and Contemporary Perspectives* 1 (1987), 21–52. I thank JAI Press for permission to use this material and Vicky Caron and Judith Friedlander for their helpful comments.

ABBREVIATIONS

ACIP Association consistoriale israélite de Paris Archives
AI *Archives Israélites*
AIU Alliance israélite universelle
APP Archives de la Préfecture de Police (Paris)
Asile Société philanthropique de l'Asile israélite de Paris
UI *L'Univers Israélite*

1. For France see David Weinberg, *A Community on Trial: The Jews of Paris in the 1930s* (Chicago: University of Chicago Press, 1977); Paula Hyman, *From Dreyfus to Vichy: The Remaking of French Jewry* (New York: Columbia University Press, 1979); Jacques Adler, *The Jews of Paris and the Final Solution: Communal Response and Internal Conflicts, 1940–1944* (New York: Oxford University Press, 1987); and Nancy L. Green, *The Pletzl of Paris: Jewish Immigrant Workers in the Belle Epoque* (New York: Holmes and Meier, 1985). For England and Germany see Jerry White, *Rothschild Buildings: Life in an East End Tenement Block, 1887–1920* (London: Routledge & Kegan Paul, 1980); William Fishman, *East End Jewish Radicals, 1875–1914* (London: Duckworth, 1975); Lloyd P. Gartner, *The*

Jewish Immigrant in England, 1870–1914 (London: Simon Publications, 1973); Steven Aschheim, *Brothers and Strangers: The Eastern European Jew in Germany and German Jewish Consciousness, 1800–1923* (Madison: University of Wisconsin Press, 1983); Jack Wertheimer, *Unwelcome Strangers: East European Jews in Imperial Germany* (New York: Oxford University Press, 1987). For the United States see Morris Rischin, *The Promised City: New York's Jews, 1870–1914* (New York: Corinth, 1964), esp. ch. 6; Ronald Sanders, *The Downtown Jews* (New York: New American Library, 1976); Irving Howe, *World of Our Fathers* (New York: Simon and Schuster, 1976).

2. John H. Weiss, "Origins of the French Welfare State: Poor Relief in the Third Republic, 1871–1914," *French Historical Studies* 13 (Spring 1983), 47–78; François Ewald, *L'état providence* (Paris: Grasset et Fasquelle, 1986); Cissie Fairchilds, *Poverty and Charity in Aix-en-Provence, 1640–1789* (Baltimore: Johns Hopkins University Press, 1976); Alan Forrest, *The French Revolution and the Poor* (New York: St. Martin's Press, 1981); Rachel Fuchs, *Abandoned Children: Foundlings and Child Welfare in Nineteenth-Century France* (Albany: State University of New York Press, 1984); Bronislaw Geremek, *La potence et la pitié: L'Europe et les pauvres du Moyen-Age à nos jours* (Paris: Gallimard, 1987); Jean-Pierre Gutton, *La société et les pauvres en Europe (XVI–XVIIIe siècles)* (Paris: PUF, 1974); Olwen Hufton, *The Poor of Eighteenth-Century France, 1750–1789* (Oxford: Clarendon Press, 1974); Colin Jones, *Charity and Bienfaisance: The Treatment of the Poor in the Montpellier Region, 1740–1815* (Cambridge, Eng.: Cambridge University Press, 1982); Ann-Louise Shapiro, *Housing the Poor of Paris, 1850–1902* (Madison: University of Wisconsin Press, 1985); Judith F. Stone, *The Search for Social Peace: Reform Legislation in France, 1890–1914* (Albany: State University of New York Press, 1985); and for England, where much has been written about the origins of the poor law, see, for example, W. K. Jordan, *Philanthropy in England, 1480–1660* (London: Allen & Unwin, 1959); and David Owen, *English Philanthropy, 1660–1960* (Cambridge, Mass.: Harvard University Press, 1964).

3. Jean-Paul Clébert, *L'incendie du Bazar de la charité* (Paris: Denoël, 1978), 68.

4. Paris, Bibliothèque de l'Histoire de la Ville de Paris, Ochs Collection (newspaper clippings), D1218–34 (1892–1900), particularly *Le Figaro* of August 24 and 25, 1892, and *Le Paris*, of August 23 and 25, 1892.

5. *Le Jour* (Paris), July 25, 1893. See also *L'Intransigeant* (Paris), July 25, 1893; *L'Eclair* (Paris), July 25, 1893; *XIXe siècle* (Paris), July 25, 1893; Paul Pottier, "Essai sur le prolétariat juif en France," *Revue des Revues*, 3d ser., 28 (March 1899), 484–85.

6. See articles in *L'Intransigeant*, August 27 and 28, 1892, and in Drumont's *La Libre Parole* (Paris), August 5, 23, and 24, 1892.

7. And, theoretically, most "Jewish" philanthropic works were also open to non-Jews. Thus the *AI*, February 21, 1895, lauding a Jewish soup kitchen in the Marais quarter of Paris, went so far as to argue, "In the poor neighborhoods, Jewish soup is very popular, and stomachs are refractory to the anti-Semitism which rages among the upper and better-off classes." (Chicken soup takes on even wider curative powers, joining the fight against anti-Semitism!) When the Fondation Rothschild supported a nondenominational subsidized housing

project, however, the *AI* reproached it for ignoring the poor Jewish workers in the Marais (February 29, 1912).

8. These two years are the only ones for which comparative information is available. Furthermore, as Third Republic statistics do not reflect religion, we must extrapolate from nationality data for Russians and Romanians, of whom the Jews were estimated to comprise 75 and 100 percent of the immigrants, respectively. See my Ph.D. dissertation, "Class Struggle in the Pletzl: Jewish Immigrant Workers in Paris, 1881–1914" (University of Chicago, 1980), Appendixes A and D, and page 157, for more detail. *Annuaire statistique de la ville de Paris, année 1886* (Paris: Imprimerie Municipale, 1888), 608, gives the comparative data for 1883 and 1886.

9. See the excellent and by now classic study of this period by Michael R. Marrus, *The Politics of Assimilation: A Study of the French Jewish Community at the Time of the Dreyfus Affair* (Oxford: Oxford University Press, 1971); along with Phyllis Albert, *The Modernization of French Jewry: Consistory and Community in the Nineteenth Century* (Hanover, N.H.: University Press of New England, 1977); Patrick Girard, *Les juifs de France de 1789 à 1860: De l'émancipation à l'égalité* (Paris: Calmann-Lévy, 1976); Doris Ben-Simon Donath, *Social-démographie des juifs de France et d'Algérie, 1867–1907* (Paris: Publications Orientalistes de France, 1976); David Cohen, *La promotion des juifs à l'époque du Second Empire*, 2 vols. (Aix-en-Provence: Publications de l'Université de Provence, 1980). More specifically on immigrants, natives, and philanthropy in this period see Hyman, *From Dreyfus to Vichy*, 120–32, who sees World War I as the turning point.

10. Jordan, *Philanthropy in England*, 155.

11. *AI*, May 15, 1900. See the classic work on Jewish philanthropy by Ephraïm Frisch, *An Historical Survey of Jewish Philanthropy* (New York: Macmillan, 1924), which interprets the ideal as reality, at least up to the nineteenth century. See also Joseph Lehmann, "Assistance publique et privée dans l'antique législation juive," *Revue des Etudes Juives* 35 (July–September 1897), i–xxxviii; L. K. Amitai, *La sociologie selon la législation juive appliquée à l'époque moderne* (Paris: Librairie Fischbacher, 1905); and Salo Baron, *The Jewish Community: Its History and Structure to the American Revolution*, 3 vols. (Philadelphia: Jewish Publication Society, 1942), esp. 2:319–25. For the contemporary period, see, e.g., Gerald Tulchinsky, "Immigration and Charity in the Montreal Jewish Community before 1890," *Histoire Sociale/Social History* 16 (November 1983), 378–79; Milton Goldin, *Why They Give: American Jews and Their Philanthropies* (New York: Macmillan, 1976). In addition, official histories exist for most organizations.

12. Zadoc Kahn, *Sermons et allocutions*, 3d ser., 3 vols. (Paris: A. Durlacher, 1894), 2:238. See also David Owen's discussion (*English Philanthropy*, ch. 6) of philanthropy as a compensation for religion, and some religious leaders' worries that philanthropy would become a substitute for religion. See also Oscar Handlin, *A Continuing Task: The American Jewish Joint Distribution Committee, 1914–1964* (New York: Random House, 1964), 116–17; and Goldin, *Why They Give*, 172, describing the problem of reconciling Judaism with American lifestyles: American Jews "found [that] the quasi-American conviction that money can solve

any problem could be tastefully joined to the ancient concept of *zedakah*." An even more pessimistic view of Jewish welfare is seen by Zosa Szajkowski, *Poverty and Social Welfare among French Jews, 1800–80* (New York: Editions Historiques Franco-Juives, 1954).

13. Maxim DuCamp, *Paris bienfaisant* (Paris: Hachette, 1888), 440. See Michael Marrus's discussion of Zadoc Kahn's notion of the "community of suffering," *Politics of Assimilation*, 28, 49, 77, 82–83.

14. The Consistory was set up by Napoleon as the official intermediary body between Jews and the state.

15. Université populaire juive, *Compte rendu et statuts, 1902–3* (Paris: Imprimerie N. L. Danzig, 1904); Wolf Speiser, *Kalendar* (Paris: N.p., 1910), 56.

16. *UI*, February 15, 1907.

17. *UI*, July 16, 1883. A similar discussion of education of the Jewish poor, but a century earlier and in England, is in Todd Endelman, *The Jews of Georgian England, 1714–1830: Tradition and Change in a Liberal Society* (Philadelphia: Jewish Publication Society of America, 1979), ch. 7.

18. Narcisse Leven, *Cinquante ans d'histoire—l'Alliance israélite universelle*, 2 vols. (Paris: Félix Alcan, 1911–20), 2:527.

19. *UI*, March 13, 1908. See also J. [Iouda] Tchernoff, *Dans le creuset des civilisations*, 4 vols. (Paris: Editions Rieder, 1937), 4:281; and *AI*, March 5, 1902, and January 21, 1904.

20. *UI*, December 20, 1907.

21. *AI*, March 24, 1881.

22. E.g., *AI*, December 17, 1885, and November 1, 1894.

23. See, for example, Léon Kahn, *Les professions manuelles et les institutions de patronage* (Paris: A. Durlacher, 1885); Zosa Szajkowski, "Yidishe Fakhshuln in Frankraykh in 19tn Yorhundert," *YIVO-Bleter* 42 (1962), 81–120; and Ecole du travail, *Comptes rendus*, 1880–1918; Albert, *Modernization of French Jewry*; Girard, *Les juifs de France*; and Lee Shai Weissbach's interesting article, placing Jewish apprenticeship programs in the larger context of similar French programs, "The Jewish Elite and the Children of the Poor: Jewish Apprenticeship Programs in Nineteenth-Century France," *AJS Review* 12 (Spring 1987), 123–42.

24. Outgoing letter, June 15, 1882, Register BB50, p. 11101, ACIP.

25. Michel Rudnianski and Patrick Girard, "Les relations entre israélites français et juifs russes," 2 vols., vol. 1, "1860–1890" (Rudnianski), vol. 2, "1890–1905" (Girard) (Maîtrise, U.E.R. d'Histoire, Université de Paris I, 1971–72), 2:206–7; *AI*, December 13, 1888.

26. *UI*, October 26, 1906. See also *UI*, January 26, 1906, and December 17, 1909; ACIP, B91, File "L'Atelier"; and Hyman, *From Dreyfus to Vichy*, 124–25.

27. Now known as CASIP, the Comité d'action sociale israélite de Paris. See Comité de bienfaisance israélite de Paris, *Assemblées générales* (1881–1920); Léon Kahn, *Le Comité de bienfaisance* (Paris: A. Durlacher, 1889). The name changes of this organization seem to correspond to prevailing linguistic trends and influences. If the original emphasis on "encouragement" is reminiscent of the language of debate over the emancipation of the Jews, the term "Comité de bienfaisance," taken on in 1855, was perhaps a late reference to French revolu-

tionary ideology. See Isser Wolloch, "From Charity to Welfare in Revolutionary Paris," *Journal of Modern History* 58 (December 1986), 779–812, on the "comités de bienfaisance" generated "from below" during the Revolution.

28. Outgoing letter, December 4, 1884, Register BB52, p. 12074, ACIP.

29. Kahn, *Les sociétés de secours mutuels* (Paris: A. Durlacher, 1887), 150–51; Szajkowski, "Fakhshuln," 120.

30. AIU Archives, France IH1: Sociétés, File "Refuge du Plessis-Piquet."

31. Comité de bienfaisance to AIU, January 5, 1894, April 10, 1894, and January 22, 1895, France IH1, File "Comité de bienfaisance," AIU Archives.

32. AIU to Comité de bienfaisance, January 1899 and September 1906, ibid.

33. As Gareth Stedman Jones has noted, critics of philanthropy in England in the 1860s and 1870s worried lest "a large army of paupers, better informed than the charities themselves, migrate regularly from one to another" (*Outcast London: A Study in the Relationship between Classes in Victorian Society* [Oxford: Clarendon Press, 1971], 266). See Jordan, *Philanthropy in England*, 78–80; Tulchinsky, "Immigration and Charity," 377, regarding a similar fear of inciting immigrants to come to Montreal; and, for a contemporary example, "City Officials Have No Solutions for the Homeless," *New York Times*, October 10, 1984, p. B4.

34. *Le Paris*, August 27, 1892; see also *Le Matin*, July 28, 1893. For an example of how a psychiatrist, Henry Meige, explained that "nervous Jewish pilgrims" were encouraged by world Jewish organizations, see Jan Goldstein, "The Wandering Jew and the Problem of Psychiatric Anti-Semitism in Fin-de-siècle France," *Journal of Contemporary History* 20 (1985), 541.

35. Maurice Didion, *Les salariés étrangers en France* (Paris: V. Giard and E. Brière, 1911), 100–101; see Gérard Noiriel, *Le creuset français* (Paris: Seuil, 1988), 111–15, on the distinction made between French and foreigners, based on length of stay, in social legislation.

36. Quoted in Girard, *Les juifs de France*, 122.

37. Amitai, *La sociologie selon la législation juive*, 105. Maxim DuCamp devoted an entire chapter to "false poverty" in *Paris bienfaisant*. Cissie Fairchilds traces the distinction between the deserving and undeserving poor back to the seventeenth century in France, *Poverty and Charity*, 29. See also Owen, *English Philanthropy*, 110–12; Jordan, *Philanthropy in England*, 151–54; and Jones, *Charity and Bienfaisance*, 251, 272–74.

38. Comité de bienfaisance, *Assemblée générale* (1907), 10.

39. *AI*, December 23, 1909.

40. Ibid., first page editorial entitled "Contre les mendiants ambulants."

41. A century later there are still calls for a "guichet unique" by the president of the Union nationale des bureaux d'aide sociale (*Le Monde* [Paris], April 22–23, 1984).

42. Neil Evans, "Urbanisation, Elite Attitudes and Philanthropy: Cardiff, 1850–1914," *International Review of Social History* 27 (1982), 315. See also Owen, *English Philanthropy*, ch. 8; Fairchilds, *Poverty and Charity*, 29; Weiss, "Origins of the French Welfare State," 53–54, noting that disorganization was seen to encourage "les industries de la fausse indigence." *L'Univers Israélite* put it bluntly on

September 26, 1913: "Organization would cost less than the current disorganization."

43. *AI*, October 18, 1900.

44. *AI*, October 6, 1892, and July 27, 1893; and *UI*, September 26, 1913.

45. *AI*, April 19, 1888. Theodor Herzl minced no words in analyzing this preoccupation: "Some of these charity institutions are created not for but against the persecuted Jews. Remove the paupers as quickly and as far away as possible. And thus, many an apparent friend of the Jews turns out, on closer examination, to be no more than an anti-Semite of Jewish origin in philanthropist's clothing" (*The Jewish State*, in Arthur Hertzberg, ed., *The Zionist Idea* [New York: Atheneum, 1975], 212). See also Weinberg, *Community on Trial*, 265; and Michel Foucault's classic analysis of "renfermement" (enclosing) of the poor to keep them from infecting a healthy society, in *Folie et déraison: Histoire de la folie à l'âge classique* (Paris: Librairie Plon, 1961), ch. 2.

46. The right of residence was regulated through the *herem hayyishub* (ban of settlement). The major work on this topic is Louis Rabinowitz, *The Herem Hayyishub* (London: E. Goldston, 1945), a fascinating account of this "immigration legislation" acting as a trade monopoly for medieval Jewish communities. See also Baron, *Jewish Community*, 2:4–17, 322–23, 3:98–104; Arcadius Kahan, "The Early Modern Period," in Nachum Gross, ed., *Economic History of the Jews* (New York: Schocken, 1976), 74–75; S. M. Dubnow's classic introduction to the *kahal* in eastern Europe, *History of the Jews in Russia and Poland*, trans. I. Friedlaender, 3 vols. (New York: KTAV Publishing House, 1975), 3:188–98. Cf. Michael Walzer, *Spheres of Justice* (Oxford: Basil Blackwell, 1983), esp. ch. 2 on membership.

47. *UI*, July 16, 1883.

48. Interview, Sarah (and Abraham) Uhafti, Fontenay-sous-Bois, October 27, 1978.

49. *UI*, May 5, 1911.

50. *AI*, May 26, 1887.

51. *AI*, April 18, 1889. The *Alliance Israélite* was indignant that the indigents were taking advantage of the Pesach motto: "Let he who is hungry come and eat."

52. André Billy and Moïse Twersky, *L'épopée de Ménaché Foïgel*, 3 vols. (Paris: Plon, 1927–28), 2:34.

53. *AI*, August 10, 1882, February 7, 1883, May 6, 1885.

54. Comité de bienfaisance to AIU, March 12, 1894, France IH1, File "Comité de bienfaisance," AIU Archives; reports, August 8–12, 1905, BA1709, File "Groupe des émigrés juifs de Paris," APP, resulting in several arrests; Comité de bienfaisance, *Assemblée générale* (1905–6), 11. For other instances when the Welfare Committee had to have recourse to police protection, see Outgoing letters, February 15, March 19, 1883, and February 18, 1889, Registers BB50, pp. 11366 and 11408, and BB57, p. 13746, ACIP; cf. Hyman, *From Dreyfus to Vichy*, 120.

55. Rudnianski and Girard, "Les relations entre israélites français et juifs russes," 2 (Girard):206–7; *AI*, December 13, 1888.

56. *UI*, January 10, 1896.

57. By 1913 the school had sixty-five students. See *UI*, September 12, 1913; APP, BA 1708, "La Table d'hôte des émigrés," "Pièces communes."

58. APP, BA1708, "Bureau russe du travail"; and report, October 14, 1912, BA1324, "Affaires concernant la Russie," APP.
59. Novochelski to AIU, January 23, 1888, France D51: Emigration—Divers, AIU Archives.
60. ACIP, B60, B65.
61. Doris Ben-Simon Donath used consistorial burial statistics for tracking immigrants (*Social-démographie des juifs*). See also Michael Weisser's book on Jewish *landsmanshaftn* in the United States, *A Brotherhood of Memory* (New York: Basic Books, 1985).
62. See, for example, the by-laws of the Société religieuse de secours mutuels des tailleurs russes "L'Amitié Fraternelle" dite "Ahavath Reim," ACIP, B60, B65; cf. Zosa Szajkowski, "Dos yidishe gezelshaftlekhe lebn in Pariz tsum yor 1939," *Yidn in Frankraykh*, ed. E. Tcherikower, 2 vols. (New York: YIVO, 1942), 2:226–27; Green, *Pletzl of Paris*, ch. 6.
63. Asile, *Rapports des exercices* (1905–20); AIU Archives, France IH1, File "Asile de jour israélite;" ACIP, B78, "Associations cultuelles."
64. By comparison, the Comité de bienfaisance, which did not depend on its membership for revenue, derived 45 percent of its income from collections, donations, and lotteries. The rest came mostly from investments and the sale of coupons to the poor (for bread, coal, and so on). E.g., Comité de bienfaisance, *Assemblée générale* (1904–5), 12.
65. As had Léon Novochelski, for his earlier Société de bienfaisance, although with poorer results: "The Alliance, which did so much for the Russians at the time of the emigration, will it today let those who have come to Paris die of hunger?" (Novochelski to AIU, January 23, 1888, France D51: Emigration—Divers, AIU Archives). The Alliance gave 250 francs to the society in February but in response to a similar request in October answered that it could no longer help.
66. Asile, *Rapport de l'exercice* (1905–6), 13–14, emphasis added.
67. Cf. above, note 51, the *Archives Israélites*'s reference to this Pesach precept—with indignation—at the time of the matzoh distribution fraud.
68. Asile, *Rapport de l'exercice* (1905–6), 13–14.
69. Ibid., 15.
70. And even then, not everywhere wholeheartedly. See, e.g., Baron, *Jewish Community*, 2:7–9, on the Frankfurt community's poor reception of the Chmielnicki refugees.
71. As the oft-quoted Comte Stanislas de Clermont-Tonnerre put it: "The Jew, as a nation, must be refused everything; the Jews, as individuals, may be granted everything; they must constitute neither a political body nor a corporate order within the state; it is as individuals that they may be citizens" (*Opinion*, in *La Révolution française et les juifs*, vol. 7 [Paris: EDHIS, 1968]).
72. André Spire, *Souvenirs à bâtons rompus* (Paris: Albin Michel, 1962), 38.
73. *AI*, June 2, 1887; see also *AI*, February 9, 1882, and January 31, 1884; "aucune solidarité ne tient devant la concurrence et l'intérêt," *AI*, October 31, 1901.
74. *AI*, November 8, 1894.
75. Baron, *Jewish Community*, 2:352–63; Dubnow, *History of the Jews*, 1:103–13, 188–98, 274–78, 366–71, 2:59–62; see also Michael Stanislawski, *Tsar Nicholas I and*

the Jews (Philadelphia: Jewish Publication Society, 1983); Jonathan Fraenkel, *Prophecy and Politics: Socialism, Nationalism and the Russian Jews, 1862–1917* (Cambridge, Eng.: Cambridge University Press, 1981).

76. Asile, *Rapport de l'exercice* (1905–6), 21.

77. *AI*, September 24, 1903.

78. Walzer, *Spheres of Justice*. Walzer is refuting John Rawls's more abstract notion of justice.

Michael B. Katz

8. The History of an Impudent Poor Woman in New York City from 1918 to 1923

IN 1916 the Philadelphia Society for the Organization of Charity published a poster to announce an exhibition of its work. On the poster, a woman dressed in black, her face covered with a veil, grasps the hand of a young mother in a striped shawl whose infant dozes at her feet. The veiled woman, a Society Visitor, has reached out to take the hand of the soft, meek young mother who has offered her own hand without resistance but also without force. The Society Visitor stands very slightly higher than the woman in the shawl, who looks downward, away from her benefactor. Although the women are holding each other's hands, their faces point in different directions. It is their hands, not their eyes, that meet.[1]

Charity joined women from different social classes in a drama of sacrifice and gratitude that reinforced the distance between them even as it drew them together. Charity was personal, a living relationship, contingent and voluntary, never cold, casual, or automatic. Above all, charity was private. Even as the state expanded, late nineteenth- and early twentieth-century charities fought to sharpen the line between themselves and public agencies. Afraid, they said, of the cold impersonality and corruption inherent in the public sphere, representatives of private philanthropy argued that only voluntarism could prevent charity from crossing the line between gift and entitlement. When help came from public sources, when relief was easily accessible, poor people began to claim a right to assistance; they exchanged deference for assertiveness; and they lost their will to work. Demoralization and permanent dependence followed, and distant, sullen relations between classes began to reinforce the social walls that arose amid the altered ecology of industrial cities.[2]

Despite the New Deal, the entrance of the federal government into the welfare arena, and the expansion of welfare rolls in the 1960s, these themes have not died. Public outrage is a predictable response to the assertive behavior of the poor who occupy welfare offices or demonstrate for increased benefits. The hostility to unmarried women with children on Aid to Families with Dependent Children and the fear that General Assistance aids the able-bodied point to a continued attempt to discriminate between the worthy and the unworthy poor. And the Reagan administration's expectation that private agencies can pick up the slack from federal cutbacks highlights the continued faith in voluntarism.

As it happens, these themes reflect recurrent myths more than contemporary realities. Private welfare never was adequate to the needs of dependent people in American cities, and public relief has a much older history than most people realize. Voluntarism exacted a high price for the pittance it grudgingly granted the very poor. It served as much to estrange classes as to cement them. Indeed, only the actions of the state began to make survival a human right, not a gift or a reward for good behavior.

One problem with understanding how relief or welfare functioned in the past, especially in the nineteenth and early twentieth centuries, lies in the sources. For the most part, we have the reports of agencies on their own work, counterbalanced to some extent by the acerbic observations of their enemies. The difficulty with these sources goes beyond lack of balance. Rather, it is the image they create of relief or welfare as a series of parallel vectors: urban Protestant philanthropy, child saving, poorhouses, outdoor relief, religious and ethnic societies, mothers' pensions, and so on. In truth, all these blended together into a network not very usefully described as either public or private.[3]

Seen from the vantage point of somebody who needed help, the situation appeared quite different. The sources of relief were landmarks on a complex topographical map that poor people had to learn to read in order to survive. The rules for the journey were as important as the locations of aid. For poor people had to enter and negotiate a complex series of relations with representatives of another class as they swallowed their pride and made their way through the terrain with their eyes cast downward, a word of gratitude always at the ready. Only by negotiating that terrain with them is it possible to see how relief and welfare really worked and how desperately poor people managed to survive. In the process, we will find the hollow core in the recurrent rhetorical myths that disfigure American discourse about poverty and welfare.

In most cities, by the late nineteenth century Charity Organization Societies (COS), started in England in the 1860s and introduced to America in Buffalo, New York, in 1878, attempted to rationalize charity by distinguishing between the worthy and unworthy poor, recommending appropriate courses of philanthropy to other agencies, and supervising the relief given to individual families. Their method was friendly visiting. They called on the poor in their homes; investigated their backgrounds; checked their stories with relatives, friends, neighbors, employers, landlords, and other agencies; and tried to offer constructive advice, even, when absolutely necessary, material help in the form of groceries, medicine, fuel, rent, and clothing. Charity Organization Societies compiled elaborate case histories for every client family: a narrative account of each contact by friendly visitors, reports from people questioned about the family, records of assistance given, and all correspondence and documentation. Where these files exist, and almost all have been destroyed, they offer unparalleled insight into the relations between families and welfare and into the experience of poverty in late nineteenth- and early twentieth-century America.[4]

This essay is the story of one family visited in New York City between 1918 and 1923.[5] By that time, serious challenges had begun to erode the influence of Charity Organization Societies. A new generation of reformers and charity workers (some, to be fair, from within their own ranks) had begun to challenge the societies' assumptions about individual responsibility for poverty and the dangers of public assistance, while through programs for children and, especially mothers' pensions, the state tentatively had begun to assert a new role that would be greatly expanded with the New Deal.[6]

In the years from World War I through the 1920s, charity and welfare, voluntarism and professionalism, gifts and entitlements, private and public defined the poles tugging at policy and practice. Neither, of course, ever won a complete victory, and the tensions between them were played out in the histories of individual people who needed help. This tension is what the story of the Kennedy family, told here, is partly about. It is also about the relations between women from different classes and the problem of authority in the practice of philanthropy. In the end, the story exposes the contradiction at the heart of scientific charity, the theoretical basis of the Charity Organization Society, and it offers at least two cheers for the state.[7]

The Kennedy Family: A History

On the night of December 30, 1917, Thomas Kennedy, age thirty-eight, went to load baggage at Grand Central Terminal. Told there was no baggage to unload because the trains were late, he went to the docks to look for work. At 3 A.M. he was found at the foot of an embankment, "half frozen lying up against the door of a restaurant, one leg broken in two places, some bones in his back broken, his eye badly hurt, and his face cut." He was taken to Volunteer Hospital, on Beekman and Water streets. No one ever knew with certainty what had happened to him except that he had not been drinking. His wife thought he had fallen into an unprotected excavation between South and 39th Street ferries.[8]

His wife, Delia (ten years younger than her husband), "had disobeyed her mother to come" to America from County Mayo, Ireland, in 1908, at the age of eighteen, and "left behind four brothers and two sisters." Her mother had died not long afterward, and one brother had come to the United States, where he settled in Virginia, and ran a saloon until prohibition. Delia visited him from time to time until she married. After she arrived in America, Delia supported herself through "housework, cooking, and laundry in private homes." At one point she lived for fifteen months in the home of a Mrs. Sicher, 16 East 73rd Street, a well-to-do woman with several servants, who gave her clothes and $38 a month.

Delia and Thomas Kennedy were married on October 3, 1915, in St. Boniface Church by Father Casey, also from County Mayo, of whom Delia was very fond. Their son Thomas was born nearly a year later, on September 15, 1916. At the time of Thomas, Sr.'s accident, Delia was four months pregnant. When Thomas had his accident, the Kennedys had been living for three months in four rooms on the second floor of 309 East 46th Street, which they rented for $15 a month. Before that they had lived for three months at 238 East 46th but had been evicted because Delia had taken another family in the building to court over the location of a clothesline. Even though the court had sided with Delia, the housekeeper thought she was a troublemaker and told the family to move. There "was no reason," said the housekeeper, "'why Mrs. Kennedy should not have put her line where it would not interfere with the neighbors.' She advised Mrs. K. not to take the matter into Court but Mrs. Kennedy was set on proving no one could get ahead of her." The housekeeper had been offended, too, by the way Mrs. Kennedy treated her husband. She made him "do things that a man ought not to do. For instance, when he came home tired she made him go down in the basement to drop wood, and made him fetch and carry for her; was always at him to take the baby carriage up and down for her, etc."

The Kennedys had met trouble at their previous address, 739 2nd Avenue, as well. The housekeeper there remembered Delia well. "Her first comment was, Mrs. Kennedy was a very impudent woman." Delia had accused the Italian janitress "of letting her children steal the pillows of her baby carriage. The janitress raised a stool to strike Mrs. K. when some neighbors intervened. Mrs. K. had the janitress summoned to Court." The janitress served three days and was fined $15.

When their baby was born, the Kennedys had been living on the fourth floor of 316 East 49th Street, but the stairs there had proved difficult, which is why the family had moved. There the housekeeper defended the Kennedys. They were quiet people. Delia was "not a strong woman," and Thomas was "not a drinking man." They had paid their rent regularly. Nonetheless, the COS Visitor who interviewed the housekeeper thought there was more to the story. The housekeeper was "not very communicative" and said she "wouldn't tell anything to injure another person."

Thomas Kennedy, born in County Longford, Ireland, had come to America in 1904 and lived since then in New York City. One of his sisters lived on 138th Street; she had two children but had to work because her husband was a drunk who did not support her. Thomas and this sister had quarreled and, as a consequence, saw little of each other. Another sister, married to a stableman, also lived in New York City. Thomas had worked at the Grand Central baggage depot for several years. He was, according to his supervisor, Mr. Stack ("an unusually nice man"), a "nice fellow," who had "gotten into bad repute on 1 or 2 occasions." By that, Mr. Stack meant he had been drinking too much. Stack told him he would have to stop, and he did, but he started again around the time his son was born. Stack fired him for his drinking, and Thomas went to work for American Express. After a while, he returned and asked to be taken on again. Stack told him he would have to take night work, "which at first he didn't want," for "at least 6 months to punish him and make him understand he meant business." Thomas took the work and was "perfectly straight" during the months before his accident.

Delia did not know that Thomas once had contracted syphilis, and no one ever told her. After the birth of Thomas, however, when she developed breast abscesses, the hospital took a Wasserman test, which proved negative. Nonetheless, the abscesses were serious, and she had to return to Bellevue Hospital, where she stayed for four months and had five operations on her breasts. (It was about this time that her husband started drinking again.) Although he had not infected his wife, his history of syphilis complicated Thomas's treatment after his accident. It was "not possible to give him any medication by injection as whenever an injection is made a sore results." Able to take only liquid food, he slipped in and out of consciousness, his condition worsened, and on February 17, 1918, Thomas Kennedy died.[9]

When Thomas first had been hurt, the family had a few days' supply of coal on hand. St. Boniface Church sent its visitor, Mr. McGuinness, who gave them $2 for groceries. Neighbors brought up food and asked Delia to eat with them. The Milk Station gave her two quarts of milk a day for her baby. A "friend" brought her $1, which she used for carfare to the hospital, and another neighbor in her building also gave her carfare. A woman she had met only in the park came to her rooms with $1 for the insurance premium. When the rental agent came for the rent, which he did not expect to collect, he served Mrs. Kennedy with an eviction notice. But one of her husband's workmates, who was visiting to find out how the family was managing, went back to work to take up a collection. He went first to Mr. Stack, who told him "it would not do for one of the officials to start it" and made his contribution later. In all, Thomas's workmates contributed between $20 and $40, which was enough to pay the family's rent for the next month at least.

On January 29, the Baby Health Station (a division of the New York Department of Health) asked the Charity Organization Society to investigate the condition of the family. The COS Visitor went first to the family's home, where she interviewed Delia, and from there began a circuit of former landlords, employers, hospitals, charities, and relatives. She even had the COS investigation bureau check to see if the Kennedys had been legally married. Two days later, Delia appeared at the COS District Office to say she wanted "no assistance from the COS because she did not understand that one had to 'go' through such a great deal of red tape." She asserted that "she was not ashamed of anything in her life, but she did not think in order to receive a little help one had to have one's relatives and references looked up."[10]

Undeterred, the COS Visitor continued her rounds. At St. Boniface, Mr. McGuinness said that he would continue to send $2 a week for groceries and, as well, one hundred pounds of coal. When the COS Visitor told him that Thomas probably would not recover, McGuinness suggested that Delia and her baby move to a cheaper place. Maybe, he said, she could find someone to share an apartment. Given the demands on the parish, he did not know if he could help. Certainly $15 each month was out of the question.

On February 2 the Visitor had an order of groceries sent to the Kennedys, and on February 4 she went back to visit. She found Delia on her way out. Her cousin, a motorman, had given her money for rent, but she refused to give the Visitor his name or address. She was in a hurry. Her husband, she said, was dying. The Visitor said the District Office would pay for milk and asked why she had not been to the Milk Station (part of the Baby Health Station) to collect it. Delia, who was "excited and overwrought and . . . extremely rude," said she had had "a dispute" with the nurse there, who had tried to make her pay for one of the two bottles of milk.

The Visitor went to the Milk Station to try to sort out the dispute. There, a Mrs. Olds (probably one of the social workers attached to the Milk Station) confirmed that Delia had become "higly incensed" when asked to pay for one quart. She was "very disagreeable, swore at Mrs. Olds," and told her she did not believe her reasons for asking for payment. She did, however, pay for one of the two quarts that she took away. To make matters worse, Mrs. Olds had asked Delia what she thought about "moving into cheaper rooms." Delia responded that "she did not have to move at the bidding of Mrs. Olds or Visitor from D[istrict]. O[ffice]. as the social service nurse at the hospital was paying her rent." When questioned about the new coat she was wearing, Delia said it was a gift from her sister-in-law, with whom she now was on speaking terms. Mrs. Olds "was quite disgusted" and thought Delia "ought not have any more help until she showed a different spirit." On the same day, the COS agreed to cut off Delia's free milk. The nurse at the Milk Station, Miss Maher, "was most apologetic" to the COS "for referring" the family. She felt that Delia was "most insulting" and that "nothing ought to be done for her." In fact, Delia had been giving conflicting stories to nurses, Visitors, and social workers, and Miss Maher thought this a "good case to drop."

When the Visitor telephoned the Volunteer Hospital, she found that it had been helping the family. Three times the hospital social worker had given Mrs. Kennedy $5 for groceries and had paid a month's rent. The social worker, naturally, was "surprised" to learn that the church also had been paying for groceries and that the Milk Station had been giving the family milk. She, too, complained about Delia's behavior. She was "very rude when offered the grocery order. She did not like help in that way, preferring to have the money given to her." The social worker also told the COS that Delia had engaged a lawyer to sue the construction company and the city for negligence in her husband's death. The lawyer, whom the COS tracked down with some trouble, thought the case would be difficult because there were no witnesses.

By March, Delia, now a widow, was a candidate for a widow's pension from the Board of Child Welfare, which entered the case for the first time. Its initial act was to visit one of Thomas's sisters, who was in no "position to help," although she sympathized with Delia, with whom she was on friendly terms. Nonetheless, she realized "that strangers have had difficulty in getting along" with her "because she has a high strung spirit." But she meant "well, is a good mother, and was an excellent wife." Nor could Thomas's other sister help financially. She had three school-age children and had to work herself. These relatives could not "take her into their home as it would surely make family trouble if she were a permanent guest." Unless some help arrived soon, Delia would have to "commit her child." The board's visitor, Miss DeKoster, asked the COS to help the family until the pension started.[11]

Her husband's death and her accumulating financial difficulty chastened Delia, at least temporarily. On March 11 she appeared at the COS District Office "dressed in a very good looking black coat and a black sailor hat heavily draped with a mourning veil." She "appeared very docile and gentle in comparison with her former attitude" toward the COS. She had just received an eviction notice and had to appear in court on Friday to ask for an extension. She wanted help and advice. The COS advised her to take cheaper rooms in the Bronx near her relatives and, in the meantime, to go to court to request an extension on her rent. The COS decided to pay to move her and to give her a month's rent, and the court gave her a brief extension to find another place to live.

After her appearance in court, the COS Visitor called on Delia and told her to look for rooms in the Bronx and not to pay more than $12 a month. Although she now claimed to be anxious to leave her current rooms, Delia said she would not be able to find three satisfactory rooms for $12. Finally, Delia agreed to look and to report back by 9 A.M. the following day. Although the Visitor found her current apartment "dirty and disorderly" (which was not characteristic of Delia's housekeeping, according to other reports), the "baby was sweet and clean." Despite a cold, it seemed "very well." Delia was very proud of young Thomas, who, she said, looked like his father, "a fine looking man," and she "brought out a photo" of her late husband to show the Visitor.

The next day the COS paid a grocery bill for the family for $1.68. When

Delia appeared at the District Office on Saturday, she reported that she had been unable to find three rooms for $12. While she was in the office, the Visitor telephoned the Bronx district and learned of a suitable place. Delia refused to look at it. She was, she said, "going home" and "would make no further effort to do as Society requested." Nonetheless, she "was advised to go and look at the room and report her decision to D.O. on Monday morning, March 18th at 9 o'clock." The COS Visitor telephoned Miss DeKoster at the Board of Child Welfare, who promised to watch conditions in the family and "see what plan" Delia made. Delia did not go to look at the rooms. Later, she claimed the reason for her rudeness and her refusal was fatigue. At the time she was several months pregnant.

Apparently, once again her neighbors took up a collection, and Delia could pay her rent for one more month. As it seemed likely that her pension would start soon, the Milk Station reversed its position and urged that milk be given her until the allowance started. Even with the allowance, which was $13 a month, Miss DeKoster pointed out that Delia still would not have enough money to live. Pregnant and not too well, she was not strong enough to work to supplement it. The church should be asked to help, and the Save-a-Home Fund had become interested. The situation would improve when the baby was born because Delia's pension would increase to $26 each month. In the meantime, the COS paid another grocery bill for $1.81.

When Delia's pension began on April 16, 1918, the COS called the Milk Station at once and told it to stop the free milk, and Delia's COS file was marked closed. So it remained for almost exactly two years, during which time she apparently managed by making occasional forays to private sources and, when she was strong enough, by working to supplement her pension. In April 1920, she asked the nurse in charge of social service at the Sichers' (her old employer) company for help, and the nurse requested a report on the family from the COS. In August 1920, the Association for Improving the Condition of the Poor (AICP) telephoned for a report because the case had been referred to it. The youngest child, Rita, was sick in Bellevue Dispensary and Delia could not work. The Board of Child Welfare had asked the AICP to supplement her pension until September first, when they could increase it themselves. In the same month, the Salvation Army also asked for information about the family.

Delia and her children apparently survived the crisis because nothing was heard of them for another two years. In April 1922, the Social Service Department of St. Bartholomew's Protestant Episcopal Church asked the

COS for information on the family. Its social worker wanted to "place the children and send the mother away temporarily." Somehow, Delia once again avoided disaster and managed to keep her children. A year and a half later, in August 1923, the mother of a woman for whom she had worked and who had given her milk asked the COS to investigate Delia. She suspected that Delia really did not need help.

So one more time a COS Visitor trudged off to visit Delia, who still was living at 309 East 46th Street, her address when her husband had died five years earlier. Now, however, Delia and her two children lived in two rooms. The building was old but "in fairly good repair." The kitchen, which also served "as living room," had "outside windows." The bedroom was "lighted by a side window" and had "a large door into the living room. Both rooms were clean, comfortably furnished and homelike." Delia now was "quite cordial" and claimed to be "managing very well at present and needed no assistance from COS." The children, Thomas and Rita, were "rather attractive children, but neither is particularly robust. They were both well dressed." Delia claimed that Rita always had been well but that Thomas, several pounds underweight, was under a doctor's care at Bellevue Dispensary.

She still received a pension of $26 a month from the Board of Child Welfare, which she supplemented by office cleaning in the early morning at 342 Madison Avenue. She earned $10 a week. She hoped the free milk from her former employer would continue because she had a $60 bill from a private dentist. Playing out an old script one more time, the COS Visitor suggested that Delia have her work done at a free clinic at the College of Dental and Oral Surgery. But Delia said she had been to a clinic once and found it unsatisfactory. She would not go back. "She thanked the Visitor for her interest but seemed quite able and anxious to make her own plans." There are no more entries in her file.

Themes in the History of the Kennedy Family

Many of the great themes in the relations between families and welfare echo through the Kennedys' experience. Although a number of them should be noted, the Kennedy story is an especially vivid illustration of the problem of authority in philanthropy and the contradictions at the heart of scientific charity.

First, it is important to stress that, like so many other cases, the Kennedys' history shows how ordinary working-class families slipped into dependence. In their case the precipitating cause was an accident. Thomas Kennedy was a hardworking, steady man, whose wages barely kept his family above destitution. As long as he worked, they managed to eat and pay the rent, but they were unable to save anything for emergencies. When he had an accident and died, his widow and child were left with no money and no source of income. Accidents like the one that Thomas met, moreover, were not freak instances in working-class experience, rare examples of very bad luck. Instead, they happened often because they were rooted in the conditions of work and life. In Thomas Kennedy's case these conditions were irregular night work and the lack of ordinances forcing cities and construction companies to erect adequate protection around their excavations. Dependence of the sort experienced by the Kennedys, in short, was part of the structure of working-class life.

At least as important as accident was sickness. In the Kennedys' experience, it was not the sickness of a husband and father that brought the family to destitution but the illness and weakness of Delia Kennedy when she became the head of her family. She was not strong enough to work until a year or two after her husband died. Even then, the periodic illnesses of her children forced her into temporary dependence when she had to stay home from work to care for them, and her own need for dental work forced her to seek charity as well.

Their recurrent need for assistance was one important factor that kept the Kennedys within one small section of New York City. Their experience was more like the poor trapped in East London, described by Gareth Stedman Jones, than that of the men in motion of American social history. They had moved frequently but within the same neighborhood. One reason, certainly, was their proximity to Grand Central Station, where Thomas Kennedy worked; another was the network of friends, neighbors, and sources of potential help that they constructed over time. Indeed, Delia Kennedy's refusal to leave midtown Manhattan for the Bronx, even though her husband's sisters lived there, underlined the importance to her of her neighborhood.[12]

Neighbors, friends, and workmates played an extraordinarily important part in the Kennedys' story. When Thomas Kennedy was hurt, neighbors and friends immediately offered not only sympathy but food, carfare, and insurance money. None of those who helped the Kennedys, it is important to remember, themselves had very much to spare. When the Kennedys were about to be evicted for the first time, Thomas's workmates took up a collection to pay the rent. Some months later, when Delia Kennedy, a widow with no money, was about to be moved to the Bronx by the Charity Organization Society, again neighbors raised rent money for her. She seems to have asked directly for very little of this help. When neighbors, even an acquaintance she made in the park, or her husband's workmates heard of her problems, they helped spontaneously.

The Kennedys received less help from their relatives, who were themselves very poor. Relations with Thomas's two sisters were strained. Thomas had quarreled with one, and the families appeared to have little to do with each other until his accident, when they drew closer, and one sister gave clothes to Delia Kennedy. Nonetheless, Thomas's sisters praised his wife and clearly recognized that, had they the resources, the responsibility to aid the family would have been theirs. A cousin, whose identity eluded the Charity Organization Society's investigations, does appear to have helped the family with rent on at least one occasion. Whether he provided assistance more often—a source of aid kept secret by Delia Kennedy—remains unknown.

Like most COS case histories, the Kennedys' story is about the relations between women as much as about those between neighbors and kin. Most COS clients and most Visitors were women. As in few other places, the case histories show the relations between women from different social classes in action. These, inevitably, were full of tension, pulled by the poles of class and gender. Visitors were missionaries from the bourgeoisie, intruders into the world of the poor, investigators and judges, under orders to ascertain character, ferret out fraud, and separate the worthy from the unworthy applicants. By definition, their relations with their clients were asymmetrical; power lay clearly on one side. At the same time, as women, Visitors confronted other women suffering from sickness and destitution, anxious about their children, struggling to keep their families alive and together. Their clients suffered because they were women: unable to find work at decent wages; dependent on husbands who sometimes drank or disappeared, suffered accidents, could not find work, or died; and often sick themselves from childbirth, undernourishment, and fatigue. How did the Visitors respond? Were they pulled more strongly by the poles of class, which gave official definition to their role, or by those of gender? With the Visitors who dealt with Delia Kennedy, it seems, the pull of role and class was strongest. The case records are remarkable for the lack of sympathy in language or tone. Not a drop of sentiment squeezes through the dry narration and frequent condemnation. There is no indication of any empathy between the Visitors and Delia, no appreciation of why she might rather not move to the Bronx, no clue that her illness, the death of her husband, or her poverty touched Visitors enough to override her impudent and assertive manner.[13]

Thomas and Delia Kennedy in no way brought their dependence on themselves. Thomas appears to have been a devoted family man, willing to work hard, able to control his drinking. He cracked only when the baby was born and his wife was hospitalized for months with breast abscesses. The knowledge of his own history of syphilis, which he had kept from his wife, must have been a source of great anxiety and guilt. But he should not be blamed for his disease itself. For, with low wages, undoubtedly trying to save enough to start his own family, not married until he was thirty-six, most of his sexual contact probably was with prostitutes.

Delia Kennedy was tough, fiery, proud, and full of argument. At times she probably was unreasonable. Certainly, she did not always tell the whole truth. But who can blame her for withholding information about some of the assistance given her from the prying questions of the COS Visitor? Fiercely independent, she was determined to have her due, and she knew how to use the courts to get it. (Indeed, her story points to the use of the courts by working-class people to settle disputes between neighbors and kin.) A good mother and housekeeper, with a sense of style (reflected in the COS Visitor's comments on her clothes), Delia did not have an ounce of deference. She also refused to allow the conventional sexual division of labor to trap her completely, as a former landlady's critical comment on her treatment of her husband illustrates. Nonetheless, Delia clearly cared deeply for her husband and admired him.[14]

The great issues in her story concern authority and deference. Consider the assumptions implicit in the decision of medical authorities and the COS not to tell Delia that Thomas once had contracted syphilis. They clearly believed they had the capacity and authority to decide what was best for her. Their actions reflected the belief that patients or clients were like children, incapable of making correct decisions or dealing with unpleasant information. The same assumptions underlay the decision of the COS that Delia should move to the Bronx, whether she wanted to or not.

The COS was willing to work hard to assist families with serious problems. But its price was gratitude and deference. As Gareth Stedman Jones has written, charity was a gift, and gifts have peculiar qualities. First, they are voluntary sacrifices; second, they almost always are "symbols of prestige." To receive a gift without payment is "to become a client and subservient." Third, gifts are "a method of social control. To give, for whatever motives, generally imposes an obligation upon the receiver. In order to receive, one must behave in an acceptable manner, if only by expressing gratitude and humility." Fourth, "a gift is a relationship between persons." When it is depersonalized, "a gift loses its defining features." This is what had happened in British and American cities by the latter part of the nineteenth century. In New York as well as in London, Charity Organization Societies were a response to what Stedman Jones has called the "deformation of the gift":

> The gift as sacrifice no longer implied the gift that would lead the poor in the path of virtue. The separation of classes had produced the deformation of the gift. The original integrity of the gift relationship had been replaced by a promiscuous compound of indiscriminate alms giving and a careless Poor Law relief. In either case, the relationship between persons had disappeared, and with it the elements of prestige, subordination, and obligation.[15]

When Delia asserted her entitlement to aid, rejected the advice of COS agents and public social workers, and became angry instead of deferential, she violated the contract implicit in both private and public philanthropy. She refused to understand that charity was supposed to reinforce asymmetrical social relations between classes. Either charity was a strategy of class control, or it was a menace. The deference of clients was the sign that it worked.

Not all gifts bound individuals together with sacrifice and gratitude. For Delia received many gifts from her peers. Friends, neighbors, and her late husband's workmates stretched their thin resources to give her money for rent, food, and insurance. Their reasons, surely, had nothing to do with deference or subordination. Indeed, their generosity points to the variation in the meaning of gifts by class. Gifts exchanged within classes cannot be understood in the same way as those between them. To explain gifts within the working class, one need not retreat to a romantic altruism that stretches human nature. It is more likely that assisting one's peers in times of trouble was a pervasive, accepted obligation, carried out with little reflection or moralizing. Even so, it was a custom that rested on an expectation of reciprocity, if not from the recipient then from someone else. Working-class life was full of accidents, tragedies, and periods of hardship. Virtually everyone could expect to need help sometime. In these circumstances, gifts to needy friends and neighbors were a kind of insurance, part of a circulating fund on which working-class families could expect to draw when their turn arrived. As such, the gift relation within the working class was un-mediated by moralism or expectations of gratitude. Instead, it carried with it only the expectation of reciprocity, though not necessarily from the recipient. Small gifts were a form of exchange within working-class net-works, an adaptive response to the inadequacy of the state, the limitations of charity, and the structure of working-class life.[16]

There are two remarkable aspects to this emphasis on deference in Delia's history. One was its diffusion beyond the boundaries of private charity. The reaction of public social workers in the Milk Station clearly points to the absence of any sharp line separating their expectations from those of the COS agents. The second is the persistence of deference as a strategy of social control long after it made any sense. Deference might have been an appropriate strategy for a town or village, but its assumption of the possibility of intimate, personal contacts—of the widespread power of individual influence and example—was ludicrous in industrial cities. The ecology of residence, the size of workplaces, the emerging politics of class, the very size of cities, made deference a hopeless strategy of control, even when it was redeployed with such vigor in the 1870s.

Based as it was on close personal contacts between classes and the reestablishment of deferential social relations, scientific charity was not, as its sponsors argued, a modern and forward-looking movement. To the contrary, it was a futile attempt to recreate an evanescent and illusory past. Nonetheless, it had its uses as a way of legitimizing cutbacks in expenses for relief (and they happened almost everywhere between the 1870s and the 1890s), assuaging guilt about poverty and fears of social disorder, and avoiding a frontal confrontation with the structural roots of dependence. These serviceable qualities sustained scientific charity for decades, rein-forced its transmutation into casework (which, after all, retains much the same model of social relations, even when the agent holds a master of social work degree and is literate in Freud), and reappeared to undergird the 1980s war on welfare whose assumptions were about as realistic as its nineteenth-century predecessor.[17]

Charity Organization Societies sought to break the dependence of their clients on relief. Through counseling and judicious aid, they hoped to restore them to independence. For this reason, they stressed the superiority of private over public relief. Public relief promoted false notions of entitle-ment, and entitlements bred permanent dependence; they broke class relations; they led ultimately to assertiveness and militancy in the deference of spurious rights. By contrast, private relief was a gift, the very opposite of entitlement, earned through appropriate behavior and gratitude.

Here was the great contradiction at the core of scientific charity. Its ostensible goal was personal independence, but it sought deference and gratitude. The price of continued COS support was docility. The ideal client took COS advice without hesitation and said thank you. The price of support, in other words, was continued and even intensified dependence. In fact, independence, the putative goal, was punished.

This is what the relation of Delia Kennedy to the COS shows so clearly. Delia was in every way, except one, a worthy case. She was a poor widow with a child, reduced to dependence through no fault of her own, a good mother who usually kept her house clean and did not drink. She certainly deserved help. But she refused to show gratitude; she had no deference. She fought with her neighbors, objected to the COS investigation of her character, had a clear sense of what help she should receive, and asserted her rights loudly. Only once, when she was truly desperate, did she hold her temper and show the COS the docility it sought. As a consequence, the COS and the other charities that dealt with Delia disliked her intensely. Her lack of gratitude and her assertiveness angered them, and, as punishment, they cut off her baby's free milk.

Delia survived because she knew how to play the network of private and public sources of aid that spread throughout New York City. There were many potential sources of small amounts of aid: neighbors, kin, former employers, the Catholic church (which helped her very much), and both public and private agencies. Welfare was a loosely coordinated network that is not usefully described as either public or private. Agencies of both sorts and even individuals (such as the mother of Delia's former employer, who asked the COS to investigate to see if she was worthy of the free milk supplied by her daughter) tried to cooperate with and reinforce each other. Their cooperation and coordination were imperfect. Despite the efforts of the COS, and later Social Service Exchanges, to rationalize and systematize relief activity, some sources always slipped through the net, and it remained possible for clever people, like Delia Kennedy, to conceal some of her sources of assistance.[18]

In New York City, after 1916 the new element in welfare was the mothers' pension, administered by a Board of Child Welfare independent of the city's other relief apparatus. Although pensions were given only after an investigation proved the applicant worthy, although they were small, they were of extraordinary importance. They were one of the first halting steps taken by the state toward an entitlement, a recognition that some classes of people deserved regular aid by virtue of their condition. They also made it possible for some families to survive without the intrusive charity of the COS or similar agencies. For the pensions did not prohibit recipients from working. To the contrary, authorities assumed that women would supplement them. They were an incentive to work and gain independence. With two children and a $10 a week job, Delia Kennedy managed an income of over $60 a month, not affluence, not even comfort, but independence. Pensions, therefore, undercut the equation between charity and deference; they superseded the definition of relief as a gift. They fostered the idea of entitlement. As such, they completely undercut the principles of scientific charity. They threatened to make obsolete, even offensive, the COS and its ideal of a hierarchical social order bound together through deference. That is undoubtedly why the COS opposed mothers' pensions so bitterly. Inadequate as they were, they were the advance troops of an army that could transform charity into welfare.

For Delia Kennedy, it was her pension, not the advice and charity of the COS, that enabled her to land on her feet and establish a modest independence. With her job cleaning offices, she could cope with temporary emergencies by going to former employers or neighbors for occasional help. She could thank the COS Visitor for her interest and show her the door. In spite of, not because of, the COS, her story has, if not a happy, at least a modestly satisfactory ending.

Notes

1. The poster is reproduced on the cover of my book *Poverty and Policy in American History* (New York: Academic Press, 1983).
2. For statements of the theory of scientific charity and charity organization, see Josephine Shaw Lowell, *Public Relief and Private Charity* (New York: Putnam, 1884), and S. Humphreys Gurteen, *A Handbook of Charity Organization* (Buffalo, N.Y.: privately published, 1882).
3. As an example of criticism of organized charity, see Konrad Bercovici, *Crimes of Charity* (New York: Knopf, 1917). Books that deal with only one aspect of the question of dependence are Paul Boyer, *Urban Masses and Moral Order in America, 1820–1940* (Cambridge, Mass.: Harvard University Press, 1978); Gerald Grob, *Mental Institutions in America: Social Policy to 1875* (New York: Free Press, 1973); David J. Rothman, *The Discovery of the Asylum: Social Order and Disorder in the New Republic* (Boston: Little, Brown, 1971); and Roy Lubove, *The*

Struggle for Social Security, 1900–1935 (Cambridge, Mass.: Harvard University Press, 1968).

4. By the late nineteenth and early twentieth centuries, the larger Charity Organization Societies did much more than investigate and sometimes relieve needy people. The larger ones created labor exchanges, did research, supported various progressive reforms, published monographs, participated in social work education, and, sometimes, took an active role in local politics. Their activities were divided into different departments, however, which, in the case of New York, were almost separate organizations. The apparatus of relief and investigation appears to have been remarkably resilient to newer trends in what, by the second decade of the twentieth century, had come to be thought of as social work. The best source for the history of charity organization is Frank Dekker Watson, *The Charity Organization Movement in the United States: A Study in American Philanthropy* (New York: Macmillan, 1922).

5. It is difficult to find out who visited the family whose story is told here. Each set of notes on a visit or other contact is initialed, but this does not help very much because the Charity Organization Society did not list its entire staff. In 1917 the budget summary points out that sixty-five people worked in the District Office, but the listing of COS staff in the annual report includes only the district secretaries. (Until 1909, the district secretaries were called district agents. The change of term signified an expanded role because in the same year their decision-making power over individual cases, which had been circumscribed by their district committees, was expanded.) This leaves most of the paid staff unaccounted for. Thus it is possible that the family was visited by a paid agent. The COS had 693 volunteer visitors in 1918. Interestingly, their names are all listed. The initials on the record do not match those of any visitor. Nonetheless, this is not evidence that none of them was in charge of the case. The reason is that married visitors (and all visitors were women) were listed in the report by their husbands' names. They might well have used their own first names, however, in initialing the notes of their visits. In the text I have chosen to call the people who visited the family Visitors rather than agents. Whether or not they were paid employees, "visitor" is the designation they used when they described themselves. It is possible that the reason the COS did not list its complete staff is that it wanted to preserve its image as a volunteer organization ([New York] Charity Organization Society, *Annual Report*, Thirty-Fifth Year, October 1, 1916, to September 30, 1917, *Charity Organization Bulletin* 222 [April 3, 1918], 14; COS, *Annual Report*, April 2, 1918, pp. 6, 84; Lillian Brandt, *Growth and Development of AICP and C.O.S. [A Preliminary and Exploratory Report]*, Report to the Committee on the Institute of Welfare Research, Community Service Society of New York, 1942, p. 229).

6. On the expansion of government activity in welfare before the New Deal, see Lubove, *Struggle for Social Security*; Susan Tiffin, *In Whose Best Interest? Child Welfare Reform in the Progressive Era* (Westport, Conn.: Greenwood, 1982); LeRoy Ashby, *Saving the Waifs: Reformers and Dependent Children, 1890–1917* (Philadelphia: Temple University Press, 1984); James T. Patterson, *America's Struggle against Poverty, 1900–1980* (Cambridge, Mass.: Harvard University

Press, 1980); Ann Shola Orloff and Theda Skocpol, "Why Not Equal Protection? Explaining the Politics of Public Social Welfare in Britain and the United States, 1880s–1920s," paper presented at the annual meeting of the American Sociological Association, Detroit, Michigan, September 2, 1983; and Michael B. Katz, *In the Shadow of the Poorhouse: A Social History of Welfare in America* (New York: Basic Books, 1986), chs. 6–8.

7. There is a great deal of material on the New York COS in Watson, *Charity Organization*. See also Lillian Brandt, "The Charity Organization Society of the City of New York, 1882–1907," in [New York Charity Organization Society,] *Twenty-Fifth Annual Report for the Year Ending September Thirtieth Nineteen Hundred and Seven* (New York: United Charities Building, 1907), and Brandt, *Growth and Development*. For an account of New York in this period, which includes an examination of the active political role played by the COS, see David C. Hammack, *Power and Society: Greater New York at the Turn of the Century* (New York: Russell Sage Foundation, 1982), 151.

8. The narrative is constructed from case 2053 in the Community Services Society Collection in the Rare Book Room in Butler Library, Columbia University. Names have been changed to protect privacy. All unnoted quotations are from the case records.

9. In the early part of the twentieth century, a patient who had been treated and showed no signs of syphilis for five years was not considered infectious and could marry. There is no information about how long before his marriage Thomas had contracted syphilis. The drugs used to treat Thomas's final injury could have caused his syphilitic symptoms to flare up when first injected. I am indebted for this information to Dr. Barbara Bates (private communication).

10. On the history of Baby Health Stations and Milk Stations in New York, see S. Josephine Baker, *Fighting for Life* (New York: Macmillan, 1939), 126–46, and Sheila M. Rothman, *Women's Proper Place: A History of Changing Ideals and Practices, 1870 to the Present* (New York: Basic Books, 1978), 124–27.

11. On the introduction of pensions for mothers or widows in New York State, see David M. Schneider and Albert Deutsch, *The History of Public Welfare in New York State 1867–1940* (Chicago: University of Chicago Press, 1941), 180–83.

12. Gareth Stedman Jones, *Outcast London: A Study in the Relationship between Classes in Victorian Society* (Oxford: Clarendon Press, 1971), 81–88; Stephan Thernstrom and Peter Knights, "Men in Motion: Some Data and Speculations about Urban Population Mobility in Nineteenth-Century America," *Journal of Interdisciplinary History* 1 (1970), 18–19.

13. The lack of sympathy in the case records could be a result of the Visitors' dislike or of agency policy. Certainly, much more sympathy was reflected in the handling of the one case in Philadelphia that I analyzed in *Poverty and Policy* (pp. 18–54). "Mrs. Sullivan" in Philadelphia, however, behaved in a far more deferential way than Delia. Only the analysis of many more cases will resolve the question.

14. The use of the courts to settle disputes between working-class people in the nineteenth century is dealt with in detail by Allen Steinberg in "The Criminal Courts and the Transformation of Criminal Justice in Philadelphia 1815–1874"

(Ph.D. dissertation, Columbia University, 1983). It is also touched on in Michael B. Katz, Michael J. Doucet, and Mark J. Stern, *The Social Organization of Early Industrial Capitalism* (Cambridge, Mass.: Harvard University Press, 1982), 228–40.

15. Stedman Jones, *Outcast London*, 251–52. See the remarkably similar definition in Lowell, *Public Relief*, 88–89.

16. E. Wight Bakke, *The Unemployed Worker: A Study of the Task of Making a Living without a Job* (New Haven: Yale University Press, 1940), 26–29, points out the way the class of the giver affected the meaning of gifts to the working-class people he studied. On exchange theory and its application to working-class family life, see Michael Anderson, *Family Structure in Nineteenth-Century Lancashire* (Cambridge, Eng.: Cambridge University Press, 1971), passim.

17. I treat the war on welfare during the Reagan era in *Shadow of the Poorhouse*, ch. 10. For an extended discussion of contemporary ideas on poverty, see my *The Undeserving Poor: From the War on Poverty to the War on Welfare* (New York: Pantheon, 1990). I treat the assault on outdoor relief in the late nineteenth century in *Shadow*, 46–52. See also Frederic Almy, "The Relation between Public and Private Charities," *Charities Review* 9 (1899), 2–30, pt. 2, 65–71; and Seth Lowe, "The Problem of Pauperism in the Cities of Brooklyn and New York," [New York] Sixth Annual Conference of Charities (1879), *Proceedings*, 200–10.

18. The variety of charities that existed in New York can be seen by looking at the *Charities Directory* published each year by the Charity Organization Society. In New York at this time the COS operated the Social Service Exchange.

Contributors

Bruce Bellingham is Assistant Professor of Sociology at Florida State University. He has published articles on child abandonment and child saving in mid-nineteenth-century New York City, which form part of a larger project based on the records of the New York Children's Aid Society.

Rachel G. Fuchs is Associate Professor of History at Arizona State University. She is the author of *Abandoned Children: Foundlings and Child Welfare in Nineteenth-Century France* (New York, 1984) and a forthcoming book, *Poor and Pregnant in Paris: Strategies for Survival in the Nineteenth Century* (Rutgers University Press).

Nancy L. Green is chef de travaux (assistant professor) at the Ecole des Hautes Etudes en Sciences Sociales in Paris. She is the author of *The Pletzl of Paris: Jewish Immigrant Workers in the Belle Epoque* (New York, 1986) and currently working on a comparative social history of immigrant labor in the garment industries of Paris and New York.

Michael B. Katz is Professor of History and Director of the Urban Studies Program at the University of Pennsylvania. He has written and edited books on education, poverty, urban life, and social policy in America and Canada. His most recent book is *The Undeserving Poor: From the War on Poverty to the War on Welfare* (New York, 1990).

Lynn Hollen Lees is Professor of History at the University of Pennsylvania. She is the author of *Exiles of Erin: Irish Migrants in Nineteenth-Century London* (Ithaca, 1979) and other works on urban society and is currently working on a book-length study of working-class experience of the Poor Law in nineteenth-century England.

Catharina Lis is Professor of History at the Free University of Brussels. She is the author of *Social Change and the Laboring Poor: Antwerp, 1770–1860* (New Haven, 1986) and is currently working on a book entitled *Social Control from Below: Urban Families and Their Unruly Members in Eighteenth-Century Brabant and Flanders*, in collaboration with Hugo Soly.

Peter Mandler is Assistant Professor of History at Princeton University. He is the author of *Aristocratic Government in the Age of Reform: Whigs and Liberals, 1830–52* (Oxford, 1990) and has most recently written on the making of the New Poor Law in England.

Ellen Ross is Associate Professor of Women's Studies at Ramapo College of New Jersey. She has published many articles on poor and working-class women in late nineteenth-century London, forming part of a larger project to appear as *"In Time of Trouble": Wives and Mothers in Working-Class London, 1870–1918* (Oxford University Press).

Hugo Soly is Professor of Early Modern History at the Free University of Brussels. He is the author (with Catharina Lis) of *Poverty and Capitalism in Pre-Industrial Europe* (Atlantic Highlands, N.J., 1979) and is preparing with Lis a book titled *Social Control from Below: Urban Families and Their Unruly Members in Eighteenth-Century Brabant and Flanders*.

Index